TERROR
IN THE CRADLE
OF LIBERTY

TERROR
IN THE CRADLE
OF LIBERTY

HOW BOSTON BECAME A CENTER
FOR ISLAMIC EXTREMISM

ILYA I. FEOKTISTOV

BOOKS

New York • London

First American edition published in 2019 by Encounter Books,
an activity of Encounter for Culture and Education, Inc.,
a nonprofit, tax exempt corporation.
Encounter Books website address: www.encounterbooks.com

Manufactured in the United States and printed on
acid-free paper. The paper used in this publication meets
the minimum requirements of ANSI/NISO Z39.48–1992
(R 1997) (*Permanence of Paper*).

FIRST AMERICAN EDITION

LIBRARY OF CONGRESS CATALOGING-IN-PUBLICATION DATA
Names: Feoktistov, Ilya I., 1982– author.
Title: Terror in the cradle of liberty : how Boston became a center
for Islamic extremism / Ilya I. Feoktistov.
Description: New York : Encounter Books, [2019] |
Includes bibliographical references and index.
Identifiers: LCCN 2019019752 (print) | LCCN 2019980107 (ebook) |
ISBN 9781641770767 (hardcover) | ISBN 9781641770774 (ebook)
Subjects: LCSH: Muslims—Massachusetts—Boston. |
Islamic fundamentalism—Massachusetts—Boston. | Tsarnaev, Dzhokhar. |
Tsarnaev, Tamerlan. | Islamic Society of Boston. | Mosques—Massachusetts—Boston. |
Radicalization. | Terrorism—Religious aspects—Islam.
Classification: LCC BP67.U62 M44 2019 (print) |
LCC BP67.U62 (ebook) | DDC 363.32509744/61—dc23
LC record available at https://lccn.loc.gov/2019019752
LC ebook record available at https://lccn.loc.gov/2019980107

Dedication

To my dear mother, Anna, in whose final company I had spent a wonderful summer writing this book. May her memory be a blessing to this world forever.

CONTENTS

INTRODUCTION

I did not want to come into the office on Patriots' Day 2013. Also known as Marathon Monday, it is an official holiday in Massachusetts. Its center of festivities is on Boylston Street in Back Bay, where the runners in the Boston Marathon have been reaching the finish line since Patriots' Day 1897. I happened to live just one street over from the final stretch and for the past few years, I had spent the day on the Boylston Street sidewalks and in its bars with thousands of spectators as hundreds of runners hustled by for hours, finish line in sight. But this year, while my friends were having drinks on the sidewalk patio at Abe and Louie's, I was stuck in an office building. We had scheduled a fairly mundane "catch-up-and-planning" meeting at Americans for Peace and Tolerance, a Boston-based national security nonprofit that I had co-founded in 2008 with human rights activist Charles Jacobs and documentary film producer Avi Goldwasser. I was getting more and more annoyed as the meeting dragged on.

Three hours after winner Lelisa Desisa ran by, a third of the runners were still on the course, with small packs of them coming steadily down Boylston to cheers of encouragement from the sidewalks. Suddenly, my friends heard a boom from the direction of the finish line, about three hundred yards ahead, and a cloud of smoke began to form above the crowds. The screams were at first indistinguishable from the cheering. Then, as they stood on their patio chairs to peer out over the heads of the crowd toward the finish line, another explosion went off in the crowd right in front of them, in another cloud of smoke and a spray of blood.

My friends would become much more interested in my line of work after that day, as would several national media outlets. For much of the previous decade, a group of concerned Boston civic leaders, which would ultimately coalesce into our organization, had been warning other leaders and the public about a network of al-Qaeda–connected Islamist extremists that has been fundraising for terrorist causes and radicalizing Muslim youths in Massachusetts since before the September 11, 2001, attacks. Our thoughts, as we found out the identities of the bombers, were all the same: we had failed.

This story starts in 2002, half a year after ten 9/11 hijackers left Boston's Logan Airport and crashed their two planes into the Twin Towers. In April 2002, a small mosque called the Islamic Society of Boston (ISB), located in Cambridge's Central Square between Harvard and MIT, posted an appeal on its website's bulletin board: "Chechen Refugee Family needs temporary place to live until they complete their permanent refugee status in the US. Husband has good business knowledge, automechanic experience and construction."

Those willing to help the family were asked to contact a Toronto-based woman named Maret Tsarnaeva. Her brother Anzor, his wife Zubeidat, and their eight-year-old son Dzhokhar had just come to Boston. They were homeless and helpless in a place very different from their Caucasian homeland. Ultimately, the family settled in a small apartment a block away from the ISB's Cambridge mosque. Dzhokhar's brother, sixteen-year-old Tamerlan, and his two sisters, Bella and Ailina, soon joined them there. The family, which was not religious when it arrived in America, began attending the ISB mosque; and several of its members started to turn increasingly fundamentalist.

Later in 2002, a Boston businessman and philanthropist named Bill Sapers was attending what he believed to be a routine meeting of the Roxbury Community College Foundation, where he served as vice chairman. Roxbury Community College is part of the Massachusetts state university system, serving a largely African American population in the Boston neighborhood for which it was named. The Foundation raises money from private donors for scholarships and program support at the college.

In the middle of a discussion about fundraising, Sapers heard some surprising news: the college's vice president announced that the Roxbury Community College would soon be replacing a campus parking lot with a multistory garage. Sapers thought that was strange. "Why do we want to build a garage over the parking lot?" he told me he remembered asking. "We have plenty of parking spaces, and most of our students live nearby. We could spend that money on more important things."

He then got an even bigger surprise: "It isn't costing us anything," the vice president replied. "It's being built by Saudi Arabia. It's for the mosque next door."

"What mosque?" Sapers wondered.

This was the first time Sapers had heard about a plan to build a nearby mosque as a major expansion of the Cambridge-based Islamic Society of Boston. He had been under the impression that the city-owned land adjacent to the college was being reserved for a potential expansion of the RCC campus. But when he tried to dig deeper, he ran up against a brick wall. Neither the college president—Dr. Grace Brown—nor anyone at the Massachusetts Department of Higher Education would tell him when this decision had been made, or why the plan for a garage had not been vetted previously. Running out of options, he asked investigative journalist Tamar Morad to look into the matter and offer her investigation to the *Boston Globe* for publication. The article would be written, but it would never appear. The *Globe* killed it.

• • •

Eleven years later, Tamerlan and Dzhokhar blew up two homemade bombs at the Boston Marathon, killing three people and wounding 264. Hiding inside a boat in a suburban backyard after a rampage that had already cost his older brother and an MIT police officer their lives, Dzhokhar wrote a message on the boat's hull:

> I bear witness that there is no God but Allah and that Muhammad is his messenger. Our actions came with a message and that is La Illaha Illalah [there is no god but Allah]. The U.S. Government is killing our innocent civilians but most of you already know that. As a Muslim I can't stand to see such evil go unpunished, we Muslims are one body, you hurt one you hurt us all....know you are fighting men who look into the barrel of your gun and see heaven, now how can you compete with that. We are promised victory and we will surely get it.

The stories of the Tsarnaev brothers have been told in countless places, including the John Joseph Moakley United States Courthouse in Boston's trendy Seaport neighborhood, where Dzhokhar was sentenced to death for his role in the bombing. But the story of the mosque the Tsarnaevs attended during their increasing radicalization—and of the radicals who own and control it—has been mostly ignored. Few know that since shortly after the Tsarnaev family arrived in Boston, Boston's top political, law enforcement, and religious leaders knew about the ISB's connections to terrorism and Islamist radicalism, but refused to tell the public as they continued to embrace the mosque's owners out of selfish political and pecuniary motivations. As the evidence in the following chapters will show, the ISB has been, since the 1980s, the primary front group for Muslim Brotherhood activists living in New England. The Muslim Brotherhood, founded in Egypt in March 1928, is one of the oldest and largest Islamist extremist organizations in the world and has spawned terror groups from al-Qaeda and the Islamic State to Hamas, as well as affiliates in countries across the world, including the United States. Events that happened in Boston and people who live or had lived in the area have played a surprisingly large role in the histories of all these infamous groups, as this book documents.

Almost no one knows that the City of Boston, under Mayor Thomas Menino, had fleeced its taxpayers by selling off prime real estate at a fraction of its value to the owners of the ISB for the construction of an extremist mosque. Indeed, some of the most prominent political and community leaders in Massachusetts, including some of the top leaders of the local Jewish community, have, until the present, embraced and actively supported the anti-Semitic, anti-American, and pro-terrorist owners of the ISB. The ISB's owners have exploited the good intentions of these Boston leaders, their belief in the ideology of multiculturalism, and their honorable desire to welcome immigrants—such as myself—to Boston.

This failure of leadership extends to Massachusetts law enforcement agencies, as well as to the local offices of their federal counterparts. In helping a group of ISB-affiliated Muslim immigrants obtain access to financial services, for example, Massachusetts attorney general Maura Healey might have unwittingly aided a terrorist-fundraising conspiracy by ISB owners and donors to violate federal bank secrecy and money-laundering laws. Many other local elites simply didn't listen to warnings then; and they're still not listening now. Since you've bought this book, hopefully you will.

PART ONE

DISCOVERY

CHAPTER 1

MANY SURPRISES

One year after Bill Sapers learned about the Roxbury mega-mosque project, in October 2003, Charles Jacobs and Avi Goldwasser were walking back from lunch to the offices of The David Project, a pro-Israel group they had recently founded together. Charles was the president; Avi was executive director. They were startled by a front-page article in a newspaper vending machine titled "Radical Islam: Outspoken cleric, jailed activist tied to new Hub mosque." This was not the article Sapers had commissioned, however, and it was not in the *Boston Globe*. It was in the city's "other" newspaper, the tabloid *Boston Herald*. Although Tamar Morad, the journalist Bill Sapers hired, had discovered many of the allegations listed in the *Herald* article; not only did the *Boston Globe* kill Morad's article, it also refused to sell the article to Sapers, or even back to the author herself for publication elsewhere. Morad had written her article the same year that the *Globe*'s Spotlight team was reporting its Pulitzer Prize–winning exposés on the sex abuse scandals in the Boston Catholic archdiocese. But the *Globe* did not want to touch a scandal involving a mosque and the Islamic religion. On its own initiative, however, after Sapers tipped it off to the story, the *Herald* was picking up the slack.

The revelations in this and subsequent *Herald* articles were disturbing. A group called the Islamic Society of Boston (ISB), which already owned a small mosque across the Charles River in Cambridge, was building a mega-mosque in the Boston neighborhood of Roxbury. It was to be the largest mosque on the east coast and it had the staunch support of then Boston mayor Thomas Menino. Yet, at the same time, the mosque had deep and troubling connections to Islamic extremism and terror.

According to the *Herald's* 2003 reporting, the ISB had direct and significant links to the Muslim Brotherhood and other radical and terrorist entities. A prominent Muslim American activist who had recently been arrested by British authorities while catching a connecting flight in London on his way to Syria had organized the ISB as a Massachusetts corporation back in 1982. When he was arrested in 2003, the activist, Abdulrahman Alamoudi, was carrying a suitcase stuffed with $340,000 in undeclared cash. After being extradited back to America, Alamoudi was charged with plotting a terrorist conspiracy with Libya to assassinate then Saudi Crown Prince Abdullah. In 2004, he pled guilty to the charges and is currently finishing out a seventeen-year sentence in federal prison.

During the judicial process, federal authorities alleged that he was also one of the most important al-Qaeda fundraisers in the United States. Federal court evidence has shown that Alamoudi was a top leader within the American Muslim Brotherhood, and had founded twelve Brotherhood front groups in the United States. He was also an active supporter of terrorism against Israel. As the Second Intifada broke out in 2000, Alamoudi was videotaped at a rally in D.C.'s Lafayette Park addressing America's president: "Hear that, Bill Clinton, we are all supporters of Hamas, *Allahu Akbar*. I wish they added that I am also a supporter of Hezbollah."

Such was the nature of the man who founded the mega-mosque about to be built in Boston, on city-owned land right next door to Roxbury Community College.

Alamoudi was not the only ISB leader whose troubling connections were revealed by the *Herald's* reporting. The *Herald* discovered that a board of six trustees entirely owned and controlled all of the ISB's property, including the mosque in Cambridge and the new mega-mosque location, under a charitable land trust known simply as the Islamic Society of Boston Trust (ISB Trust). None of the trustees actually lived in the Boston area at the time, and the chairman of that board, Egypt-based pharmaceutical executive Osama Kandil, was also identified by the *Herald's* research as a Muslim Brotherhood leader. In the late 1970s, while studying in Boston, Kandil had co-founded a Muslim Brotherhood front group called the Muslim Arab Youth Association (MAYA), along with Osama bin Laden's nephew, Abdullah bin Laden. MAYA's constitution made its radical aims entirely clear: "In the heart of America, in the depths of corruption and ruin and moral deprivation, an elite of Muslim youth is holding fast to the teachings of Allah." In 2004, the U.S. Customs Service named Kandil as a member of the "SAFA Group," a loose network of interlocking businesses and charities operating out of Herndon, Virginia, accused of laundering and transferring funds to terrorist groups. Kandil and Alamoudi were also two of the four directors of an organization called Taibah International Aid Association, which was designated as a terrorist-fundraising group by the U.S. Treasury Department's Office of Foreign Assets Control (OFAC) in 2004.

The *Herald* also reported that the treasurer of the ISB Trust, Walid Fitaihi, had been playing a confidence game with Boston's Jewish community leaders. Fitaihi, who came to Boston from Jeddah, Saudi Arabia to attend Harvard Medical School, was a wealthy heir to a century-old Saudi jewelry empire and the largest single source of funding for the new mega-mosque's construction. The *Herald* discovered that Fitaihi had been writing articles in Arabic-language newspapers expressing violent anti-Semitic sentiments. Writing in the London-based *Al-Sharq al Awsat* in 2000, Fitaihi wrote that Jews will be "scourged" because of their "oppression, murder, and rape of the worshippers of Allah." According to Fitaihi's article, the Jews

> have perpetrated the worst of evils and they have brought the
> worst corruption to the earth....They have incurred Allah's wrath
> and they have been afflicted with misery. That is because they
> continuously rejected the Signs of Allah and were after slaying
> the Prophets...and this resulted from their disobedience and their
> habit of transgression.

Fitaihi made a prediction about the future prospects of American Jews: "Their covenant with America is the strongest possible in the US, but it is weaker than they think, and one day their covenant with the people will be cut off."

To Charles and Avi, this seemed like a strange sentiment coming from a man who, since the 9/11 attacks, had been at the forefront of the ISB's outreach efforts to the Jewish community as the ISB's interfaith outreach director. Fitaihi actively courted Jewish leaders, and, as a result, was invited to address the congregation of Boston's largest synagogue, Temple Israel. He had also developed an interfaith partnership with the New England branch of the Anti-Defamation League. Neither the ADL nor Temple Israel's Rabbi Friedman seem to have done any vetting of Fitaihi. After the 9/11 attacks, Rabbi Friedman, along with the JCRC and the ADL's Boston branch, began an official relationship with the Islamic Society of Boston (ISB).

Charles has often said that he sympathizes with Rabbi Friedman's motives. It was a fair and decent thing to do, to tell the Muslims of Boston that in their hour of deep communal worry and uncertainty, Jewish leaders would stand with them in support and interfaith fellowship. Fitaihi certainly didn't see it that way. He had an ulterior motive for the interfaith outreach he was doing, quite unlike Rabbi Friedman's kindhearted (if "kumbaya") one. Writing in the Egyptian newspaper *Al Ahram Al-Arabi*, on November 11, 2001, exactly two months after the 9/11 attacks, Fitaihi gloated about how the Jews have been reaching out to him out of fear:

> The Muslim community in the U.S....and in Boston in particular, has begun to trouble the Zionist lobby....Despite the attacks of distortion coordinated by the Zionist lobby, to which it has recruited many of the influential media, there are initial signs that the intensive campaign of education about Islam has begun to bear fruit. For example, the rate of converts to Islam since September 11 has doubled...For this reason, the Jewish institutions have begun to contact Muslim institutions and have called on us to hold dialogues with them and cooperate [with them]. They are afraid of the outcome of the Islamic-Christian dialogue through the churches, the mosques, and the universities...

Temple Israel and the ADL's failure to see through Fitaihi's moderate and friendly façade would soon become a major source of contention in the Boston Jewish community that festers to this day. When Bill Sapers first saw the allegations against Fitaihi, he couldn't believe what he read. He was a member of Temple Israel, and here was his own rabbi inviting a vicious anti-Semite into the place where he and his family worshipped.

But the most alarming revelation in the *Boston Herald* article was the identity of another person on the ISB Trust board of trustees—one of the most vicious anti-Semites in the world, the "Theologian of Terror," as the Anti-Defamation League has termed him—Sheikh Yusuf al-Qaradawi. Qaradawi is the spiritual leader of the Muslim Brotherhood and one of the most influential extremist voices in the Muslim world. He is banned from entering several countries, including Egypt and the United States, but, from his redoubt in Qatar, Qaradawi has for years been issuing fatwas to the Muslim world. He has called on Muslims to carry out suicide bombings against Israeli civilians, to kill U.S. soldiers in Iraq, to execute homosexuals, and to beat wives who become "disobedient." He has claimed that God sent Hitler to punish the Jews, and that Hitler had "managed to put them in their place." He has called for Muslims to build nuclear weapons to "terrorize their enemies" and has claimed that he hopes to "die a virtuous death like a jihad warrior, with the head severed from the body" by exploding himself among the Jews of Israel. His influence has been magnified by his regular broadcasts on Al Jazeera, through which he reaches millions of viewers around the Muslim world with sermons like the one broadcast by Al Jazeera on January 9, 2009.

"Oh Allah, take your enemies, the enemies of Islam," Qaradawi screamed from the pulpit on the Qatari satellite channel's video feed:

> Oh Allah, take the Jews, the treacherous aggressors. Oh Allah, take
> this profligate, cunning, arrogant band of people. Oh Allah, they
> have spread much tyranny and corruption in the land. Pour Your
> wrath upon them, oh our God. Lie in wait for them....Oh Allah,
> take this oppressive, tyrannical band of people. Oh Allah, take this
> oppressive, Jewish, Zionist band of people. Oh Allah, do not spare
> a single one of them. Oh Allah, count their numbers, and kill them,
> down to the very last one.

This murderous terrorist was to be an honored dignitary at the ISB mega-mosque. The ISB listed Qaradawi as one of its trustees from 1993 until 2001, touting his endorsement of the mosque project with a video-taped message at a 2002 fundraiser and a letter published in its fundraising brochure. Qaradawi's fundraising appeal for the ISB had to be videotaped because he was banned from the United States for his terrorist activity.

What in the world was this man doing on the board of a massive mosque being built in the Cradle of Liberty?

But the news would only get worse. Over the next several months, the *Boston Herald* reported on precisely *how* the ISB had obtained the city-owned land in Roxbury, even against highly placed competitors for the property, among them Harvard and Northeastern Universities. The ISB, as it turned out, had a number of advantages over all other bidders; and one such advantage was a dedicated member with inside connections at Boston City Hall.

Muhammad Ali Salaam is a Panamanian immigrant, a convert to Islam, and a prominent member of the ISB. In the late 1990s, he was serving as the deputy director of special projects of the Boston Redevelopment Authority (BRA). The BRA was created in 1957 to combat the urban blight and decay then rampant in many neighborhoods of Boston. It has counterparts in most of the big cities in the country, all of them products of the urgent desire for "urban renewal," which began in the 1950s, and which has enriched many well-connected developers in Boston and elsewhere. Like most urban-renewal agencies, the BRA was substantially under the control of the mayor. At its founding, the BRA was given jurisdiction over various public properties and acquired large swaths of formerly private real estate through eminent domain. The condemned land included the property on which the ISB's Roxbury mega-mosque would be built.

Internal BRA documents show that Ali Salaam joined the ISB as a leader and donor, fell deeply under the sway of the ISB's extremist board of trustees, and began working on a scheme to transfer city-owned land to the ISB for far below market price. While representing the city in negotiating the land deal for the mosque project, Ali Salaam also donated $11,690 of his own money to the project. In an email to four of the ISB's trustees, the public servant was obsequious in his praise of his new religious mentors:

[A]s individuals you each have a commanding presence that can
best be described as awesome; and you cannot perhaps imagine
the impression that you make when you come together. I sincerely
believe this to be a blessing from Allah. Therefore, each of you
should strive to be mindful of this. My admiration for ISB is based
upon the example that each of you reflect in your love for each
other and the knowledge of Islam that each of you command. I can

only hope that by associating with ISB, I might absorb some of this knowledge and also be an example to others and with the help of Allah, bring others to Islam.

As a BRA official, Ali Salaam was tasked with directly overseeing the deal *between* the BRA and the ISB; yet so taken was he with his "awesome" trustees and their "love for each other," that he ended up completely merging his roles as both city official and ISB official. For example, in the winter of 1999–2000, Ali Salaam, at the invitation of the ISB trustees, took part in an ISB fundraising trip to the Middle East, dedicated specifically to the mosque project. He joined the delegation in his capacity as a BRA official, receiving permission to do so from BRA director Paul McCann—after promising to reimburse the authority for his travel costs. An ISB newsletter from February 2000 describes Ali Salaam's role on the delegation, while in his official capacity, as working "hard during Ramadan to solicit funds from overseas. Dr. Walid [Fitaihi]…took on Saudi. Dr. Muhammad Amr and Muhammad Ali Salaam took on other Gulf states."

In December 2000, ISB leaders and Ali Salaam wrote a letter to Roxbury Community College president Grace Brown. The letter—written on BRA stationery and signed by Ali Salaam, Yousef Abou-Allaban, and Walid Fitaihi—offered the RCC a donation of $10,000 to be used at President Brown's discretion. The letter also asked that the source of the donation remain anonymous. Bill Sapers believed that this $10,000 was meant to guarantee that President Brown would not raise objections to the sale of land that the college was counting on for its future expansion.

In a confidential memorandum from February 1999, written on BRA letterhead, Ali Salaam advised the ISB trustees on how to obtain favorable terms from the BRA, referring to the City of Boston as "they" and to the ISB as "we." Having merged his public servant and ISB member roles into one, Ali Salaam had in effect negotiated the land deal with himself. It turned out to be a great deal for the ISB, but a loss for Boston taxpayers, raising serious questions of government involvement with religion combined with the typical municipal real estate corruption of a big city.

The BRA valued the city land in Roxbury (2.04 acres) at $2,010,966 in March 2000. Yet three months later, the BRA agreed to sell it to the ISB for $401,187.50, only $175,000 of which the ISB would pay in cash, promising to make up the rest with a package of public "benefits" that never materialized. The public benefits the ISB promised to provide as part of the deal included a number of promises that raised even more questions about the entanglement of the city with a religious organization. The ISB promised to deliver a series of lectures at the Roxbury Community College "on various aspects of Islam" and to give five thousand books on Islamic law and the history of Islam to the college's library. There were also promises to maintain a nearby playground and the Clarence "Jeep" Jones Park.

The ISB never made good on any of these public benefits. Considering the type of books and lectures that the ISB's trustees would have donated, that failure might have turned out to be a blessing in disguise. But whether delivered or not, the ISB's promise to involve itself in the RCC's curriculum only added to the questions already prompted by the discounted sale of the land. Why was the City of Boston accepting as a "public benefit" a series of lectures on Islam, at a public college, orchestrated by a radical Islamic organization? The First Amendment's Establishment Clause requires that government officials neither aid, inhibit, nor entangle themselves with religion, government agencies cannot subsidize potential proselytizing efforts, something that the BRA's own lawyer recognized. In 1989, when the ISB-BRA deal was first being discussed, BRA counsel Tom Farrell warned that the deal could violate the Anti-Establishment Clause of the First Amendment. Muhammad Ali Salaam chose to ignore this warning.

In interviews for a fundraising video the ISB produced for the mega-mosque project in 2000, ISB leaders even bragged about the great deal they had secured from Boston taxpayers. The ISB's executive director, Yousef Abou-Allaban, with a childish grin on his face, was caught in a publicity outtake, saying that "[w]ith the blessing of Allah..., we were able to get the land from the City of Boston almost free of charge." At this point his grin turned to a giggle, and he said, somewhat sheepishly, "I'll probably have to rephrase that." Walid Fitaihi, the ISB's anti-Semitic treasurer, was not so easily embarrassed:

This is very unique project, because it's probably the only project in the United States in which the city itself, the City of Boston in this particular project, is supporting the project. They're donating, they're actually donating—assigning—a piece of land in a very unique prominent location behind Northeastern University for the Muslims to build the largest cultural center [in the United States] with only a nominal fee. So it's unique because it's coming from within.

But nowhere was the ISB's triumphalism more boldly on display than in the fundraising brochure that featured Yusuf al-Qaradawi's endorsement. In a section titled "Land in Exchange for Proselytism for Islam," the ISB bragged:

> The city of Boston had shown its real support for the project when it allocated the land for the [Islamic Society of Boston] in exchange for a symbolic fee despite competition from Harvard and Northeastern University to buy the land. This grant is an acknowledgment of the role of the Association [ISB], and an appreciation of its importance and the credibility of its members. In exchange for this grant, the Association [ISB] has committed itself to providing social and cultural services to the local community. It is the intention, with Allah's permission, that the main part of these activities will be geared toward proselytism and teaching about Islam.

CHAPTER 2

HELP BILL

Charles and Avi were deeply troubled by the *Boston Herald* articles. The fact that the ISB already had an established mosque in Cambridge was worrisome enough. Now it would be expanding to a massive $23 million edifice in a neighborhood where there were few Muslims but many potential converts among the African American community. There were already a number of unofficial "storefront" mosques in Roxbury, some ministered to by amateur "imams" with little formal training—but also few financial or ideological ties to the fundamentalists in the Middle East or South Asia. What kind of Islam would be taught at this massive mosque? Would it become a center of radicalization? A place where Boston's Muslims would be taught to hate Christians, Jews, and Israel? Given who would be running it, all evidence suggested that this is exactly what the center would become. Doing something to stop a radical Islamic institution from threatening the Jewish community was imperative. Charles and Avi began organizing a David Project task force to lobby Jewish leadership, as well as to warn Boston's citizens about the ISB and its inside deal with their city's government.

Meanwhile, Bill Sapers, the first concerned citizen to discover the planned mosque project and its extremist backers, had been fighting a lonely battle. He had reached out to as many movers and shakers as he could—Boston mayor Thomas Menino; the leaders of the Roxbury Community College; the Massachusetts Department of Higher Education—detailing his concerns about the ISB's extremist leadership and Boston's apparent support for that leadership. His letters and phone calls went unanswered. And so Sapers joined the David Project task force, helping it to develop, over a period of several weeks, a three-part strategy to expose the ISB and its questionable land deal with the City of Boston.

The first part in this strategy was mostly clear. The ISB was bragging about how Muhammad Ali Salaam had successfully flouted the separation of church and state, using his position as a public official to enrich his mosque, all for the purpose of "proselytism for Islam." Challenging the mosque deal on constitutional grounds seemed like an obvious direction to take.

The second part would expose the anti-Semitism professed by the ISB's leaders. Boston has one of the largest and most politically involved Jewish communities in the United States. Boston's iconic Zakim Bridge is named after a New England regional director of the ADL. There is a large Holocaust memorial steps away from the site of the Boston Massacre and Boston City Hall; and there are many Jewish politicians inside Boston City Hall. With one ISB trustee—Qaradawi—inciting Muslims to kill all the Jews in the world, and another—Fitahi—anticipating that the American public would soon turn against the Jews, the ISB's planned radicalization center posed an obvious risk to Boston's Jewish community. The David Project task force assumed that Boston Jewish leaders would join the effort to counter this threat to a community they've been entrusted with protecting. That would turn out to be a major miscalculation.

The third part of the strategy was a media campaign to mobilize citizens of Massachusetts alarmed by the radical ISB mosque project. This effort assembled a diverse group: Jews, Roman Catholics, Episcopalians, and atheists. And then, a quite unexpected person reached out to the task force.

Sheikh Ahmed Subhy Mansour is an Egyptian Islamic theologian with a doctorate from Al Azhar University. As the premiere center of Sunni Muslim scholarship in the world, Al Azhar is often called "the Vatican of Islam," and Sheikh Mansour joined its faculty soon after earning his degree. But as a professor, Mansour taught a reformist theology that excluded some of the more violent and intolerant trends within Islamic thought. To spread his message, he founded a religious reform movement called the Quranists, and co-founded the secular Egyptian political party *Al Mostaqbal* (The Future), with prominent newspaper columnist Farag Fouda.

Unfortunately, Al Azhar, like many other Islamic institutions in Egypt, was under the thumb of the Muslim Brotherhood and also had a significant number of scholars loyal to the Wahhabi school of Islam imported from Saudi Arabia. Sheikh Mansour's partner, Farag Fouda, was declared an apostate by Al Azhar clerics, and assassinated outside the party's offices by two members of a Muslim Brotherhood splinter group, *al-Gama'a al-Islamiyya*. Sheikh Mansour was pushed out of his professorship and, as a bone thrown to the Brotherhood by then-president Hosni Mubarak, was jailed and tortured by secular government authorities.

After his release, Sheikh Mansour received asylum in the United States and was accepted into the Scholars at Risk Program at Harvard Law School. through the help of Islam scholar and Harvard alumnus Daniel Pipes. One night, shortly after he arrived in Cambridge, he and his wife Monera went for a walk around the neighborhood. As the time of the Muslim evening prayer was approaching, they saw a mosque and decided to go inside to pray. It was the Islamic Society of Boston's original Cambridge mosque, on Prospect Street, about a mile from the Harvard Law School campus.

While waiting for his wife to finish the women's prayer upstairs, Mansour scanned the mosque's bookshelves and noticed that they were filled with Muslim Brotherhood literature—books and pamphlets that he says were "full of hatred for the Jews, the Christians, and for America." He realized that the same extremist movement that had jailed and tortured him in Egypt had gotten to America before him, and that he was now in its Cambridge headquarters. Mansour told me how he felt when he understood where he was: "I felt scared because I discovered that I am in the wrong place. When these people recognize me, I will be in trouble. So I prayed quickly and went downstairs and called my wife and we escaped from this mosque."

When Sheikh Mansour told Daniel Pipes about the hateful Muslim Brotherhood literature he saw at the ISB's Cambridge mosque, Daniel Pipes suggested that he ought to get in touch with the David Project task force. And so the coalition for a public media campaign was born, in October 2004, a year after the original *Boston Herald* report. Named "Citizens for Peace and Tolerance," the coalition was led by Sheik Mansour;

Steve Cohen, a Jewish Harvard-trained lawyer; and Dennis Hale, a member of the political science department at Boston College and a lay leader in his Episcopal parish church. It was officially dedicated to "educating members of the public concerning the consequences of hat[r]ed and bigotry among the diverse religious and ethnic communities."

Dennis Hale, who was named president of CPT, had been involved in politics since his student days at Oberlin College, where he was a member of Students for a Democratic Society and the editor of a student political journal, *The Activist*. In his senior year, he co-edited an anthology of student writing entitled *The New Student Left*, which was published by Beacon Press in 1966. After receiving his PhD from the City University of New York, Hale began teaching at Boston College, focusing his teaching and writing on the experience of citizenship in modern states, and in particular in the United States. But Hale's attention was drawn by the 9/11 attacks to the phenomenon of modern terrorism, and to the links between religious and political extremism. Soon he was studying the politics of the Middle East in the context of the foreign policy challenges facing the United States. When the group went public, he summed up his concern about the ISB with a question that drove all of his colleagues in CPT: "Will this Islamic Center, under this leadership, be a force for peace and tolerance—or will it become a jihad academy?"

Charles Jacobs, who midwifed the CPT board's formation, claims that, while it was easy to find a Christian director, and even a Muslim one, it was much harder to find a brave Boston Jew. He found one in Steve Cohen, a Harvard-trained lawyer who started his career in litigation, then shifted for a number of years to community advocacy for low and moderate income housing in Boston. Eventually, he founded a real estate development agency. Before settling into his career in Cambridge, Cohen traveled extensively in the Middle East, working on a farm in Morocco and living with the Berbers of the Atlas Mountains. He studied Islam in Istanbul, and traveled around Egypt and Jordan.

But when Cohen first heard about the ISB through the *Herald* articles, he was worried:

> The Muslim community is building a mosque, a large mosque in
> Roxbury. No problem. That's great. The issue was that we had a
> religious organization in our midst that we think may have been

advocating extremist views about women, about homosexuals, about
Jews, about Christians, about non-Orthodox Muslims, and nobody
was aware of these views. And, not only were they not aware of
these views, but the city of Boston was subsidizing them and helping them without the slightest bit of investigation into who it was
that they were actually subsidizing. We just wanted to get that word
out.

As Citizens for Peace and Tolerance prepared to get the word out during
the summer of 2004, they began their own investigation into the ISB in
order to supplement the *Herald*'s reporting and build a compelling case to
be presented in public. For help in this effort, Bill Sapers reached out to
noted terrorism expert Steven Emerson and put him in touch with the
David Project and CPT.

Steven Emerson was the first American journalist to recognize the
threat to American society from Islamic extremism. In the early 1990s, he
was a special investigative correspondent for CNN, specializing in foreign
terrorism. While staying at a hotel on assignment, he stumbled across a
national conference of Muslim Brotherhood–affiliated organizations based
in the United States. Before the first World Trade Center bombing in
1993, when the American establishment still viewed Islamic fundamentalists as the colorful local allies who had helped defeat the Soviet Union in
Afghanistan, Muslim Brotherhood activists had no reason to be secretive
in their activity. But with the Soviet Union gone, they had already shifted
focus to a new enemy: Western civilization, with America and Israel being
the primary targets.

Emerson left CNN to produce an investigative documentary describing what he discovered after he stumbled across the conference. The documentary debuted on the PBS Frontline news show as *Terrorists Among Us:
Jihad in America* and won the 1994 George Polk Award for best television
documentary, as well as the Investigative Reporters and Editors award for
best investigative reporting. Standing in front of the Twin Towers, Emerson
warned that the first World Trade Center bombing was just the beginning
of a determined war by radical Islam against America. By September 11,
2001, Emerson had published numerous books and articles on terrorism
in America, one of which, *American Jihad: The Terrorists Living among
Us*, inspired the *New York Times*' Ethan Bronner to write: "[Emerson] is

an investigator who has performed a genuine service...His information should be taken seriously." When his predictions came true in the final destruction of the Twin Towers, Emerson was invited to testify numerous times before Congressional investigative committees, and the information he accumulated was also instrumental in many post-9/11 terrorism prosecutions. Emerson's investigations were especially significant in the Holy Land Foundation case, which became the largest terrorism financing trial in U.S. history, in terms of the numbers of co-defendants and co-conspirators involved.

After Bill Sapers reached out to him, Emerson prepared an extensive report on the Islamic Society of Boston that added significantly to the *Boston Herald*'s findings of Islamist ideology and support for terrorism being promoted at the ISB. Emerson and his organization, the Investigative Project on Terrorism, traced the ISB's origins to a group of foreign students at Harvard, MIT, and other Boston-area colleges, many of whom had become Muslim Brotherhood members back home in Egypt, where the Muslim Brotherhood originated, or in other Muslim-majority countries. These local students began organizing in New England as part of the national Muslim Students Association, which Emerson had identified as the first Muslim Brotherhood front group in the United States. While some such students went back overseas after graduating, some chose to stay in New England for good. These students—Fitaihi, Kandil, and others—formed the ISB as part of a national organization of U.S. citizen and permanent resident Muslim Brotherhood members: the Islamic Society of North America (ISNA). Throughout their efforts, top Muslim Brotherhood leaders like Yusuf Qaradawi directed them from abroad.

For most of the umbrella group's existence, Emerson has been keeping tabs on the Islamic Society of North America (ISNA) and its affiliates, like the ISB. He has documented its Wahhabi funding; so extensive that, at times, Saudi Arabia was ISNA's largest source of income. Emerson has also documented the ideology promoted by ISNA and its leaders, which is anti-Semitic and intolerant of nonfundamentalist Islamic practices. Worst of all, ISNA leaders and publications indoctrinate American students with hatred for the United States and visions of a worldwide Islamic theocracy. And, according to Emerson, who pulled the ISB's tax records, the ISB told the Internal Revenue Service that it is part of ISNA when it sought nonprofit status for tax purposes.

Armed with more evidence against the ISB, Citizens for Peace and Tolerance prepared to go public with their concerns in October 2004. Meanwhile, the David Project task force was continuing with the other element of its strategy to confront the ISB mega-mosque project. As a lawyer, real estate developer, and dedicated civil libertarian, Steven Cohen immediately recognized the separation of church and state issues raised by the land deal between the City of Boston and the ISB. Cohen felt that "the notion of the city...subsidizing a religious group in the construction of their place of worship crosses the line. It's not even close. It is unconstitutional and it violates our whole system of values."

Cohen and his fellow activists felt that a significant legal challenge could be raised against the transfer to the ISB of public land, at a substantial discount, for the purpose of constructing a house of worship. It was a government subsidy to religion in the form of a reduced price and an inside deal for prime taxpayer real estate. As it happened, there was a potential plaintiff with the standing as a City of Boston municipal taxpayer to bring such a case to court. James Policastro lived on the east side of Mission Hill in the Roxbury neighborhood, about five hundred yards from where the ISB's new mosque was to be built.

An Italian American Catholic by birth, he says he was always less religious than spiritual. Ironically, since he and everyone else involved with CPT would soon be accused of anti-Muslim bigotry, Policastro's spiritual quest drew him in an ecumenical direction, and he was so inspired by Sufi Muslim thought that he sent his children to a Sufi school. He knew that a mosque was going into that vacant lot for years before Bill Sapers ever heard about the project, and he didn't think much about it. But as a building contractor, he knew a bit about how the city operated whenever public property changed hands, and he was not a fan of the process. A few years before, he had sued the city over a sweetheart deal it made with the Catholic Church for another piece of city-owned property in his neighborhood. Drawing on his long experience with the city and its shifty real estate practices, he became very suspicious of this BRA/ISB partnership, describing it bluntly as an "illegal way of doing business...and this particular case is just one of...scores that have been done over the years and really aren't in the best interest of the [city's] taxpayers," benefitting "a politically favored group of one sort or another. It's been a real eye opener for me, a very educational process, but the initial impulse was really to expose what

I felt was business as usual, how business gets done in Boston, and perhaps seek some redress from the courts so that it wouldn't continue to happen."

Policastro agreed to be the plaintiff, and the legal preparation for a case against the BRA began. Meanwhile, the second part of the David Project task force's strategy—to enlist the help of Boston Jewish community leaders in confronting the anti-Semitic leadership of the ISB—was running into major obstacles.

CHAPTER 3

THE SILENCE
OF THE LAMBS

O
n a cold day in early 2004, Charles Jacobs and Avi Goldwasser met
with several Jewish community leaders in New England. Present at
this meeting were Robert Leikind, then executive director of the Anti-
Defamation League's (ADL) New England branch; Larry Lowenthal,
then executive director of the American Jewish Committee's (AJC) Boston
office; and Alan Ronkin, the "number 2" at the Jewish Community Relations
Council (JCRC), sitting in for its executive director, Nancy Kaufman. Barry
Shrage, then president of the Combined Jewish Philanthropies of Greater
Boston and the titular head of the Boston Jewish community could not
come but sent word that he would follow up on the results of the meeting. Charles and Avi laid out what they knew about extremism and Jew
hatred at the ISB and asked for leadership and guidance from the people
in attendance. The response was immensely discouraging. The ADL's Rob
Leikind expressed concerns and was interested in exploring legal action.
But the rest insisted on a circular argument that dialogue with the ISB was
the only answer, and that, in any case, the ISB was not nearly as bad as the
Boston Herald made it out to be in its reporting. After all, the ISB's lead-
ers had for a long time been inviting Jewish leaders to interfaith dialogue.
The AJC's Larry Lowenthal had attended many a barbeque at the ISB's
leaders' homes, who, he said, were absolutely charming. At the same time,
Lowenthal wondered why these leaders never invited him to address the
ISB congregation, like the ISB's leaders were invited to address Jewish ones.

By the end of the meeting, it was very clear that all of the groups and leaders in attendance had long since been co-opted as allies of the ISB's leaders, *years* before the *Boston Herald* report. And nothing in the reports had changed their prevailing views. Rob Leikind of the ADL had already been working with Walid Fitaihi on joint interfaith anti-hate projects. Larry Lowenthal of the AJC had been invited by the ISB to hold joint interfaith dialogue sessions. Nancy Kaufman of the JCRC had been working closely with the ISB through the Greater Boston Interfaith Organization (GBIO)—an ecumenical coalition of left-wing clergy. The GBIO is a project of Industrial Areas Foundation, founded by none other than Saul Alinsky, the far-left community organizer who had a major impact on President Barack Obama and not-president Hillary Clinton. Alinsky famously wrote the leftist community organizer's bible, *Rules for Radicals*, and prefaced it with an acknowledgment Lucifer as "the very first radical."

Having first co-opted Boston's indigenous black Muslim leaders, then the black Christian clergy, and then the city's many powerful main-line Protestant churches, the ISB was a powerful presence at the GBIO. Kaufman, who had spent the previous fifteen years moving the JCRC toward the GBIO's radical agenda, had no desire to rock the boat.

Barry Shrage of the CJP, meanwhile, was afraid of losing the good graces of Boston mayor Menino, who was a strong supporter both of the ISB mosque project and of Shrage's causes at CJP, on whose support a lot of CJP's philanthropic activity depended. Menino was also famous for not taking criticism kindly. Charles told me that he tried several times to change Shrage's mind, to no avail. "I said, 'Barry, this is a very dangerous thing. It's the most dangerous thing for the Jewish community and you've got to tell the mayor what you know about the ISB.'"

When Shrage asked Charles what he could possibly say to the mayor, Charles replied:

> You have to say something like this: "We are the Jews. We've been
> in Boston for a long time and we've done a lot of good. We helped
> fund the revolution. We built and support many of the hospitals
> in this city. We are among the largest Boston philanthropists. You,
> mayor, can't bring these people down on our heads. Allow me to
> show you who the ISB's leaders are, and what a danger they pose to

all of Boston, but first to the Jewish community." But Barry flat-out refused to do it. At some point he said to Charles: "You want me to start a Jewish jihad."

Charles was disheartened and angry, and complained for days to colleagues about Boston's "top Jewish leader refusing to protect his own community." He once told me, before the 2013 marathon bombing, that if anything bad happened in Boston due to the ISB's presence, "it's on Barry. He had the only realistic chance to convince Boston's leaders that the ISB should not be embraced."

Charles was even more upset that some Boston Jewish leaders had become *the most visible* public champions of the ISB. He felt that this was particularly dangerous. Non-Jewish Bostonians might reasonably have the expectation that the Jews, who have the most skin in the game, would know more than anybody else about the threat of Islamic extremism to peaceful coexistence. Yet instead of raising warning flags, they gave the ISB a kosher seal of approval that opened the gates for these extremists to enter the city. "If something happens, God forbid, the Jewish community could be blamed," he worried. How would people react if they knew that "the Jews" actually knew about the ISB's terrorist connections, did not warn the city, and instead gave the ISB the "good housekeeping seal of approval" to radicalize Boston's Muslim youths.

Yet the most common reaction from Boston's Jewish leadership to Charles's exhortations was a return to circular reasoning: "Don't you believe in dialogue?" Avi has explained this impulse with the old allegory: everything looks like a nail when the only tool you have is a hammer. Religious hatred, according to the Jewish liberal worldview, is the result of ignorance; and ignorance is dissolved by education and dialogue. The idea is that when you talk to people, they are no longer stereotypes but actual human beings. This approach had worked fairly well after the Holocaust in combating Christian anti-Semitism. And what were the Muslims of the ISB, basically, but just another religious group who did not understand the Jews, but only because they had never really encountered them in a face-to-face dialogue? Polite dialogue in private was basically the only tool that these leaders knew how to use. According to Charles, "The assumption that all people want peaceful coexistence and positive-sum interactions is an act of faith for many that is hard to shake."

After Fitaihi's anti-Semitic writings came to light in a *Boston Herald* article titled "Mosque leader's message of hate," most Jewish leaders took in stride the revelation that they had been covering for Islamic anti-Semites all these years. The very same day the article was published, flooded with calls from alarmed Boston Jews, the ADL decided to act. Unfortunately, the action consisted of Rob Leikind and ADL New England board chair Ginny MacDowell writing a private and polite letter, in which they described their concerns about Fitahi but assured the ISB of their continued good wishes. Having let the ISB know their alarm, the ADL leaders even reassured the ISB that they were eager to defend the mosque when local Jews called to complain. "Needless to say," they wrote, "these allegations are extremely troubling and not surprisingly we are receiving many inquiries from concerned citizens about them. We recognize that friends and neighbors of goodwill are associated with the Islamic Society of Boston and are urging that people not jump to conclusions and instead allow you the opportunity to respond."

The ISB sent a response a day later. Fitaihi was not mentioned once in the letter, and neither was the substance of his anti-Semitic writing. Instead the ADL was reminded that the ISB collaborated on "a campaign called 'Outnumber the Hate' which condemned hate crime and bigotry of any kind." The ISB told the ADL that "we are confident that our activities are above reproach," and that "the views of any individual member, supporter or trustee of the Islamic Society of Boston are expressly their own and do not represent the views of the organization." The ISB promised to "investigate these most recent allegations to determine their veracity."

Leikind dutifully waited for three weeks for the ISB to investigate. He received no response. He sent another letter on March 29 and didn't hear back until May 4, when the ISB sent another generic statement against bigotry, again without mentioning Fitaihi. Finally, more than two months later, Leikind sent another letter that was much blunter and to the point. Writing on July 15, 2004, he was joined by Rabbi Ron Friedman of Boston's largest synagogue, the reform Temple Israel. Friedman had been the rabbi who spent the most time in dialogue with Fitaihi. Rabbi Friedman had even invited Fitahi to give a speech at his synagogue—and was now under serious pressure from congregants like Bill Sapers to explain how the rabbi could have been deceived and why he, in turn, had deceived the entire congregation. In the new letter, the Jewish leaders wrote, "This matter is also disconcerting because Dr. Fitaihi served as a representative for the ISB at many interfaith gatherings after 9/11. He was actively welcomed into the community and repeatedly professed his desire to build warm and trusting relations with other faith communities. Yet, even as he was doing this, the so far unrefuted information available to us indicates that he was writing letters that appear to have conveyed a far more intolerant view." The letter ended with a lament that the ISB has not been returning ADL's phone calls, along with another polite request for "clarification."

After receiving this letter, the ISB finally addressed the Fitaihi issue directly: but they did so by claiming that his anti-Semitic articles didn't actually exist; that the claims were completely made up by ill-wishers. Then, when the original articles were produced, the ISB claimed they had been mistranslated. After Harvard Arabic Professor Ahmed al-Rahim certified that the translations were accurate, and that "[t]he anti-Semitism exhibited in his writings is the same whether it is in Arabic or English," the ISB insisted that Fitaihi's writings were not aimed at "all Jews," but only Israelis.

Throughout the back-and-forth with the ISB, leaders of the ADL and other Jewish organizations kept the Jewish community in the dark, assuring concerned community members that everything was OK. Fitaihi eventually agreed to apologize, privately, in a meeting with Jewish leaders—including the JCRC's Nancy Kaufman—that was closed to the public. A David Project staffer was very forcefully asked to leave when a Jewish leader identified him. And, by arrangement, the apology was never publicized—neither by Boston's Jewish community nor its Muslim community. The Jews of Boston would simply have to rely on their leaders' private judgment.

While the effort to spur the Jewish community leadership to action was going nowhere, the legal challenge and media campaign efforts were moving forward throughout the summer of 2004. They were officially launched in October.

On September 29, 2004, James Policastro filed his lawsuit against the Boston Redevelopment Authority, alleging violations of the Establishment Clause of the U.S. Constitution. On October 6, 2014, Dennis Hale, Steven Cohen, and Ahmed Mansour officially launched Citizens for Peace and Tolerance with a press conference. They outlined their concerns about the ISB's extremist trustees, its ties to the Muslim Brotherhood and terrorism, as well as the City of Boston's unconstitutional provision of city land to the ISB at a discounted price.

The media campaign and the lawsuit began to have an effect. Both the *Boston Herald* and the *Boston Globe* covered the story in a steady drumbeat that resulted in twelve articles between them in the month of October alone. Major outlets like the Associated Press also picked up the story and took it international. Jonathan Wells, the reporter who wrote the original *Herald* articles, was now at Boston's local Fox 25 affiliate, and he worked with Fox 25's investigative reporter Mike Beaudet to produce three investigative segments for the channel's evening news show throughout October and November 2004. These featured some of the new information about the ISB's questionable background discovered by the David Project task force or provided by Steven Emerson.

• • •

I read the news reports about the ISB up at Dartmouth College, two hours north of Boston in Hanover, New Hampshire, where I was starting my junior year. My major was in molecular biology and biochemistry, but national security issues and the phenomenon of Islamist extremism had started to compete for my attention after the start of the Palestinians' Second Intifada in September 2000 and the 9/11 attacks one year later.

Both events happened while I was studying at an international boarding school in Hong Kong, the Li Po Chun United World College—one of over a dozen United World Colleges around the world. The school had, at least back then, a thoroughly globalist leftist bent. The mantra of the place was "international understanding," and sixty-nine of the seventy-one nations represented among the student body, from Sudan to the United Kingdom, got exactly that. The United States and Israel—not so much. When teachers and students wanted to say something nice about my background, they stressed my Russian origin. "You're not really an American, you're from Russia," was a frequent excuse after someone insulted Americans in my presence.

I arrived at the school just ahead of the start of the Intifada in late August 2000, and so did Marwan from the Palestinian territories. This sounds like a clichéd farce, but it's true: Marwan's first order of business was to ask the teacher in charge of his dorm building whether the Jews slept in the same rooms as everyone else, and to announce, Borat-style, but in all seriousness, that he refuses to share a room with a Jew. Then, he began explaining how much he admires Hitler. And yet, the school refused to discipline him in any way beyond a stern private talk. It would have been too politically incorrect—and perhaps physically dangerous—to punish him. Within weeks, Marwan solved the school's unpleasant problem himself when he went back to Jenin to fight in the Intifada as soon as Arafat launched it.

My best friends at the school were a Muslim Afghani refugee who grew up in the Netherlands and a Hindu Tamil from South Africa. In general, the students were mostly awesome and the faculty was overwhelmingly doctrinaire. My English teacher, who was otherwise a very nice person, had renounced her American citizenship because she despised the country.

Being on the other side of the globe from the contiguous United States in the immediate aftermath of 9/11 was tough enough. The recriminations against America and the nearest Americans at hand by a unanimously hostile leftist faculty at my Hong Kong school were tougher. It was as if fifteen Americans had crashed hijacked planes into the tallest building in Afghanistan, all seventeen floors of it, instead of fifteen Saudis doing the same into American landmarks. It was also personal:

"*You* had it coming!"

"*You* can't prove it was Osama Bin Laden."

"*Your* people have been killing Muslims for decades."

"*Your* own CIA did it."

"I heard all *you* Jews didn't show up for work in the World Trade Center that morning."

That last one came from a Pakistani student who was a big fan of 9/11 conspiracy theories and found out about them from the Pakistani press almost as quickly as they were being concocted in real time during the months following the attacks. In another open display of hatred, as we were watching the attacks in real time, an Islamist Jordanian girl who wore a hijab and who had recently gone on an anti-Semitic rant against the school's Israeli students, was openly weeping. Touched, I told her I appreciated her grief for American lives lost in what was obviously to her and to me an attack in the name of her ideology. She told me she couldn't care less about American lives. She was sad that America was now going to massacre her people. Many more Jordanians would be killed in the years ahead by her fellow Islamists than by Americans, including thirty-six guests and the fathers of the bride and groom murdered at a Palestinian wedding party in Amman, as well as a Jordanian Air Force fighter pilot burned alive inside a cage by the Islamic State.

All of this was pretty shocking to experience at nineteen, as was learning about the true hatred at the core of Islamist extremism and the immoral support for it by the globalist left. I spoke up, I complained, I challenged the teachers constantly in front of fellow students. I was expelled from the school three months before graduation for sneaking my girlfriend into my dorm room. Fair punishment or ideological retribution? Reasonable minds might differ.

Anti-Semitism and anti-Americanism from leftists and Islamists at an international school in Hong Kong was one thing; but I never would have imagined that I would encounter genocidal anti-Semitic hatred on an idyllic rural Ivy League campus. By the end of my sophomore year, in 2004, I had become president of the Dartmouth Israel Public Affairs Committee and AIPAC's campus liaison at the College. While researching the history of anti-Israel activity on campus—as AIPAC asked its campus activists to do back then—I came across the website of the Al Nur Dartmouth Muslim Students Association.

Thanks to the pioneering work of Palestinian Media Watch and the Middle East Media Research Institute, I had seen the pre-YouTube-age online videos of fire-breathing Middle Eastern imams yelling about killing Jews in the name of Allah. But, racism in the American South, where my family moved from Siberia when I was ten years old, had seemed back then to be a more immediate threat. I also knew, vaguely, that some of what the Middle Eastern imams were yelling came directly from Islamic scripture, including the infamous line about the Jews hiding behind trees and the Muslims killing them as part of the Islamic version of Armageddon.

I didn't think I'd find that line published by my Muslim classmates on their student group's website. I definitely didn't think that the website would also feature modern commentary by a Pakistani fundamentalist interpreting the passage with relevance for this day and age. According to the Dartmouth Muslim student group's commentator:

When Allah wills, He will give mastery to the Muslims. He will
help them even by means of plants and stones which will assist the

Muslims against the Jews by informing them about the where-
abouts of the Jews. The Jews have predominance over the Muslims
in spite of the fact that they are a minority. But according to this
true narration, the situation will definitely change before the Day of
Resurrection, and the Muslims will dominate the Jews.

The commentator gave a hint as to how this might be accomplished:

In the present-day world, archery has lost its value as it has been
replaced by other inventions like tanks, guns, missiles, atom bombs,
etc. In the present-day context, the injunction of the Noble Koran
[is] to acquire [the] power [and] means [of] manufacturing and
possession of all these devices. It is incumbent on the Muslims that
they equip themselves with all this material and show no careless-
ness in this regard[.] It is incumbent upon the Muslims to over-
power the might and power of the infidels for the glorification of
Islam.

Such hatred, and it being so close to home, reminded me of Marwan, the
Palestinian erstwhile student at my school in Hong Kong who didn't want
to share a room with Jews and who went off to fight in the Second Intifada.
As I wrote back then in the Dartmouth student newspaper: "How can we
expect the Muslim Palestinians to peacefully live side by side with the Jews
in Israel when the Dartmouth Muslim Students Association website calls
for wholesale murder of Jews by Muslims? And how can moderate and
peaceful Muslims deny the false accusations that all Muslims are violent
and hate non-Muslims when the public voice of the Muslim students at
an Ivy League institution seems to suggest otherwise?"

After I published my article in the Dartmouth student newspaper, the
college's Hillel rabbi, Edward Boraz, asked to meet with me. I came into
that meeting thinking that he wanted to find out more about the materials
on the Al Nur website, which impacted the safety of the whole campus
Jewish community. Instead, his first question was: "What motivated you
to go digging through the Al Nur website?" It took me a while to figure
out what was going on, but I was shocked when I realized that the Hillel
rabbi was accusing me of Islamophobia for exposing the vicious Jew-hatred
my classmates decided to put on their website. He did not care about the

Jew-hatred—his concern was for the people who promoted it. Yet another early adult life lesson learned.

The news coming out of Boston about the ISB added to the vague feeling that the anti-Semitic and anti-American hatred I first encountered among foreign Islamists and the globalist left in Hong Kong was now spreading into New England.

· · ·

Meanwhile, I had not been the only one following the news about the ISB. The burst of coverage finally attracted the attention of an elected Boston city government official who was not afraid to stand up to Mayor Menino and the Boston Redevelopment Authority on the issue of the city's problematic land deal with the ISB.

Jerry McDermott grew up in the Boston neighborhood of Allston-Brighton, original home of Aerosmith, and of Michael Bloomberg as a baby. In 2002, he was elected to represent Allston-Brighton on the Boston City Council. Before being elected to the city council, he had spent twelve years as a realtor. After his stint on the council, he would go on to become the executive director for the North Shore branch of Habitat for Humanity. Reading about the city's land deal with the ISB, McDermott immediately saw red flags. As McDermott recounted to me in a thick Boston Irish accent:

> Having some real estate background I saw the price of the land—a city of Boston asset—and then saw what it was being sold for. And that certainly alarmed me. It set off all kinds of questions. And I think my knee jerk reaction probably was much like any taxpayer who wondered why the City of Boston would give away a piece of land that valuable to any group who can afford a twenty-two million dollar building.

Twenty-two million was the proposed cost of the ISB mosque's construction.

McDermott was the chairman of the Boston City Council's Post Audit and Oversight Committee, and he called for a hearing to publicly review the ISB land deal, questioning whether it had been concluded with the best interests of the Boston taxpayers in mind. His goal was to ensure that the ISB paid the full market value of the land—the difference between the $2 million at which it was appraised and the $175,000 that the ISB paid for it.

"Certainly we could use it for all the social service programs that the City is always saying they don't have enough money for," he told me. "Clean up the streets. Clean the parks. Hire some new police officers or firefighters or teachers, or do something, but certainly get the full market value."

As things stood in November 2004, the David Project, after half a year of efforts to challenge the ISB's expansion, had racked up a series of accomplishments. The ISB was on the defense across all fields. Its carefully cultivated relationships with the Jewish community and the broader interfaith organizations of Boston were under strain, though definitely far from ruptured. Its public image had taken hit after hit, with the negative press about its connections to Islamic extremism and terrorism showing no signs of ebbing. Boston's legislature was actively investigating the sweetheart deal the ISB got from the city for the land on which its mega-mosque was being built. Included in that investigation was a look at the role of BRA deputy director and ISB member Muhammad Ali Salaam in arranging the deal. The question of whether the deal was even constitutional under the Establishment Clause was now being litigated in a Massachusetts court.

But the individuals and organizations that joined the David Project task force had no idea what they were getting themselves into. The Islamic Society of Boston would strike back to defend its interests in a way that put on full display the power, ingenuity, and ruthless cynicism of the Muslim Brotherhood movement in the United States.

CHAPTER 4

THE ISB STRIKES BACK

Dennis Hale summed up what happened next: "We hoped that by forming Citizens for Peace and Tolerance, holding our press conference, we would get somebody's attention. We did. We got sued."

It was apparently the Fox 25 coverage that touched a nerve. The ISB's leadership wasn't just being written about; now their faces were being splashed across the evening news. Reporter Mike Beaudet had tracked ISB executive director Yousef Abou-Allaban down with a video camera and did an early morning ambush interview in Abou-Allaban's driveway as he headed to work at his psychiatry practice. Abou-Allaban's psychiatry practice office sign and building façade were also broadcast as B-roll. If the ISB leadership had any hope that the story would fade away, that hope was now gone. And the story had now ignited a Boston City Council investigation of the Boston Redevelopment Authority. So, on May 12, 2005, ISB chairman of the board Osama Kandil and ISB executive director Yousef Abou-Allaban filed a defamation lawsuit against Fox 25.

The lawsuit proceeded through its discovery phase during the summer and fall of 2005. In this phase of civil litigation, plaintiffs and defendants use the subpoena powers of the court to request relevant documents from the other side in order to build their respective cases. The ISB was able to subpoena communications between Fox 25 reporters and members of the David Project task force on the mosque. These revealed the extensive planning that went into the launch of the Citizens for Peace and Tolerance media campaign and Jim Policastro's lawsuit in the fall of 2004. Based on this information, on October 31, 2005, the ISB joined Kandil and Abou-Allaban's lawsuit as an additional plaintiff, and a total of seventeen individuals and organizations were added as defendants. They were Fox 25 and the *Boston Herald*; six journalists from these news organizations who worked on the ISB story; the David Project and its executive director, Anna Kolodner; Bill Sapers and Steven Emerson; as well as Citizens for Peace and Tolerance and its directors, Dennis Hale and Steven Cohen. Ultimately, Ahmed Mansour would be added as the final defendant. The complaint alleged eleven counts of defamation, civil conspiracy, and violation of civil rights. Steven Emerson was served with the lawsuit at the U.S. Capitol in D.C., where he had just given testimony on Saudi-funded extremism in America at the invitation of the Senate.

According to the ISB's complaint, the David Project task force and the journalists working with it committed

> unlawful actions in joining together in a concerted, well-coordinated effort to intimidate Plaintiffs, who are members of the Boston-area Muslim community, to deprive them of their basic rights of free association and the free exercise of their religion guaranteed by the Constitutions of the United States of America and the Commonwealth of Massachusetts.

The complaint went on to state the particular injuries the ISB allegedly suffered:

> The Defendants' campaign has substantially delayed the completion of the ISB's Project. In the wake of the Defendants' attack, donations to the ISB have decreased and many of the ISB's worshippers are reluctant to exercise their religious rights at the ISB, fearing that they too will be branded as terrorists or supporters of terrorism.

Jeff Robbins, a partner at the major Boston law firm Mintz Levin, would represent the David Project in the lawsuit. Robbins was involved in the Jewish community, had followed the David Project's campaign to expose the ISB, and had ambitions of a leadership role in the Jewish community. Robbins believed that the case was going to be a "slugfest," as he termed it, but claimed that he felt compelled to get involved in this fight for free speech out of principle. He minced no words in describing what he thought of the ISB's lawsuit:

"What was, in fact, going on in this case was enormously simple. It was, in my view, an attempt by the Islamic Society of Boston, funded by money from the Middle East, and directed by folks in Washington, D.C., to intimidate several newspapers and private citizens and nonprofits who had had the temerity to criticize the Islamic Society and certain Islamic leaders associated with the Islamic society.

"It was difficult not to conclude that this was all about bullying and about intimidation, and not about any legitimate claim to have been defamed."

Floyd Abrams, one of America's top First Amendment lawyers, felt pretty much the same way as Robbins did when he was introduced to the case. Abrams had successfully represented the *New York Times* in the landmark Pentagon Papers case against the Nixon administration in 1971, and went on to handle many other groundbreaking free speech cases in the following decades. As one of Abrams's colleagues has written about him, "the modern history of the freedom of the press in this country is intimately associated with the career and work of Floyd Abrams." Abrams became the attorney for Steven Emerson and Bill Sapers. He felt that the ISB was misusing the courts and predicted that it would pay a price for it.

It turned out that these hunches were on target. Far from being genuinely aggrieved by slanderous accusations, or being denied the right to worship, the ISB's goals in this lawsuit had been to shut down criticism from the start, when its leaders first came up with the idea. On November 17, 2004, after the flurry of Fox 25 news stories on the ISB's ties to extremism and terror, ISB executive director Yousef Abou-Allaban got an email from Nabeel Khudairi, a local optometrist. Khudairi was active with the Islamic Council of New England, an umbrella group consisting of all mosques and other Islamic organizations in the Boston area. This email seems to have been the origin of the lawsuit idea. Khudairi told Abou-Allaban: "I also suggest the ISB thwart the FOX Libel-and-Sleaze recklessness with a lawsuit."

According to Khudairi, "If FOX is being sued for this story, it stands to reason that they will be prevented from reporting on the story further while the case is in court." The strategy Khudairi outlined seemed clear:

Silence the ISB's critics by abusing libel laws to deny freedom of speech to those media and political activists who dare to stand in the way of the ISB's extremist agenda. Ultimately, prevailing in the lawsuit wouldn't even really be that important. The process would be punishment enough for the ISB's critics.

Unfortunately, the strategy worked exactly as Khudairi predicted it would. Defense lawyers are very risk-averse when it comes to the behavior of their clients. The lawyers for Fox 25 and the *Boston Herald* prevailed upon their clients to cease reporting on the ISB's extremism in order to limit their legal risk, even as more and more information about the ISB's deep involvement with terrorist causes came out during trial. Since the beginning of its coverage in November 2003, the *Boston Herald* had printed nineteen articles exploring the ISB's extremist background. After the lawsuit was filed in November 2005, the *Herald* continued reporting on various aspects of the ISB's land deal with the Boston Redevelopment Authority, as well as on the ISB's libel lawsuit, but its reporting on the ISB's extremism ceased immediately and permanently right up until the present day.

Steven Cohen believes that the *Herald* and Fox 25

weren't interested in litigating this lawsuit. They weren't interested in defending on the merits. They would've been happy to settle quickly and extricate themselves and the ISB assumed that we would do likewise. We, however, were more motivated than the media defendants and at least for a period, we sought to address the underlying principles raised by this lawsuit.

Cohen, a Harvard-trained lawyer himself, felt that the lawsuit strategy pursued by the various legal teams focused too much on technical legal arguments in order to extricate the defendants from the lawsuit as quickly as possible. In the end, the judge wasn't swayed by any of these arguments. Cohen was not surprised, and believed that if he had been defending the David Project, he would have approached the case in a very different way:

Instead of spending over a million dollars on legal fees, on nice legal technical arguments and interesting First Amendment points,

THE ISB STRIKES BACK

we would have handled this litigation on the basis of the merits, which is: What allegations have you folks made and what basis is there for those allegations? In other words, we would have been talking about who the leaders are of the Islamic Society of Boston, what they preach, what their history has been, we would've been talking about the reason that we were concerned and we would've put all of the individuals associated with the Islamic Society of Boston in the docket. They would've been questioned. They would've been cross-examined. We would have learned, and the city of the Boston and the public would have learned a great deal more than we know today.

Charles agreed, but he was stymied from challenging Robbins by the David Project's board. He later lamented: "Robbins had the board mesmerized. But I always imagine if the case had been about who these guys were, who funded them, and what they preached, instead of about technicalities. The ISB would not—and should not—have escaped public scrutiny as easily as it did."

Not only were the merits of the case never discussed in court, the David Project and Citizens for Peace and Tolerance were told by Jeff Robbins and his team at Mintz Levin not to make any public statements about the case because judges do not like parties playing politics with the issues being litigated in their courts. Charles believes it was a major opportunity lost. With the ISB launching a political campaign in the name of religious freedom, and labeling its critics as Islamophobes and racists; those critics were forced to be silent. Indeed, as the lawsuit progressed, the ISB was counterattacking across all the other fronts opened up by the David Project, and it was winning.

The ISB understood very clearly the importance of controlling the narrative. As soon as Bill Sapers started digging into the ISB's deal with the City of Boston in late 2002, the ISB began hiring, one after the other, some of the most high-profile public relations and strategic communications firms in the city. The ISB spent tens of thousands of dollars on its PR efforts. At least five PR firms ended up working for the ISB: Rendon Group, Liberty Square Group, the Nicolazzo and Associates crisis communication group, Farrah Consulting Group, and Howell Communications. Perhaps not coincidentally, because of client conflict of interest rules, none of these top Boston firms was available to help the defendants.

The PR firms had extensive connections within city and state government, and among major Boston media outlets, especially the *Boston Globe*. The *Globe* became the ISB's biggest booster in the media. In 2002, the ISB's then outreach director, Salma Kazmi, was instrumental in convincing the *Globe* to kill the article on the ISB written by Tamar Morad, which the *Globe* had commissioned and paid for. Two weeks after the Citizens for Peace and Tolerance press conference, the *Boston Globe* unleashed a two-day counteroffensive on behalf of the ISB with a prominent article on each day that read pretty much like verbatim ISB PR language. "Islamic group repudiates trustee's anti-Semitic quotes," read the first day's headline. "Islamic group denies ties to extremists" was the headline the following day.

The second day's coverage also included an editorial called "A Moderating Mosque," based on the *Globe* editors' conversation with what the editorial called the "new leadership of the embattled Islamic Society of Boston." The *Globe*'s editors took all of the ISB's claims at face value and reported them as fact, writing, for example, that

> Dr. Yousef Abou-Allaban, chairman of a newly constituted board of directors, promises transparency. The center, he says, is fully under the control of a seven-person local board. Radical and Jihadist speakers will not be provided forums. Donations are scrutinized for ties to possible terror networks. One such donation of $10,000 has already been rejected. And mosque members maintain open relations with local law enforcement, including the FBI.

The ISB leaders had convinced the *Globe* editors that the organization had turned over a new leaf and that the mosque's leadership was

> saying clearly that it wants to join the family of forward-looking religious institutions in the city....The point now, they say, is to move ahead and assume a place as a moderating influence and welcoming presence. There is evidence that the Islamic Society of Boston means to do just that....Bostonians of all faiths should welcome the new mosque and encourage the responsible members to prevail.

All of the promises that the ISB made to the *Boston Globe*'s editors turned out to be false. But the most barefaced ISB lie promoted by the *Globe*—that the organization was now under "new leadership"—was also the main justification the *Globe* used to make its rosy predictions that the ISB will change its ways and become more moderate going forward. That lie could have been easily disproved with a minimum of journalistic effort.

The ISB's trustees had good reasons to want to stay in the shadows. Many of them, such as the trust's chairman, Osama Kandil, and the trust's treasurer, Walid Fitaihi, had serious blemishes on their records, first revealed by *Herald* and Fox 25 reporting. These blemishes weren't going away. In fact, many of the trustees had decided to leave the United States, at least while the lawsuit proceeded, and were living in places like Saudi Arabia, Egypt, and Qatar until things cooled down stateside. But these trustees did not want to leave behind their control of the ISB mosques and the extremist ideology preached there. So, they came up with a shell game.

The ISB Corporation, the legal entity organized in 1982 under Massachusetts corporate law by al-Qaeda financier Abdulrahman Alamoudi, was the original empty shell in this game. It neither legally owns nor in any way controls anything tangible that actually makes up the physical "ISB." The legal title to every tiny bit of the ISB's real and movable property: the land, the buildings, the money in the bank accounts, even the toilet paper in the mosques' bathrooms—all of it—is owned by an entirely different legal entity, the Islamic Society of Boston Trust (ISB Trust).

The ISB Trust exists under Massachusetts trust law, as a matter of official and public record, with the declaration and terms of the trust easily accessible online. According to the trust's terms, the trustees "shall have full power to deal in or with the Trust estate as they see fit," and to change the trust's beneficiaries as they see fit. The empty-shell ISB Corporation, therefore, exists merely as the trust's at-will beneficiary. So it really does not matter who sits on the ISB Corporation's board of directors. Such a board has no more power over the actual, physical "ISB" property than a trust fund kid usually has to raid her nest egg for a big cocaine party.

The Roxbury ISBCC mosque construction project was certainly not "fully under the control" of the new empty-shell ISB Corporation's board of directors, as the *Globe* had told its readers. The directors' role was clearly circumscribed in a legal agreement between the directors and the ISB

Trust, in which the real purpose for the board's creation was laid out: "The Trustees," read the agreement,

> in recognition of their own personal circumstances, which have required the majority of the Trustees to relocate from their previous homes in Greater Boston to various locations overseas, hereby approve the creation, effective June 1, 2004, of a new Board of Directors of the ISB...to serve as a temporary local governing Board of Directors of the ISB...

Although ISB spokesmen insisted to the *Globe* that the newly created local board of directors fully controlled the ISB, the agreement made it clear that all financial, governance, and decision-making authority remained with the ISB Trustees. The directors' allowance was set at $10,000.

Running this shell game, the ISB trustees can always rotate new front men on and off the ISB Corporation's board of directors, trotting fresh faces out in front of the media as the ISB's "new leadership" whenever the ISB brand needs a new makeover. Or, as they ultimately did with the Roxbury ISBCC mosque when it opened, the trustees can add another empty shell to the game, with a new name and a new certificate of incorporation, whose peculiar appearance out of nowhere the *Globe* and other Boston media will be guaranteed to buy without questions.

Absent in this whole scheme is any role for the actual ISB members— that is, ordinary congregants. ISB members do not get a voice through any director or trustee elections. Most of them probably don't even know who their mosques' actual heads are. This makes the ISB fundamentally different from the religious institutions that most Christians and Jews are familiar with, with their vestries, temple boards, and other lay governing committees.

It would have been very easy for the *Globe*'s editors to fact-check and falsify the ISB's claims to them. The *Globe*'s Spotlight Team is the oldest continuously operating investigative journalism unit in the country. Just a few years earlier, the Spotlight Team did not shy away from controversy when it came to uncovering abuses within another religious institution in Boston—the Catholic Church—and were rewarded for their journalistic curiosity with the 2003 Pulitzer Prize for Public Service. The 2015 film

Spotlight, which won that year's Oscar for both Best Picture and Best Original Screenplay, memorialized this investigation. Charles and I would meet with the storied Spotlight Team on July 8, 2009, and would quickly realize that journalistic curiosity was not the prime motivating force behind the *Globe*'s coverage of the ISB. I still have the PowerPoint slides I showed them, all eighty-nine of them. What was supposed to be a half-hour meeting stretched into an almost two-hour presentation about the ISB's connections to Islamist extremism and terror. The Spotlight Team seemed intrigued and asked many questions. The story went nowhere.

Since 9/11, the *Globe*'s editorial policy has seemed to be based on a narrative that American Muslims constitute a "vulnerable minority," who must be protected from criticism—even if such protection involves suppressing certain facts in its coverage and promoting certain dogmatic ideas—that Western culture is racist, that Islam is the religion of peace, that Muslims are victims. As Dennis Hale put it:

> They are reluctant to criticize what they consider to be a vulner-
> able religious minority, because then they will sound like bigots, or
> worse, they'll sound like conservatives, which is an even worse thing
> to happen to you if you're a liberal.

In Hale's experience, "They believed everything the leaders of the ISB told them and nothing that we told them."

Those media that continued publishing stories not helpful to the ISB's PR narrative faced aggressive legal intimidation by the ISB's lawyers. The *Boston Herald* and Fox 25 were already silenced by the ongoing legal litigation. Boston's Jewish newspaper, the *Jewish Advocate*, continued honest coverage of the ISB and still gave Charles Jacobs a platform on its op-ed page. In retaliation, the ISB subpoenaed the *Advocate*'s communications with the David Project and Citizens for Peace and Tolerance. This had a chilling effect on the *Jewish Advocate*'s reporting. Even the ability of the defendants' lawyers to talk about the ISB's case was being aggressively challenged. When Jeff Robbins, the lawyer for the David Project and Citizens for Peace and Tolerance, appeared on Boston commentator Michael Graham's talk radio show to discuss the case, he was shocked at how quickly the ISB's lawyers went after the show's producers:

The ISB's lawyers, after I had been asked to go on a radio show
to talk about the case – within, I think, hours of my appearance
of that show – subpoenaed the tapes of my appearance from the
radio station, following it up with a letter warning the radio station
that they should keep meticulous records of every reference on
that show to the ISB or this matter and that they would be held
accountable. Well, that of course, was an effort to intimidate them
and an effort to intimidate me.

An ISB lawyer wrote to the radio host, Michael Graham:

> Your statements were false, defamatory, irresponsible, and only
> serve to further the agenda of those bigots amongst us who are
> intent upon painting entire communities in intolerant, broad brush
> strokes. [. . .] You would be well served to review the entire public
> record concerning this matter before you broadcast further false
> and defamatory information to your listening audience. Should you
> persist in ignoring information in the public record, my clients will
> have little choice but to protect their legal rights. Please instruct
> your show's producer to keep and maintain the master copy of
> yesterday and today's radio program as well as any future radio
> programs which concern, reference, or mention the ISB.

Graham later told me:

> I do know that when I received a subpoena, not just saying 'We
> want to hear what you said on the air,' but "we want to see who you
> talk to off the air and we want to see your show notes." There were a
> lot of talk show hosts, I received emails, I can't remember now how
> many, but I received quite a few emails of people going, "You're kid-
> ding me right? They did not do that to you right?" I said, "Yeah of
> course they did." "What did you do?" I told them to kiss my burka,
> I'm not gonna give my freakin' show notes to somebody, I don't
> even give my show notes to my boss.

The ISB's leaders and their consultants were experts at cynically manipulating the ideological pressure points of Boston's left-leaning media.

THE ISB STRIKES BACK

Writing in an email to ISB executive director Yousef Abou-Allaban, Boston University professor of mass communications Abdel-Rehman Mohamed gave careful instructions on engineering the race and gender makeup of an image-building press conference the ISB gave in December 2004:

> As I explained, the event has to be super-managed. I will be happy to help in the design of the format, content of messages and style of delivery in particular, as well as the orchestration and flow of the program in general. I suggest that the program presenter should be an indigenous WHITE or African American WOMAN. I suggest that there should be either a Pakistani or Arab Woman who gives a statement as part of the speakers (to negate the stereo-typing). One of the area Imams should be a speaker, I suggest either of the 2 Talibs [two Boston African American imams]. As for the child, I suggest my 12 years old son Ihab because of his color [the Mohamed family is Sudanese], articulate rendering, command of both the Arabic and American English language in which he writes poetry; and his public composure. He had also debated the Fox programs in his school and won the hearts and minds of his class mates who ended up condemning Fox....This is a very crucial matter that there should be rehearsals.

The first step of redefining the narrative was to convince Boston's liberal media that claims of ISB's extremism weren't true. The ISB invested a massive amount of energy into press conferences and outreach efforts led by articulate and sympathetic figureheads. Pleasant women and precocious children of carefully chosen skin color giving extensively rehearsed speeches about peace and love were an effective camouflage for the ISB mosques' extremist and hateful owners. The logical next step that followed was to promote to the media the idea that those making these claims about the ISB were Islamophobic bigots who spread lies about the ISB out of their hatred for Muslims. How could the ISB's critics be suspicious of the women and children trotted out by the ISB—sweet little girls in hijabs who just want to worship in peace? More and more stories promoting this narrative appeared in the Boston media, especially after the ISB filed its lawsuit alleging an Islamophobic conspiracy to deprive its members of their civil rights. And if the ISB's critics were truly bigots, then, it follows, their voices should not be given a platform at all.

As Dennis Hale worried would happen, that is exactly what the Boston media had begun to conclude. "The *Boston Globe* has been closed to us from the very beginning," he said to me.

> During the lawsuit, in response to an article that they wrote that mentions Citizens for Peace and Tolerance, we sent a letter to the *Globe* clarifying some of the things in their article, signed by me, by Steve Cohen, by Ahmed Mansour – they wouldn't publish it. Imagine that. They mention us in their own news article and then they won't publish a letter from us. We have been denied the kind of forum that the ISB routinely gets from the public media and from the city....Even the *Metro*, the subway newspaper, wouldn't publish my letter, and when you can't get into the free subway newspaper, you are really shut out....So it's very hard for us to tell our side of the story, and when we do, sometimes I'm sure people simply dismiss us as the bigots they think we are.

With help from media outlets like the *Boston Globe*, the ISB's media campaign was very successful in neutralizing the David Project's resource-starved and lawyer-constrained media strategy. Meanwhile, the David Project's effort to get the Jewish community leadership on its side—which had been an uphill battle from the beginning—was running into even more trouble. With the ISB's lawsuit shifting the focus from its own extremism to claims of bigotry hurled at its critics, Jewish leaders had become paralyzed. According to Charles Jacobs, "They feared being called Islamophobes. They feared being called bigots. They didn't want to fight, and they didn't know what to do."

For Cohen, betrayal by the Jewish leadership stung the most. "There were many troublesome things about this lawsuit," he said.

> The fact that the suit was brought is troublesome, the way the courts dealt with it was troublesome, the way the press dealt with it was upsetting, but most upsetting of all was the way the Jewish community of Boston reacted to this lawsuit—and in particular the leadership of the Jewish community. All too often, we were made

out to be racists and Islamophobes, and we thought that the Jewish community and its leadership above all would understand our claims, would give us the benefit of the doubt; they would at least investigate the allegations we were making and if they had done so, they would have found that there was a solid factual basis. They didn't do that. They didn't give us the support that we needed and that we deserved. They unfortunately backed off in what amounts to an inoffensive politically correct posture, afraid to offend. They let us down.

Barry Shrage, the president of the Combined Jewish Philanthropies, raised $1 billion for Jewish causes over the course of his tenure. He has always been a strong supporter of Israel, of ensuring Jewish continuity in New England, and of helping the less fortunate of any race or religion. As Charles wrote in the *Jewish Journal* when Shrage retired from the helm of CJP in 2017, "Barry was a fine peacetime leader, good for a community secure in its position in society; but American Jewry is less and less politically secure. Barry's ready and empathetic smile, as well as his great networking and fundraising skills were worse than worthless when external enemies began threatening the community he led. His welcoming smile extended to our enemies, and they took full advantage of it."

Charles Jacobs remembers a meeting with Barry Shrage, Nancy Kaufman, and other CJP/JCRC leaders, at which Jeff Robbins grew increasingly enraged at the JCRC's continuing attempts at outreach to the ISB, and its continuing reluctance to take a public stand: "What are you doing, Barry? They're suing us. We're Jews. You have to help us," Jacobs remembers Robbins thundering. One of the JCRC leaders, startled by the furious tone, burst into tears and ran out of the room. After she was gone, Robbins continued in one of his trademark male anatomy metaphors: "This is pretty flaccid leadership, Barry." According to Jacobs, Shrage visibly blushed in response but did nothing.

Robbins expressed his opinion of Kaufman in a late 2007 email to Charles:

Put simply, her record of purporting to "direct" pro-Israel advocacy over the last 15 years that I have been involved in it here is one of ineptitude, somnolescence, covering up inaction, pretense, and sub-mediocre strategic, tactical and operational performance.

As Robbins later complained to Avi Goldwasser and me:

> The reaction of the Jewish community leadership to the lawsuit
> was troublingly a disposition to view this as something on which
> one should not take sides, which was curious. After all, the evi-
> dence was that certain ISB leaders had supported the murder of
> Jews, and engaged in the most virulently anti-Semitic of writings.
> Under those circumstances, you might imagine when there were
> certain folks in the Jewish community that had the courage to
> raise those issues and they were sued for their troubles; that some-
> thing about the notion of "never again" would penetrate people's
> minds and they would see, with some clarity, what was going on
> here.

Although the Jewish organizational leadership was extremely reluctant to take sides, this fact did not stop defenders of the mosque project from aiming their anger at Jews in general. As Daniel Greenfield at *FrontPage Magazine* has observed, "Leftist [and I would say Islamist] anti-Semitism identifies Jews with an ideological abstraction and then attacks the actual people," who are said to constitute a monolithic conspiracy. Emails sent among ISB leaders and their Islamist allies indicate that they saw most of the organized Jewish community in the same light: as an abstract enemy force oozing the miasma of Islamophobia from their leafy suburbs. It was as if it didn't matter that most of the "organized Jewish community" in Boston was actually on the side of the ISB, or at least taking a neutral position on the controversy.

For example, on July 5, 2006, Nabeel Khudairi, the Boston Muslim activist who first came up with the idea to silence ISB's critics by filing a lawsuit, sent an email to fifty local Islamic leaders, including Boston City official Mohammed Ali Salaam, in which he forwarded a long rant by an active local anti-Semitic conspiracy theorist named Joachim Martillo. Khudairi's email included Martillo's demand that the *Boston Globe* "inves-tigate whether major Boston Jewish community organizations are engaged in [a] criminal conspiracy." Martillo claimed that the Judaism of Boston's

Jewish community "certainly deserves serious criticism, for it consists for the most part of ethnic narcissism, Holocaust obsession and worship of the State of Israel to the point of disloyalty to the USA."

Khudairi's email also included Martillo's proposal to expand the ISB's legal efforts, pitched to the American Civil Liberties Union, which would target "individuals and organizations associated with the Combined Jewish Philanthropies." This new lawsuit would

> seek relief from the organized Jewish community [consisting of] $3[–]5 million to finish the construction of the mosque, multimillions of dollars for the lack of development opportunity in Roxbury, and hundreds of millions of dollars for education to counteract the demonization that the conspirators have undertaken against the American Muslim community.

As part of their campaign against the wider Jewish community, the ISB's lawyers began to target the Anti-Defamation League with subpoenas for evidence of any contact with the David Project and other defendants in the ISB suit. The first subpoena went out in 2005, as the ADL was asking tough questions about the anti-Semitic remarks of ISB Trustee Walid Fitaihi. The second subpoena, sent out in February 2007, was a thinly veiled threat to extend the lawsuit to include the ADL as a defendant—as was a similar subpoena served to Fox 25 that resulted in the addition of the other sixteen defendants to the ISB's suit. The subpoena asked for:

> All documents, including electronic communications between the ADL and any Defendant(s)…[as well as] all documents concerning the Islamic Society of Boston, the Islamic Society of Boston Trust, Dr. Osama Kandil, Dr. Walid Fitahi, Dr. Yousef Abou-Allaban, Yousef al-Qaradawi, Abdurrahman Alamoudi or Mohammed Ali-Salaam.

Once their own organizations and personal affairs were in the crosshairs of the ISB's lawyers, Boston's Jewish leaders finally began to take a stand, rallied behind the David Project, and made a commitment to break off all interfaith collaboration with the ISB while the lawsuit continued. According to Jeff Robbins, they were flaccid no more:

Eventually, and only eventually, the mainstream Jewish organizations stood firm. The American Jewish Committee issued a strong statement. The Combined Jewish Philanthropies issued a strong statement. The ADL, while not issuing a formal statement, at least let it be known publicly that they disapproved of the lawsuit, which is perhaps the least that could be expected from an organization whose charter is to respond to the defamation of the Jewish people.

As it ramped up its attacks against the mainstream Jewish community, the ISB was able to reframe the narrative away from the issues of Islamic extremism and separation of church and state that were at the heart of the original controversy. The ISB could now portray its troubles as an extension of the Jewish-Muslim strife that had been playing out for decades in the Middle East as part of the Arab-Israeli conflict. The campaign to expose the ISB and the retaliatory lawsuit by the ISB's critics was playing out against the backdrop of the Second Intifada raging during the first five years of the twenty-first century and the dramatic Lebanon War waged by Israel against the Hezbollah terror group in the summer of 2006. The ISB was able to exploit the anti-Israel sentiments prevalent among Boston Muslims to rally many of its members by promoting the idea that Boston Jews were out to oppress Boston Muslims, just like Israeli Jews were oppressing the Palestinians. This narrative also made it seem to the majority of Bostonians who were neither Jewish nor Muslim that the ISB controversy was simply an extension of Middle Eastern beefs that didn't concern them.

Late father Raymond Helmick, a Jesuit priest and part-time faculty member in the Boston College Theology Department, was a major figure in promoting this narrative to the broader Boston community. As he said in a videotaped interview: "This is not just about the mosque in Boston, this was about the Middle East." Helmick contributed significantly to the resolution of the Northern Ireland conflict, serving as an intermediary between the Catholic and Protestant sides. Unfortunately, since 1986, Father Helmick had become deeply involved in the left-wing campaign to pressure Israel into making concessions under the guise of conflict resolution mediation.

The biases he had acquired through these inherently anti-Israel and anti-Jewish efforts would show in his approach to the ISB controversy. In an interview he gave to my organization, for example, Helmick defended the good name of Khaled Mashal, the leader of the genocidal terror group Hamas, whose charter calls for the murder of all Jews in the world. "I've talked with Khaled Mashal, the head of Hamas," he told our interviewer matter-of-factly. "He is really at great pains to say that he has great affection for Jews, that he has no problem with them, he has a problem with the occupation."

Yet when it came to the allegations made by the David Project and Citizens for Peace and Tolerance, Helmick fell back on conspiracy theories of a powerful Jewish cabal infected with an immutable hatred of innocent Muslims: "It was a number of individuals—very influential individuals as a matter of fact, very much tied in with major organizations, who were simply incapable of seeing a Muslim without seeing a terrorist."

The narrative was clear, and it was a narrative that the ISB public relations experts ran with: Despite all the evidence to the contrary, including their own words and deeds, ISB officials were portrayed as simply misunderstood lovers of tolerance, who had been smeared by a Jewish opposition incapable of seeing a Muslim without seeing a terrorist. If only there were some open-minded Jews in Boston, the ISB's allies were hinting, who would be willing to embrace the ISB, this whole misunderstanding could be mediated away. Fortunately for the ISB, there were more than enough left-wing Jews in Boston willing to enthusiastically serve this narrative.

· · ·

The Boston Workmen's Circle is an anachronistic holdover from the Jewish Bund–type socialist movements of the late nineteenth and early twentieth centuries. Formed by Bundist Jewish immigrants to the United States, the Workmen's Circle initially opposed Zionism and the creation of Israel as incompatible with its international socialist ideology. After the Six-Day War, it became a vocal opponent of Israel's presence in the disputed Palestinian territories. In Boston, it works together with an even more radical left-wing group called Jewish Voice for Peace, which promotes a one-state solution to the Arab-Israeli conflict, which would see Israel dismantled as a Jewish state and Israelis becoming minorities in an Arab-dominated "Palestine." Even the left-wing JCRC, which was itself co-founded by the Workmen's Circle, was forced to announce, in early

2019, that the Workmen's Circle could no longer remain a JCRC member organization if it continues its support for the anti-Semitic boycott, divestment, and sanctions (BDS) movement against Israel.

The leader of the Workmen's Circle, Michael Felsen, was the ISB's most active Jewish supporter at the time. He took the organization's worldview of oppressor Israeli Jews and their Palestinian victims and folded it into the local ISB controversy. Felsen thus assumed a primary role in pushing the claim in Boston that the ISB leaders were really moderate, and that they were simply victims of Jewish Islamophobes. For example, and similarly to father Helmick, Felsen has claimed access to the minds of the ISB's critics, writing that they are "incapable of believing that the vast majority of American Muslims, including the leadership of the Islamic Society of Boston Cultural Center (ISBCC), are peace-loving citizens."

Jeff Jacoby, the conservative columnist for the *Boston Globe*, wrote extensively about the ISB controversy during the lawsuit. He believes that it is, instead, people who share Felsen's leftist ideology that are incapable of believing certain realities. "It's very interesting," he's said. "There are some people who find it psychically uncomfortable to acknowledge the reality that there are some people in the world who really wish us ill and who would like to destroy us if they could. There are some people who are made deeply, deeply uncomfortable by that reality, and the way they get rid of their discomfort is by denying it, and instead focusing their hostility on those who talk about the threat."

Steve Cohen also rejects this style of deny-and-attack debate. He has said,

> I think that their ideological predispositions were such that they could not even entertain the possibility that our allegations were true. We fit into a certain familiar paradigm in their minds and perhaps it arises from the civil rights movement—that we were simply racists, that we were simply criticizing Muslims out of irrational hatred, and that idea fits so neatly into their familiar, comfortable paradigms that they didn't feel the need to look beyond it. They never looked at our evidence.

Charles Jacobs, at the behest of a fellow Jewish community member, reached out to a local reform rabbi in the hopes of engaging the rabbi in a discussion about the facts of the case. Jacobs wanted to share his documentation about the terrorism-connected ISB trustees and their ideology. The rabbi refused to look at the documents, saying that even to look at them implied bigotry in the viewer. It was as if he was asked to look at child pornography.

I asked Professor Richard Landes about the Boston Jewish left-wing love affair with the ISB. Landes is a historian of millenarian movements and a deep-thinking intellectual who has developed some very original ideas on the dynamic between Islamic extremists and the left-wing Jews who work with them. He frames this relationship dynamic in the terms of game theory, as a strategic interaction of "dupes versus demopaths." A "demopath," according to Landes, is "someone who has no commitment to the values in civil society but systematically uses the discourse of fairness and human rights in order to gain advantages."

> I would say nine out of ten times if you're nice to other people they'll be nice to you. But there are times where your being nice to other people registers as a form of weakness and calls for further violence. And so you end up with a situation in which they will systematically exploit our desire to make concessions because we think we're getting somewhere; and in fact what we're doing is digging ourselves in deeper. You're not making friends; you don't have their respect. You're being used by them.

The defining trait of the "dupes" in the demopath-dupe relationship, according to Landes, is a distorted perception of other people's mind-state—the result of what Landes calls "cognitive egocentrism," which he defines as the projection of one's own beliefs and ways of thinking upon others.

According to Landes,

> Cognitive egocentrism is when you project your mentality onto others. So in the case of leftists like Felsen, they project onto others their basic set of values which is, "we can work it out, positive-sum relations, there's some solution to this that will make us both happy and that we can both voluntarily accept. If I'm nice to you, you'll be nice to me, if I respect you, you'll respect me." So psychologically it's very hard to acknowledge that other people don't share these

values and in fact have values that by our values are bad. I mean, you know, you look at the early founders of democracy of America and they think theocracy is a bad idea and they think that tyranny and dictatorship is a bad idea. Now we're dealing with cultures in which these are not bad ideas. These are the norms and to acknowledge that by our standards these are bad cultures—we can't do that.

Felsen exemplified this phenomenon in a later interview with Americans for Peace and Tolerance, telling our interviewer:

I have to look at our president Obama, who I think really embodies very much of…the message [the] Workmen's Circle embraces…. We're all human, we need to take care of one another, we have differences, we need to understand each other's differences and express them and explore them, but let's focus on what we have in common.

Michael Felsen proved extremely useful to the ISB in helping to rehabilitate Walid Fitaihi, the ISB's anti-Semitic treasurer. As Felsen explained to our interviewer:

We were approached by representatives of the Islamic Society who told us that [Dr. Fitaihi] would like to come back to Boston from Saudi Arabia for the purpose of apologizing to the community. We said, "okay, that sounds like a very interesting thing to do, and we certainly approve of such a move"; and we were happy to host it. And we hosted it in conjunction with father Helmick and other members of the ICPL, the Interreligious Center, as well as members of the Islamic Society -- so we had about 25 people. And Dr. Fitaihi came and made his statement and there was a lot of discussion around the room and the bottom line was that I think all of us interreligiously recognized that there had been wounds—certainly on both sides between the Jewish and Muslim sides that were deep and that needed healing, and that we wanted to be proactive to try and enable that healing—to help that healing.

Fitaihi had refused to make a public apology, and the meeting Felsen described was held behind closed doors. Exactly what he said was only known to the people who attended. Yet Felsen and other leftist Jews hyped the meeting as an "apology to the media"; and the ISB got itself another effective talking point: it was "contrite" over Fitahi's anti-Semitic attacks.

. . .

Members of the David Project taskforce to confront the ISB and Citizens for Peace and Tolerance were losing major ground in the media and on the Jewish community fronts. Their lawyers forced them to minimize their public statements on the ISB during the lawsuit. The lawsuits and accusations of Islamophobia either greatly inhibited or completely silenced media outlets politically willing to report about the ISB's extremism. According to Charles, Boston Herald columnist and radio talk show host Howie Carr, arguably Boston's most outspoken and seasoned gadfly, admitted that he was muzzled by the Herald's lawyers from writing or speaking about the ISB.

Since the late 1970s, Howie Carr had been a major ink-slinging pain in the neck of murderous Boston gangster Whitey Bulger and his brother, longest-ever-serving Massachusetts State Senate president Billy Bulger, whom Carr had dubbed the "Corrupt Midget." Bulger, whose exploits inspired Jack Nicholson's character, Frank Costello, in *The Departed*, allegedly ordered his lieutenant to kill Carr. But Carr kept writing. "If the ISB can silence Howie Carr," Charles often says, "who is crazy enough to speak up?"

Meanwhile, outlets ideologically predisposed to supporting the ISB were pushing the ISB's talking points, fed to them by the ISB's PR guns-for-hire. The mainstream Jewish leadership was paralyzed by accusations of Islamophobia and fear, while the pro-ISB Jewish left in Boston had no qualms about speaking out in support of the ISB. Several dozen young leftist Jews had even formed a group called "Jews Support the Mosque," which actually raised money to be donated to the anti-Semitic ISB Trust.

On the political front, Boston city councilor Jerry McDermott was being railroaded and menaced. Neither the BRA nor the ISB showed up for the hearing of the Post Audit and Oversight Committee. McDermott held it anyway with empty chairs and name signs for BRA and ISB officials. But, that was pretty much all he could do alone, with Mayor Menino unequivocally on the side of the ISB. Jerry began to sense the hostility, as he told me:

You get a distinct feeling in City Hall when you have offended the
Mayor or the administration. This was causing a headache that I
was raising these issues. So you could feel the chill in the air. You
know when your phone calls don't go, they go unreturned for a
while. You get the looks from department heads, the looks on the
elevator. When, you're rocking the boat or upsetting the applecart,
the message is sent. It could be overtly or covertly, but the message
is sent that you're rocking the boat. So that, I would hazard to guess
that some of my colleagues didn't want to upset the applecart.

And then, Jerry began receiving threats from people, including from a
specific large donor to the ISB. He told me that this was pretty much the
last straw:

For me I realized, it didn't take me many months to realize I was
kind of out there all alone sticking my neck out, and the cavalry
wasn't going to ride in and save me. So I've got a wife and kids. I
got calls to the office harassing us and my staff. I got calls to my
house, and I realized that this was certainly, this was serious stuff.
This was hardball. I had one person, who I will not name. I know
who it was, called my house directly, just began talking saying I
have a house for you. How old are your girls? I have a house with
a big yard they could play in. Where do you live now? Where do I
live now? Well they, they know where I live, because now they've
got my number.

McDermott told me that taxi cabs began coming down his dead end
street at night, two to three every night, turning around in his driveway
and driving away. He decided to turn over his investigation to the federal
authorities in Boston.

"They just nodded and said thank you very much for the information,"
he said. "Have a nice day. And that was pretty much it. That's, that's where
it ended. But my sincere hope, and I mean this, is that the Federal government is on the ball."

That hope would be dashed.

•   •   •

Despite the ISB's advantages on all these fronts, the David Project and Citizens for Peace and Tolerance had two powerful weapons on their side: the truth and what is known in litigation as "discovery." With evident satisfaction, Jeff Robbins remembered in a later interview that "the ISB and its leadership, by filing this lawsuit, had thrown the perfect boomerang, an attack on the defendants which had come round to place the ISB and its backers in serious jeopardy." This is because, in order to win its libel case, the ISB couldn't just assert that false statements had defamed it. It had to also prove that it had suffered actual damages, for which the defendants were liable as a consequence of them making those false statements. To do so, it would have to produce evidence from its own records—opening its files not only to the defendants and their lawyers, but potentially to the wider public as well.

The ISB had overreached when it concocted a sob story, as the basis for its lawsuit's damages, about how the defendants' actions had ruined its fundraising and ability to carry out its mission. As a result, it had given the defendants' lawyers a broad range of entryways for probing into the ISB's most secret internal records. And once the lawyers began probing, they realized that what the defendants originally alleged about the ISB's ties to extremism and terrorism had merely scratched the surface of a major component of the global Islamist network, based right in Boston and centered on the ISB. As bad as the defendants thought the ISB leaders were, the organization's own records would show that they were in fact much worse than anyone had imagined.

CHAPTER 5

THE FORTY-ONE BOXES

Overall, the David Project and Citizens for Peace and Tolerance obtained about seventy thousand pages of the ISB's internal emails, fundraising and membership materials, organizational covenants, strategic memos, and—most consequentially—the entirety of the ISB's financial records between 2000 and 2007. Every electrical bill payment, every office supply bill payment, and every ISB transaction with terrorist entities—everything was now in the possession of the people the ISB had sued. In all, the discovery process produced about forty boxes of material. Fully exploring the contents was a daunting task that took several years to complete. Some things were clear immediately; other discoveries required that several pieces of the puzzle be put together before a picture could emerge.

One thing was especially clear: the ISB's claims of being financially damaged were a complete fabrication. The ISB's long-time go-to attorney, Albert Farrah, just four months before he helped file the ISB's legal complaint, wrote in an email that "[f]undraising has been robust and the ISB has $2 million in cash..." Yet in the complaint, he alleged that "the ISB has suffered monetary losses...[a]s a result of the Defendants' conspiracy," and that the ISB had been "intimidated...in its efforts to build the Mosque and Cultural Center."

More than a year earlier, on April 20, 2004, Farrah had established the "ISB Construction Account" on behalf of the ISB Trust at the Southern Bank of New Hampshire. The move out of state was probably made in order to keep the ISB's finances out of reach of any future subpoenas in Massachusetts state courts, as the ISB was already, at that early point in time, considering the option of suing its critics. Fortunately for us, the ISB's lawyers did not realize that the Southern Bank of New Hampshire had a branch just over the border in central Massachusetts, and was therefore subject to the personal jurisdiction—and therefore subpoena power—of Massachusetts's courts. That turned out to be a damaging mistake.

The New Hampshire account was set up in order to "establish a mechanism by which funds from the Account may be withdrawn to make payments due in connection with construction" of the mosque. Once subpoenaed, the bank records revealed that, within the space of fourteen months, centered precisely on the time that the David Project campaign to expose the ISB's terrorist ties was moving into high gear—the ISB had raised $4.2 million of the mosque's eventual $15.6 million price tag and deposited it into the "ISB Construction Account." Indeed, the cash flow increased exponentially immediately following what the ISB's complaint termed the campaign's "crescendo [in] a November 3, 2004 Fox TV broadcast." It might even have been the case, considering the dramatic increase in donations after the Fox 25 reports, that the ISB was able to create a successful fundraising message around its claims of victimization. Certainly, its attorney, Albert Farrah, as the manager of the account from which contractors were being paid, would have been aware of the sudden infusion of cash, even as he was making the opposite claim in court. In these and other ways, the discovery process revealed that the ISB's claims of being harmed were outrageous lies. But the real significance of the discovery documents was the story they told about the true extent of the ISB's involvement in Islamic extremism. Not only were the defendants' claims vindicated, but those claims also proved to be only the tip of the iceberg.

The ISB Trust's bank records revealed just how much the Islamic Society of Boston Cultural Center (ISBCC) mosque in Roxbury was really a Saudi project, bankrolled by the treasurer of the ISB Trust, Walid Fitaihi, and his connections back home in Saudi Arabia. The ISB had always claimed that most of the money held by the ISB Trust for the mosque's construction came from within the local Boston-area community. One of the charges its lawyers made in the libel lawsuit was that the defendants had defamed the ISB by disseminating "false information it was receiving funds 'from Wahabbis and/or Mustlem (sic) Brotherhood and/or other Saudi/Middle Eastern sources.'"

As it turned out, the ISB's own financial records showed that it received at least $8,630,523—over half of the ISB mosque's ultimate $15.6 million price tag—from Saudi and other Gulf State sources between 2000 and 2006. A full $2,387,025 of this money came from Walid Fitaihi and his father, Ahmed. This was chump change for the Fitaihis. Ahmed Fitaihi had just spent the previous decade buying up the most expensive gems on offer at Sotheby's auctions all over the world—the eighty-carat diamond he called "Jedda Bride" for seven million dollars in 1991, the five most expensive pieces of jewelry sold at the winter 1993 Sotheby's sale in St. Moritz, Switzerland, and, in 1995, the one-hundred-carat flawless "Star of Seasons" diamond in Geneva for $16.5 million—at the time, the most anyone ever paid for any piece of jewelry at any auction in the world. That one rock could have paid for the entire cost of the ISBCC, with surplus left over.

The Fitaihis were not the only Saudi bigwigs to back the ISB with their wallets. Saudi prince Bandar bin Sultan, then the Saudi ambassador to the United States, had personally given Yousef Abou-Allaban a $6,400 check. The memo line indicated the check was given on behalf of Bin Sultan's wife, Princess Haifa bint Faisal, who, at the time, happened to also be financially supporting two of the 9/11 hijackers while they were preparing their attacks in the United States. Bin Sultan also dabbled in such things himself, threatening the United Kingdom with terrorist attacks resulting in "loss of British lives on British streets" during a bribery probe into his dealings with British armaments companies.

The ISB had publicly insisted that its wealthy Saudi donors would have no say in the ideology and activities of the ISB's Roxbury mosque. Yet internal minutes from an ISB board of directors meeting on January 14, 2005, reveal that the ISB's leaders privately admitted the possibility that the ISB is "beholden to foreign donor wishes." Sure enough, when Walid Fitaihi was exposed as an anti-Semite, the ISB had very compelling reasons to stand behind him in the face of calls for his dismissal. He, his dad, and his friends in Saudi Arabia paid a large part of the new mosque's price tag, after all.

Moderate American Muslims have long claimed that Saudi and other Gulf foreign donors attach strings when they give money to American mosques, including the ability to shape the mosques' ideology, as well as their choices of imams. Dr. Zuhdi Jasser is an American Muslim of Syrian origin and the founder and president of the American Islamic Forum for Democracy. Jasser spent eleven years as a U.S. Navy doctor, including a stint as an attending physician for the United States Congress. After 9/11, Dr. Jasser began confronting the radical Islamist leaders in his own Muslim community of Phoenix, Arizona. He founded the American Islamic Forum for Democracy "as an effort to provide an American Muslim voice advocating for the preservation of the founding principles of the United States Constitution, liberty and freedom, through the separation of mosque and state."

When I asked Dr. Jasser why patriotic American Muslim leaders like him and Ahmed Mansour cannot successfully challenge Saudi-backed groups like the ISB, he complained about the influence the Saudis have over American mosques:

> The Saudi role in the American Muslim community is very interesting, and the means obviously for most of that role has been financial. But that financial contribution was not only the millions of dollars given to mosques, as in Boston or other cities around the country. It also had to do with influencing the imams and the kind of preaching that was done at those mosques. So that is why it is so hard for lay Muslims like myself to change the activist Muslim community, because the leadership is dyed-in-the-wool Islamist.

In the immediate post-9/11 years, there were many concerns about Saudi Arabia's impact on the radicalization of the American Muslim community. In 2003, experts testifying before Congress claimed that the Saudis had funded around six hundred large Islamic centers and as many as 4,800 small storefront mosques in the U.S. That same year, the United States Commission on International Religious Freedom recommended that

> Congress fund a study to determine whether and how and to the extent to which the Saudi government, members of the royal family or Saudi-funded individuals or institutions are propagating globally a religious ideology that explicitly promotes hate and violence toward members of other religious groups, including disfavored Muslims.

In 2005, Freedom House, the global human rights think tank founded by Eleanor Roosevelt, published a report titled "Saudi Publications on Hate Ideology Fill American Mosques." Nina Shea, the lead author of the report, was then the director of the Center for Religious Freedom at Freedom House. She told me that it was moderate Muslim leaders who most urged her to do her investigation:

> When friends of mine who are Muslim, in America, came to me and said, look you're doing religious freedom, you're dealing with all sorts of issues, but why aren't you speaking up for our religious freedom here at home? They said that they were being drowned out and crushed by this onslaught by Saudi Arabia, this material that is coming here, the imams that are coming here, sent here by Saudi Arabia, and saying that there should be no tolerance for Muslims like us, who are not Wahhabis, that we are not real Muslims and that we deserve to die. Of course, I asked them for samples of what they were talking about, of some of the publications that they were concerned about. And it was very shocking to me at the time to read through these documents and find out that not only were they calling for the killing of moderate Muslims, or non-Wahhabi Muslims, but they were explicitly calling for the killing of Shiites, whom they termed polytheists, and for homosexuals, and for Jews and for infidels at large, different groups of infidels. These documents were calling for war, for jihad, for militant jihad against various infidel groups, and against infidels at large and saying it was the holy duty of Muslims to do that—and these documents were being published by the government of Saudi Arabia, not just some rogue wild-eyed cleric out in the desert somewhere, but basically by the Saudi clerical establishment, by the government, even by the Air Force of Saudi Arabia.

Citizens for Peace and Tolerance discovered three of the books that Shea's investigation identified as Saudi-hate literature in the ISB's library. The ISB also featured an article on its website by controversial Saudi-hate preacher Muhammad Saleh Al-Munajjid on how a Muslim should discipline one's wife and children. Though stressing that a husband and father should use beatings only when all other means of punishment have been exhausted, the ISB's website urged members to "hang up the whip where the members of the household can see it." According to the article, "seeing the means of punishment hanging up will make those who have bad intentions refrain from indulging in bad behavior, lest they get a taste of the punishment." Wives are to be beaten if admonishing them and then refusing to sleep with them doesn't make them stop disobeying their husbands. Children are to be beaten if they don't pray. The article quotes a saying of Muhammad: "Order your children to pray when they are seven years old, and hit them if they do not do so when they are ten."

Along with the terrorist ideology, several of the Saudi and other Gulf donors to the ISB had significant financial connections to terrorism. In late 2005, Walid Fitaihi received, by Swift international wire transfer, the first installment of a $1,000,000 loan to the ISB Trust from the Islamic Development Bank (IDB) in Jeddah—courtesy of the chief of the bank's "special assistance office." The bank describes itself as "an international Islamic financing institution," established "to foster the economic develop- ment and social progress of member countries and Muslim communities individually as well as jointly in accordance with the principles of Shari'ah i.e., Islamic Law." The majority of the bank's financing at the time that it provided the loan to the ISB was contributed by the governments of Saudi Arabia, Iran, and Libya—all countries with long-standing links to international terrorism. At the beginning of the Second Intifada, the IDB was involved in financing Hamas and PLO terrorism, including payments to families of Palestinian suicide bombers, through its management of the Al Quds and Al Aqsa Funds. In August 2001, the Arab daily *Al Sharq Al Awsat* reported that the bank's president personally supervised these terror funds. The paper reported that "the IDB chief said there was no delay in paying financial assistance to the families of Palestinian martyrs."

The ISB received a $50,000 donation from the National Commercial Bank (NCB) of Saudi Arabia. Khalid Bin Mahfouz, the founder and prime benefactor of the specially designated terrorist entity, Muaffaq Foundation, founded the NCB. According to the U.S. government, a 1998 audit found that the bank transferred $3 million to Osama bin Laden through the Muaffaq Foundation.

In 2002, a relatively small donation of $1,458.56 to the ISB came by wire from a group called Lajnat al Dawa al Islamiyyah (LDI), translated as the "Islamic Call Committee." Khalid Sheikh Mohammed, the mastermind of the 9/11 attacks, used to run LDI's offices in Peshawar, Pakistan, from 1988 until 1995. In 2003, the U.S. Treasury Department's Office of Foreign Assets Control (OFAC) designated LDI as a global terrorist entity and made dealing in its assets illegal.

The ISB also claimed in its lawsuit that the defendants defamed it when they supposedly alleged that "the ISB was actually involved in raising money to support oversees [sic] terrorist groups Hamas and Hezbullah" and that "that the ISB not only disseminates extremist ideology, but that they have also taken an active role in supporting various people and organizations that have been a part of some of the most significant terrorist networks in the U.S." However, the ISB's financial records revealed large numbers of checks to Muslim charities that were shut down by the federal government and designated as terrorist entities after 9/11 due to their financial support to global terrorist groups.

For example, the ISB had written $14,907 worth of checks to the Benevolence International Foundation (BIF). BIF functioned as a fundraising and supply arm of al-Qaeda and on November 19, 2002, OFAC designated BIF as a global terrorist entity. Enaam Arnaout, BIF's chief executive officer and a member of the Board of Directors, was then convicted for operating BIF as a racketeering enterprise. Arnaout worked closely with al-Qaeda personnel to procure and deliver war materiel to mujahedeen camps in Bosnia, Chechnya, Ingushetia, Pakistan, and China. The 9/11 Commission report identified the BIF offices in Sarajevo, Bosnia as directly subservient to Osama bin Laden.

The ISB had also written at least $47,430 worth of checks to LIFE for Relief and Development, with memo lines like "Relief for Iraq." On September 18, 2006, the Detroit offices of LIFE were raided by the FBI and IRS, which seized financial and other records. LIFE's public relations coordinator, Muthanna al-Hanooti, was charged with working with Saddam Hussein's Iraqi Intelligence Services (IIS) to facilitate Hussein's operations in the United States in exchange for millions of dollars skimmed from the Oil-For-Food program. The indictment alleges that Saddam "targeted LRD [LIFE for Relief and Development] and…al Hanooti to cooperate with and serve the IIS."

One of the largest beneficiaries of ISB charitable funds, $168,331 in total between 2000 and 2007, was Islamic Relief USA, the American branch of Islamic Relief Worldwide, a British-based charity. The connection between the ISB and Islamic Relief was not just financial, but consisted of shared leadership. In 2006, one of the ISB's trustees, Mohammed Attawia, became the chairman of Islamic Relief USA's board of directors. That same year, Islamic Relief's head of operations in Gaza, Iyaz Ali, was arrested by the Israel Security Agency, admitted to providing material support to Hamas, and was subsequently deported. According to Israel, Islamic Relief's

> activities in Judea, Samaria and the Gaza Strip are carried out by social welfare organizations controlled and staffed by Hamas operatives. The intensive activities of these associations are designed to further Hamas's ideology among the Palestinian population.

In the summer of 2014, the Israeli government banned Islamic Relief Worldwide from operating in the disputed Palestinian territories due to its support for Hamas. In the fall of the same year, the United Arab Emirates designated Islamic Relief as a terrorist group due to its ties to the Muslim Brotherhood and Hamas. In 2016, Britain's HSBC, a bank that's never too shy to help terrorists and drug cartels launder money, dropped Islamic Relief Worldwide as a client due to terrorist financing concerns. The ISB mosques, however, continue to hold regular Islamic Relief USA fundraisers.

The ISB's financial support for the Holy Land Foundation (HLF) later ended up being the most significant revelation in the financial records showing the ISB's support for terrorist charities. From 2000 until December 2001, when it was designated and shut down by federal authorities, the ISB gave $14,221 to HLF. Based in Texas, the Holy Land Foundation was the largest American Muslim charity in the 1990s. Yet, according to the Treasury and Justice departments, the Holy Land Foundation, from its beginning, was a conspiracy meant to function as the primary American fundraising front for Hamas.

In 2004, a federal grand jury indicted the Holy Land Foundation and seven of its top leaders on forty-two terrorism-related charges, including conspiracy, providing material support to a foreign terrorist organization, tax evasion, and money laundering. By the time the David Project and Citizens for Peace and Tolerance's lawyers had started to dig into the ISB's financial records in 2006–7, the United States District Court for the Northern District of Texas had already set the trial of the HLF leaders for the summer of 2007. It promised to be the biggest and most consequential terrorism trial of the post-9/11 era. We were all watching very closely, and we were not disappointed.

• • •

By the spring of 2007, however, the ISB's leaders realized that their lawsuit was not turning out the way they had hoped, and might actually prove more harmful to the plaintiffs than to the defendants—despite the best efforts of the Boston media to whitewash the ISB. The ISB leaders' critical error in this case seems to have been the decision to aim their lawsuit too broadly, instead of keeping it centered on just the media. News organizations are profit-making enterprises, and would have a strong incentive to seek the cheapest resolution, including mediation and settlement favorable to the ISB. In fact, the *Boston Herald* ceased publishing articles about the ISB and its terror links as soon as the lawsuit was filed—and has refrained from saying a bad word about the ISB ever since. The *Herald* had to spend about $400,000 on its defense, and wanted no more of that.

Robbins summed up the problem in this way:

> There is a tendency on the part of the media organizations, whom the ISB had originally sued, to be somewhat timid—if not supine, then certainly not aggressive in dealing with these things. It was only, ironically, when the ISB added the nonprofits, who did not really have the resources to defend themselves, that the ISB and its backers were subjected to a serious counterattack, a counterattack which I think they didn't expect.

Robbins also speculated that the ISB might not have told its lawyers the entire truth about its actual connections to Islamic extremism and terror. He told me and Avi Goldwasser:

> One never knows whether clients tell their lawyers the truth when they bring these cases. I remember a conversation that I had with the ISB's lawyers. "You know," I said, "if you bring this case, you're going to be subjected to serious discovery. You're doing a lot of people a favor when you bring a case like this." And the ISB's lawyer

assured me that they had walked through these various scenarios with their clients and they were assured that there was nothing to hide and nothing to be concerned about. Well, that didn't turn out to be the case. I remember another conversation, well down the road, when I said to one of the ISB's lawyers, "You know, there's a Holy Land Foundation issue in this case." And he looked at me, and with all of the earnestness that he could muster, he told me that he was absolutely confident that there was no connection between the ISB and the Holy Land Foundation. Well, that didn't turn out to be quite true, either.

As the discovery process probed closer and closer to the ISB's sensitive records, the ISB's lawyers tried every legal and not-so-legal maneuver they could to avoid having its secrets revealed to the public. They tried asking the court to designate *all* of the documents obtained by the defendants during discovery as confidential, which would have shielded the material from being made public by the defendants. This strategy failed. The judge ruled that the ISB's documents must be released, due to the significant public interest in seeing the evidence in this very prominent and widely talked-about lawsuit.

The ISB had a backup plan. Even before filing its confidentiality motion, the ISB's leaders began deleting their emails. The ISB's trustees—the actual legal owners of the Cambridge mosque and of the Roxbury construction project—were all in the Middle East, well beyond the range of the subpoena powers of the Massachusetts civil courts. Yet the ISB's figurehead directors, appointed by the trustees in 2004 to shield themselves from scrutiny after the first *Boston Herald* reports, were mostly still in Massachusetts. And they were required by signed agreement with the trustees to stay in constant contact with them. According to the agreement,

> the Directors shall report regularly by telephone, email, and letter to the Trustees about the matters described herein, including furnishing the trustees with complete and accurate monthly financial reports and statements of all ISB income and expenses.

The defendants had the power to subpoena all of these reports and various communications between the ISB directors and trustees, but when the

David Project and Citizens for Peace and Tolerance asked for them, the ISB's directors said that they had nothing to produce. The ISB's directors told the David Project and CPT's lawyers point blank that they had been systematically deleting all the email exchanges between them and the ISB's overseas trustees. A motion for sanctions due to spoliation of evidence was filed by the defense and the judge was to soon rule on it.

Meanwhile, the defendants successfully challenged the ISB trustees' de facto immunity from the discovery process, which they were able to create for themselves by moving abroad during the lawsuit. The sham ISB board of directors and the ISB Trust's legal intricacies might have fooled the *Globe*, but the defendants were able to convince the judge to see through this. In the spring of 2007, the judge in the case ruled that in order for the ISB's case against the defendants to proceed, Massachusetts trust law requires that the individual trustees join the lawsuit as individual plaintiffs and submit themselves to the discovery process.

The ISB asked for time to comply with the court's demand. In truth, the ISB had no intention of complying. Instead, it used this time to stall, while three of its five trustees resigned, avoiding the need to submit to discovery. Walid Fitaihi, who had resisted all pressure to quit the ISB Trust after being exposed as an anti-Semite, filed his resignation. So did another ISB trustee living in Saudi Arabia, Ali Tobah. A trustee who had never received much scrutiny, and who was still living in Cambridge, Mohamed Attawia, was actually fired by the other trustees with an official Notice of Removal—a curious fact noted at the time by David Project and CPT attorneys, and one that would become significant later.

By May 2007, the ISB's case had deteriorated. Court sanctions for deleting emails and other records were very likely to be imposed on the ISB in the near future. And two major deadlines were coming up to comply with court orders that could have proved disastrous to the ISB. First, the court-appointed "Discovery Master" in the case ruled that Mohammed Ali Salaam, the BRA official and ISB leader who arranged an inside deal to give Boston city land to the ISB at a deep discount, was required to submit to discovery and testify at a sworn deposition in early June. Second, the ISB was to turn over all required discovery documents in its possession, also in early June.

The ISB had resisted turning over these discovery documents for over a year. All the documents that the defendants had previously received came from third parties who had no reason not to comply with the defendants' subpoenas—the ISB's banks, the ISB's accountants, the ISB's PR agencies, and so on. Now it was the ISB's turn to comply, and if it had done so, the document dump would have been the largest (at several hundred thousand pages) and the most damaging to the ISB yet.

Instead, the ISB's lawyers approached the defendants' lawyers and offered to drop the lawsuit. On May 29, 2007, the ISB's attorneys signed an agreement stipulating that all of the ISB's "claims in the action…be dismissed with prejudice, without consideration, without costs, and with all rights of appeal waived"—meaning that the ISB could never refile the suit on these same claims. The only concession the defendants agreed to was to urge James Policastro to drop his church/state lawsuit against the BRA. This lawsuit had at first seemed a promising tactic in the overall strategy to challenge the ISB's Roxbury mosque project. The separation of church and state issues raised by the deal—"land in exchange for proselytism of Islam" (in the ISB's own words)—seemed like something that could be easily challenged in court. Yet a judge had already ruled against Policastro on technical grounds. According to the ruling, Policastro had a window of time under the BRA's public comment policy to register his opposition to the land deal. He had failed to do so, and therefore had no standing to sue. As Policastro quipped in reacting to the ruling: "I didn't know there was a statute of limitations on the First Amendment."

Policastro appealed the ruling, but, considering the long odds of that appeal, dropping the case seemed a minor concession compared to the wholesale capitulation of the ISB in its lawsuit against its critics. The legal battle was over.

So, who won?

CHAPTER 6

LAWFARE AND ITS PERILS

A week after the lawsuit was dismissed, on June 6, 2007, the *Wall Street Journal* published an op-ed, "Be Careful of What You Sue For," by Floyd Abrams, the famed First Amendment lawyer who represented Steven Emerson in the ISB's lawsuit. In the op-ed, Abrams recounted the history of several failed libel suits, and concluded that suing for libel or slander "has long been a dangerous enterprise." He then turned to the ISB case specifically.

> On May 29 of this year, the potential vulnerability of a plaintiff that misuses the courts to sue for libel once again surfaced when the Islamic Society of Boston abandoned a libel action it had commenced... [.] The case was dropped. No money was paid by the defendants, no apologies offered, and no limits on their future speech imposed....While all the ultimate consequences to the Islamic Society for bringing the lawsuit remain uncertain, any adverse consequences could have been avoided by not suing in the first place.

It is clear why the ISB chose to end their lawsuit; the discovery process was exposing them to significant risks. But why did the David Project and Citizens for Peace and Tolerance agree to settle? They could have refused, demanding that they get their day in court, or at the very least to get a chance at recovering attorneys' fees. They had so much to gain by fighting the lawsuit on the merits, and in prolonging the very fruitful discovery process. In fact, many of the principal defendants were left deeply unsatisfied with its resolution, among them Steve Cohen, the Harvard-trained lawyer, who described accepting the ISB's offer as a "lost opportunity," a "failure," and a "tragedy." "Frankly," he said,

> if the Islamic Society of Boston was who they said they were, they should have welcomed this opportunity to make their case. This is exactly what we all believe in, the opportunity to get in front of the public, in front of the judge, in front of the press, in front of the people and make your case and expose yourself to cross examination. This is how truth comes out. It's a great system if it's allowed to run its course. We didn't allow it to run its course.

Unfortunately, money ended up the key factor, especially for the people who were paying it—the David Project's board of directors, which included some of the organization's largest donors. The costs of the lawsuit weren't just piling up for the ISB; they were also piling up for the defendants—who could not look to the Saudis to bail them out. Resources were limited, and financial pressures pushed the David Project's directors to welcome the opportunity to end to the lawsuit. Cohen recounted those pressures:

> There were certain individual defendants who were…scared. They were afraid that they might lose their homes [or] their life savings. They believed that we would win, but they were afraid of the horrific consequences if, God forbid, we should lose, and so they also were bringing pressure to extricate themselves from the lawsuit as quickly as possible.

The David Project's donors, especially the big donors on its board, did not want to continue paying huge legal fees for a cause they had come to see as being somewhat outside the David Project's original mission of pro-Israel advocacy. And the costs were getting bigger and bigger. By May 2007, the David Project had racked up more than a million dollars in legal fees from Robbins. The David Project had liability insurance that covered the costs of defending the organization against any potential libel claim. For the past year, however, its insurer, Zurich Insurance Company, had not been paying Mintz Levin's invoices. The law firm was looking at over half a million dollars of unpaid work, and Jeff Robbins was worried that Zurich would never pay it.

He was right to worry: three months after the ISB dropped the lawsuit, Zurich refused to pay much more than what it had paid so far, around $399,000. Zurich had commissioned an independent law firm, Mechler, to analyze Mintz Levin's work for the David Project and CPT. Mechler's analysis claimed that the company was only obligated to pay only $85,000 of the remainder. Zurich, in essence, used the "Islamophobia" claims made by the ISB as an excuse not to pay up. According to the insurance company's representative, Robbins was engaging in "affirmative actions designed to prevent the building of the mosque and community center, and not related to the defense of the defamation lawsuit filed by the ISB." Zurich also accused Robbins of padding his invoices, noting that "there were many instances of clerical work being improperly billed, [which] should be considered overhead," that is, not billed to the client in the first place.

The argument went that since so much of Robbins's investigation and discovery work was in support of this supposed ulterior motive, or even improperly billed firm overhead, Zurich was under no obligation to pay for it. The Zurich legal analysis even noted Robbins's eagerness to be in the media spotlight, where he harshly criticized the ISB, as evidence that he was playing politics and not defending against a libel accusation.

It was at this point that Jeff Robbins first betrayed his clients. Far from getting him accolades in the Jewish community as a white knight, as he had appeared to hope when he took on the case, the left-wing Jewish community in Massachusetts attacked the David Project and its lawyers. The judge in the David Project's public records lawsuit against the Boston Redevelopment Agency savaged Robbins in his opinion in the case, and implied that his clients were motivated by bigotry. Even worse, Robbins was costing the firm significant good will among leftist Massachusetts politicians, who almost unanimously supported the mosque. It is a well-known fact that Mintz Levin does major business with Massachusetts politicians. The law firm has a large lobbying arm, ML Strategies, where good will from Massachusetts politicians is the bread and butter. According to two sources closely familiar with the firm, including one who spoke against interest, Robbins's partners were furious with him for dragging the partnership into opposing Mayor Menino and his mosque; and for his public attacks on a Muslim house of worship, which tarnished the firm's image. Pressure built on Jeff Robbins to extricate himself from representing his so-called Islamophobic clients.

When Zurich refused to pay Mintz Levin's fees for representing the David Project, Jeff was in a pickle. With his partners already annoyed at the drain in resources and good will from having the ISB's enemies as the firm's clients, Jeff now had to drop the news that the firm might even have to take close to a half-million hit to its profits thanks to him. Before letting his partners know, Jeff drafted a formal written demand letter that would have been required by law as a first step to sue Zurich under the Massachusetts Consumer Protection Act. A credible threat of this type of lawsuit significantly harms an insurer's bargaining position in denying a claim, but, to his surprise, Jeff's partners wouldn't let him send it. As it turned out, Mintz Levin represents insurance companies seeking to avoid large payouts to their clients—including Liberty Mutual in asbestos litigation. As Jeff's partner, Joe Blute, wrote to Jeff on August 31, 2007, three months after the lawsuit was over:

> Jeff, the problem is simply ML being adverse to liability insurers
> on issues that we deal with in our insurance practice on behalf of
> insurers. As I understand it, and I am copying Pat Sharkey on this
> email should we need his advice, the firm's policy is not to take
> on matters that would put us in an adversarial relationship with
> liability insurers on coverage issues because of the risks of being
> embarrassed by "issue conflicts" with our clients – notably Liberty
> Mutual. That representation sometimes requires us to play the role
> that Mechler is playing here and to challenge the reasonableness
> and necessity of fees in a given case. . . [.] Because of Kim's work
> over the years and our recent work for Liberty in asbestos matters,
> ML is perceived in the industry as being closely aligned with the
> insurer side. From a practice development standpoint, given the
> relatively small number of insurers, it presents difficulties for us
> when an adversarial relationship develops with a significant player
> such as Zurich.

In other words, it would be embarrassing for the firm's insurance clients to have its lawyers publicly, in litigation against a big insurance corporation, contradict themselves on behalf of a tiny and costly client like the David Project. Pat Sharkey, Mintz Levin's legal ethics expert chimed into the conversation. However, his concern in this case was not with legal ethics, but with the firm's bottom line:

> Didn't the firm have a recent experience losing an insurer client because we were representing a client where coverage payment issues arose between the insurer/client which became a catalyst for the insurer terminating our services? Are we risking a client relationship with Zurich by sending the letter?

Joe Blute replied that, although Zurich is not a client of the firm,

> [t]he problem is the more general problem of taking positions adverse to liability insurers on issues where our clients, such as Liberty and AIG, would take different positions....This is a hot button issue, one that we have litigated on Liberty's behalf and one that is squarely presented here, i.e., a classic "issue conflict." At a minimum, it would create client relations issues with existing clients...

And so, Jeff Robbins did not send his letter threatening litigation on behalf of the David Project. Instead, he urged Charles to let him bargain for a settlement. The threat of litigation, potentially embarrassing for his firm's other clients, was off the table in the settlement negotiations, significantly lowering the David Project's bargaining power. I will not second-guess Robbins's negotiation with Zurich. He managed to get another $350,000 out of the insurer, although this still left the David Project on the hook for over a quarter of a million to Mintz Levin. But Robbins was rigidly obligated, under the Massachusetts Rules of Professional Conduct, whenever there is even an appearance of a conflict of interest between himself and a client, to disclose that conflict to the client. This includes the "issue conflict" that Mintz Levin partner Joe Blute admitted existed with the David Project, especially when the conflict of the lawyer and the client's respective interests is, as here, financial.

Jeff was obligated to inform the David Project, specifically Charles as its principal officer, of this conflict of interest and to counsel Charles to find an independent attorney for the matter in which the conflict of interest exists. Jeff did not reveal the conflict of interest to Charles. Instead, he hawked Charles for money throughout the end of 2007, complaining that he is "getting blasted, not wrongly, for balances so long after the fact," and telling Charles, "The Firm is all over me, and they are more than entitled to be unhappy." The David Project paid up, none the wiser to its attorney's betrayal of loyalty.

• • •

Meanwhile, the ISB launched its own public relations campaign to announce the end of the lawsuit. The ISB claimed victory, since it had all but succeeded in building the Roxbury mosque. The *Globe* celebrated the lawsuit's dismissal as a victory for tolerance and multiculturalism. On June 9, 2007, two weeks after it dropped all its claims against the defendants, the ISB held a daylong celebration. The celebration was dubbed the Faith and Unity March, and it concluded with a ceremonial installation of the dome cap on the Roxbury mosque's minaret—in a symbolic expression of perseverance and victory, as the first call to prayer sounded from the minaret tower.

Leading the ceremonies was a fresh young face representing a new organization, the executive director of the Muslim American Society of Boston, Bilal Kaleem. The Muslim American Society (MAS) is a national organization that had long had an unofficial presence in Boston. In 2002, MAS Boston leaders met with the ISB Trust to propose an informal merger of the two groups. According to the 2002 annual meeting notes of the ISB trustees, obtained in the ISB lawsuit discovery process: "The [ISB-MAS] relationship is a marriage and presently it is in the engagement phase. MAS shall run the day-to-day operations while the…[ISB Board of Trustees] should be entrusted to oversee security and finance."

The "marriage" relationship was consummated after the ISB's terror connections were first exposed, and a new organizational face was needed to confuse the media. The sham ISB board of directors, with its bumbling executive director, Yousef Abou-Allaban, was not going to cut it. The time came to add another empty shell to the ISB Trust's long-time game. In

October 2004, immediately following the initial Fox 25 news reports on the ISB's extremist connections, several ISB leaders incorporated the Boston branch of the Muslim American Society. Soon thereafter, MAS Boston gradually absorbed the public relations functions of the ISB, while ISB leaders assumed leadership positions in MAS Boston. In the summer of 2007, after the lawsuit was over, the ISB Board of Trustees took on three additional members, all with leadership positions in MAS. Two, Sameh El Difrawi and Hassan Al Alami, were top leaders in the Muslim American Society's Boston branch, and one, Jamal Badawi, was the founder of MAS National. At the same time, MAS Boston assumed all management responsibilities of the Islamic Society of Boston Cultural Center in Roxbury. The marriage was complete and from that point on, the ISB Trust was, again, nowhere to be seen. The ISB corporate board of directors was nominally in charge at the Cambridge mosque, and the Islamic Society of Boston Cultural Center, or ISBCC, managed by MAS Boston, became the new brand name of the Roxbury mosque. But control has always, from the beginning and until now, remained in the hands of the ISB Trust. Fitaihi's resignation as a trustee of the ISB turned out to be a con, whether to fool the *Globe* that the ISB had turned over a new leaf, or to avoid personal discovery in the lawsuit. As soon as the lawsuit was over, he was added back to the board of trustees, where he continues to remain.

The Muslim American Society, though, seemed like a poor choice for the rebranding of the Islamic Society of Boston. A month after the Boston branch of MAS was incorporated, the *Chicago Tribune* published an article revealing that the Muslim American Society was "created to be a more public face of the [Muslim] Brotherhood in the U.S.," with the goal of "achieving Islamic rule in America." The article, titled "A rare look at secretive Brotherhood in America," described how the MAS recruited thousands of American Muslims into the Muslim Brotherhood through an "active member" training program that makes the recruit "complete five years of Muslim community service and education...which urge[s] jihad, martyrdom and the creation of Islamic states." Before he was promoted to executive director of the Muslim American Society of Boston, Bilal Kaleem was the head of the MAS Boston training program in Islamic extremist indoctrination. He admitted to having gone through the training program himself, claiming that it was for him "the single most transformative experience in Islamic and personal development."

While the ISB's rebranding to MAS Boston and the choice of Kaleem as its public face was a gamble, it ended up paying off. By the time the Muslim American Society's status as the American face of the Muslim Brotherhood became known, Boston media outlets like the *Globe* were ideologically hostile to telling the truth about the ISB, or, like the *Herald*, were silenced by lawsuits and lawyers. Although he was indoctrinated in Islamic extremist ideology during his MAS training, Kaleem was, at the same time, a very attractive and charismatic spokesperson, precisely the kind of personality to bedazzle the pliant Boston media and the city's interfaith "leaders."

Kaleem, an Indian American Muslim, was born in America, grew up in Brooklyn, and got his undergraduate and master's degrees in computer science from MIT. Intelligent, handsome, and articulate, Kaleem was a potent PR weapon for the ISB. He proved to be so in his first moment in the spotlight that day in June 2007 when he successfully emceed the Faith and Unity March as a celebration of the ISB's victory over the David Project and CPT. His involvement in MAS Boston since his student days demonstrates the potential that the Muslim Brotherhood sees in America: a prime recruiting ground not only among immigrant Muslims from the Middle East and Asia, but also among those born and raised in the United States.

"This is a very happy day for us and we see it as a day of victory," announced Kaleem at the Faith and Unity March. He then introduced Yousef Abou-Allaban, the executive director of the ISB. "[T]he Islamic Society of Boston Cultural Center is pleased to announce to the community," Abou-Allaban told the gathered crowd, "its victory in protecting the right to build an Islamic Center and house of worship and to stop harassment and intimidation of Muslims in the U.S. We have stood up for our constitutional and civil rights. We have defended our principles and we have asserted our need to build a house of worship without fear of persecution. We have achieved what we set out to do."

The ISB's leaders might have failed at entirely silencing their critics, but they certainly accomplished quite a bit. As Steve Cohen noted: "Unfortunately, the way it played out in the press, it was not perceived as a victory for us and having never had the opportunity to demonstrate the truth of our allegations, the outcome was ambiguous and I think accomplished very little."

Charles remains concerned about the precedent set by the ISB's lawsuit. "The biggest danger in all of this is intimidation," he has said.

> Americans are told, "If you see something dangerous on the street now, call somebody, tell somebody if you see a strange behavior, because we're all under this threat of terrorism." Well—we saw, we called, we got sued. Who's going to call again? Who's going to speak out again?

Boston's media and civic leaders had accepted the ISB's narrative that it was a peace-loving organization under assault by bigots. Most of the city's media breathlessly reported on the ISB's minaret capping ceremony as a joyous occasion for the city and a victory of good over evil. The *Christian Science Monitor* published an article titled "Boston mosque rises above the fray." Ostensibly writing as an objective news reporter, *Christian Science Monitor* staff writer Jane Lampman portrayed the ISB's leaders as responsible and admirable community leaders, while labeling its critics—Ahmed Mansour and others at the David Project and Citizens for Peace and Tolerance—as "some people who see the Muslim presence itself as a threat and US Muslims as under suspicion."

Boston's ABC affiliate ran a special report on its flagship news program, "Channel 5 Chronicle," called "The Making of a Mosque." The lead journalist on the report, Mary Robertson, started the show with the assertion that the ISB's victory celebration was "a day of triumph for Islam in America." According to Robertson, "The message at the new mosque on this day is one of peace, tolerance, and learning to thrive . . ." She then directly attacked Charles and the David Project, pointing out that while "[to] many Boston Jews, Jacobs is a hero for keeping the ISB under scrutiny, others complained he is a trouble maker and the David Project has overstepped its bounds."

· · ·

Jacobs was indeed a hero to me, even before I knew him personally, precisely because he was a "trouble maker"—someone willing to speak truth to power. Leftist Jews at Dartmouth, like the Hillel rabbi Edward Boraz, were also calling me a troublemaker for pointing out that an Islamist student website at my college was calling for a new Holocaust. I saw such attacks as validation of my efforts. I met Charles in late spring of 2007 in New York after graduating from Dartmouth in 2006. Shortly after, he gave me a temporary summer position to research the ISB case and the tens of thousands of pages of discovery documents that it produced.

What we found out during that summer of research impelled us all to take a leap toward a permanent effort focused on the threat of Islamist extremism in New England. The ISB was here to stay in Boston. The ISBCC mosque would be built. But we would also be vigilant in keeping an eye on the ISB and exposing its efforts to indoctrinate Boston's historically moderate Muslim community. As Supreme Court Justice Louis Brandeis said: "Publicity is justly commended as a remedy for social and industrial diseases. Sunlight is said to be the best of disinfectants; electric light the most efficient policeman."

. . .

I did not fully realize how deep the failure of Jewish leadership in Boston extended. It was indisputable that Charles and the David Project had made life uncomfortable for them—forcing them to choose between defending a Jewish organization from attacks by anti-Semites, and the politically easier choice of bowing to the media narrative of Muslims being attacked by right-wing Jews. Most of them chose the easy way out.

But some Jewish leaders did not. The American Jewish Committee's Boston branch was now being led by Robert Leikind, the former executive director of the Anti-Defamation League in New England, who was deceived by the ISB's interfaith outreach, betrayed by Walid Fitaihi's anti-Semitic screeds, and threatened with legal action if the ADL continued to complain about those screeds. The American Jewish Committee (AJC) reacted to the end of the *Islamic Soc. of Boston v. David Project* litigation with a press release that slammed the ISB for bringing its predatory lawsuit in the first place. The national organization's executive director, David Harris said: "The ISB lawsuit had been a blatant attempt to chill American citizens from exercising their fundamental First Amendment rights – the right to engage in free speech, the right to raise important public policy issues and the right to communicate their concerns to the general public."

By contrast, the local Anti-Defamation League adopted a policy of saying nothing about the ISB one way or the other. Staffers in its Boston office have said that, although the ISB's anti-Semitic and Islamic extremist ties remained a significant concern for the organization, they were under strict orders to keep quiet; orders that came from the ADL's executive director, Abraham Foxman himself. The ADL's own reports identified the Muslim American Society—the new front group being represented as the fresh face of the ISB—as an organization that "has a troubling history of associations with radical organizations and individuals that promote terrorism, anti-Semitism and reject Israel's right to exist." But the ADL would not confront the MAS in Boston, and would later scrub that report from its website without explanation—or any obvious overt pressure to do so.

Most other Boston Jewish groups rushed to embrace ISB the moment the lawsuit ended. On September 12, 2007, when the first day of Ramadan coincided with the first day of Rosh Hashanah, twenty Jewish leaders and twenty Muslim leaders affiliated with the ISB signed a statement called "Building a Community of Trust":

"We, members of the Jewish and Muslim communities, seek to build trust and mutual understanding and strive to forge positive relationships between our respective communities," the Jewish-Muslim statement declared.

First on the list of the Muslim signatories was none other than Nabeel Khudairi, the man who orchestrated the ISB's lawsuit and spread anti-Semitic attacks against Boston's Jewish leaders among the Muslim community. Most of the other Muslim signatories were also problematic: a couple of al-Qaeda terrorist supporters, an alleged terrorist financier—more on them later. That did not prevent Jewish leaders from taking their claims of friendship at face value.

While most of the Jewish signatories were far-left activists like Michael Felsen of the Workmen's Circle, the list also included more prominent and politically mainstream Jewish leaders, among them Rabbi Eric Gurvis, then the president of the Massachusetts Board of Rabbis, and Rabbi Ronne Friedman, the rabbi of Boston's largest synagogue, who eagerly sought dialogue with the anti-Semitic ISB treasurer Walid Fitaihi, and now eagerly came back for seconds. Also on the list was Alan Solomont—top official of the Combined Jewish Philanthropies, nursing home operator, former chair of the Democratic National Committee, major Democrat fundraiser, Obama's ambassador to Spain, and a dean at Tufts University.

The endorsement of the ISB by these mainstream Jewish leaders gave Nancy Kaufman, the executive director of the Jewish Community Relations Council, the political leeway she needed in order to reengage with the ISB. Kaufman had been forced to keep her distance during the lawsuit, but was now under immense pressure from her liberal allies on the politically influential Greater Boston Interfaith Council (GBIO) to embrace the ISB, which had many supporters within the organization.

Shortly after the "Building a Community of Trust" statement was signed, Kaufman called for a meeting between Jewish leaders and the heads of the new ISB front group, MAS Boston, to take place at the JCRC office building in downtown Boston. Charles Jacobs sent me to attend this meeting. Most of the JCRC's top leadership was there, as well as representatives from the Workmen's Circle and other leftist groups. Most significantly, the Anti-Defamation League and the American Jewish Committee refused to attend. Bilal Kaleem and Hossam Al Jabri, respectively the director and the president of MAS Boston, represented the ISB.

Kaleem began his presentation with a speech legitimizing the Muslim Brotherhood as an idealistic organization fighting colonialism and Arab dictatorships. He claimed that Yusuf al-Qaradawi, despite his approval of suicide bombings in Israel, has still been a very positive influence on the Muslim community overall. Qaradawi might have called for the murder of all the Jews, "down to the last one," but according to Kaleem, Qaradawi's work "is very helpful to those living as minorities in the West and so you find him referenced and looked to a lot by many, including MAS."

Bilal Kaleem was thus legitimizing the most virulent Islamic sources of hatred for Jews in the world today—and only one of these Boston Jewish leaders questioned any of his assertions. In fact, another of the Jewish attendees at the meeting handed out a then-recently published article from *Foreign Policy* titled "The Moderate Muslim Brotherhood." As the title suggested, the article claimed that the extremist organization was a force for good in the Middle East. The article's assertions have since been embarrassingly demolished by the Muslim Brotherhood's subsequent behavior, which has caused it to be shunned in Muslim countries, and even banned in Saudi Arabia.

No tough questions were asked of Kaleem and Al Jabri, and many of the questions that were asked were inane. Though I hadn't planned on speaking, Nancy Kaufman suggested that I ask a question. Since I had recently learned that Hossam Al Jabri was a large donor to the Holy Land Foundation—the Hamas charity whose trial was then in progress—I decided to ask him about the case: "Mr. Al Jabri, your name appears on U.S. government exhibits in the Holy Land Foundation Hamas fundraising trial..."

"No it doesn't," he snapped back. "Not that I'm aware of."

I could feel the "stink eyes" focused on me from everywhere around the room as some of the Jewish leaders audibly groaned. These people desperately wanted to avoid conflict and had carefully cultivated their own narratives about the ISB's nature. They would not be deterred by the facts, and would attack those who raised uncomfortable questions. But I continued to press Al Jabri, the Jewish leaders' embarrassment notwithstanding: "So the question is, do you and does MAS see Hamas as a terrorist organization?"

Al Jabri refused to call Hamas a terrorist organization, launching into the usual equivocations that Hamas fanboys tend to use when asked that question:

> We do not agree with the suicide bombings and the attacks that Hamas does. Now there are many other aspects of Hamas other than this and there are many other aspects about the Israeli-Palestinian conflict that it would just be unreasonable and unethical for me to just address that piece. The Israeli-Palestinian conflict is very complicated. There is a lot of wrong that happens on both sides. We at MAS, I as president of MAS Boston, am against the suicide bombings that Hamas does but that's not the only people that bear responsibility, because there are many killings that happen from the other side that we believe are unjustified, and that we believe are unethical. So it would not make sense for me to single out Hamas in that perspective.

Only one Jewish leader challenged Al Jabri's refusal to condemn Hamas and Qaradawi. All the others seemed completely fine with his claim that there are "many aspects" to Hamas and Qaradawi that are "positive," which morally cancel out, or even overcome, the negatives. Orthodox rabbi Gershon Gewirtz from Young Israel of Brookline, however, quite eloquently destroyed that premise, telling Al Jabri:

> If someone kills, I don't care how much of a philanthropist he is. He's a murderer and I don't want to have anything to do with him. To suggest that we can look away from that for me is something that is totally beyond any level of acceptability. I just can't abide that kind of approach. If someone's a murderer, I don't feel at all guilty about it.

He challenged the JCRC's ISB/MAS guests: "I'd like your reflection on the formulation presented." Kaleem and Al Jabri dodged the challenge.

After the meeting was over, I confronted Hossam Al Jabri in front of Nancy Kaufman with the Holy Land Foundation trial exhibit identifying Al Jabri as a large donor to the Hamas front. He played dumb and she pretty much did too. She was not going to let an inconvenient truth get in the way of her interfaith embrace. Shortly thereafter, she and Bilal Kaleem teamed up to together to emcee the Greater Boston Interfaith Organization's tenth anniversary gala celebration. Leading the ceremonies with them were Boston mayor Thomas Menino, Massachusetts governor Deval Patrick, and Speaker of the House Salvatore DiMasi as honored guests. The ISB/MAS now had full backing from the JCRC and from Boston's political and religious elites. Charles Jacobs fumed, "Nancy Kaufman sold us for a mess of progressive pottage."

Back then, I had asked Richard Landes, the historian of millenarianism what he thought about my experience in that meeting with Hossam Al Jabri and Bilal Kaleem. He told me that the behavior of Jewish leaders like Nancy Kaufman and Moshe Waldoks, was basic utopianism. "Negotiations are the way to a positive-sum voluntary solution to a conflict," said Landes.

> So of course people want to negotiate. And we don't want to go to war. All these guys on the left are what I call secular millenniallists. They all want to live in a world where swords have *already* been beaten into plowshares, and spears into pruning hooks. They want to live in a world where we're all nice to each other, which would be nice, but we're not there, and to pretend that we *are* there can lead to catastrophe. You asked a challenging question and immediately

some of the Jews there came in to defend the person you were challenging. They're embarrassed by your challenge. We don't want to believe that this mosque could be, may well be, a spearhead for a ferociously anti-Western ideology.

CHAPTER 7

"THEY'RE HERE"

C harles and Avi had hired me exactly a day before the ISB dropped its lawsuit. When I found out about the news, I called Avi and asked him whether I still had my job. "The job just got bigger," was his answer. Shortly after joining the David Project, I was speaking with Bill Sapers, who was in a reflective mood and thinking about what would come next: "So they called off the lawsuit and most of us are sitting back and saying, 'Well, that's all done. We don't have to worry about a thing.' That's absolutely wrong. We've got to continue to expose them."

While the media organizations sued by the ISB folded their tents and withdrew from the battlefield, the activists at the David Project and at Citizens for Peace and Tolerance—soon to be rebranded as Americans for Peace and Tolerance (APT)—were still very far from done, and none more so than Charles Jacobs.

Charles did not give up easily. Raised in working-class Newark, New Jersey, he grew up tougher than the average middle class Jewish kid. As a student at Rutgers, he got involved with the civil rights movement and marched in Washington, where he watched Dr. Martin Luther King, Jr., give his "I Have a Dream" speech. Through the civil rights movement, he became involved in left-wing student anti-war politics as a member of Students for a Democratic Society (SDS). He remembers meeting Bill Ayers and Bernardine Dohrn at the June 1969 SDS convention, where

Ayers and Dohrn led the revolt by the ultra-radical faction of SDS that became known as the "Weather Underground" terrorist group.

Charles left the hard left when it turned against Israel. "They told me, in true Marxist fashion, that the Arab and Jewish working classes would join together and fight off the Western colonial powers—and that this would bring peace. That was the moment I realized they were delusional."

After earning a doctorate in education at Harvard University, he settled down in Boston, met his wife, and accepted a well-paying business management consulting job. He was enjoying a comfortable suburban family life when, in 1989, growing alarmed and disgusted with the *Boston Globe's* biased reporting on Israel, he and Andrea Levin formed the Boston branch of CAMERA—the Committee on Accuracy in Middle East Reporting in America. A few years later, the Boston branch would grow into the national office of the global Jewish community's most prestigious media watchdog. Charles was content to work as a business consultant and criticize media bias against Israel in his spare time.

All that changed one day in 1989 when he was reading *The Economist* on a flight back from a business trip, and noticed an article that shocked him. Hundreds of thousands of black slaves still lived in human bondage on account of their race in African countries like Mauritania and Sudan. Yet none of the leading Western human rights organizations seemed to care enough to stop this modern-day African slave trade. While still active in human rights and social justice causes, Jacobs had long abandoned leftist ideology, partly as the result of growing older and wiser, and partly due to the increasingly anti-Israel tone of the American and international left. His nonideological, purely humanitarian approach to fighting against slavery ultimately resulted in the liberation of tens of thousands of African slaves.

This made Charles Jacobs unique. Groups like Amnesty International and Human Rights Watch were never ideologically comfortable with the issue of modern-day African slavery, because the slave masters were Muslim Arabs who justified slavery through the Islamic laws of jihad and war booty. Charles concluded that rights groups in the West chose to abandon victims of non-Western oppression. He has called this phenomenon "the 'human rights complex,' where decent people in the West can be mobilized to protest every real and imagined crime perpetrated by what are seen as Western cultures, but are flummoxed, paralyzed and embarrassed when confronted by horrors committed by non-Westerners, especially if done by Muslims."

Charles has been unsparing in his criticism of the human rights establishment.

"The 'human rights movement' is a fraud," he told me.

> It exists only as a way that guilty whites can thump their chests at bad white conduct – past Western slavery, apartheid, white racism – and therefore transform themselves from spoiled rich kids, whose society, they have come to believe, despoiled the third world, into morally-purified virtuous protesters against this entire setup. So what if this leaves all those oppressed by non-Western tyrannies unspoken for? Un-championed? A small price to pay for the purification process of protesting "racism" and "Islamophobia." Silence on slavery, clitorectomies, beatings, and honor killings becomes, not a sin, but a small price paid to join the inviolable category of anti-Islamophobes. That is a badge that purges, protects, elevates, and makes you shine. But they also abandon those most in need of legitimate Western human rights help. This is a sin. Shame on them!

Appalled by the sheer magnitude of human suffering and subjugation—and by the world's indifference—Charles founded the American Anti-Slavery Group in 1994 with the Muslim Mauritanian abolitionist Mohamed Athie and the Christian Sudanese David Chand. In a July 13, 1994, op-ed in the *New York Times*, Jacobs and Athie broke the story of modern black slavery in North Africa. They described the violent slave raids of Sudan, where Arab tribesmen from the northern part of the country stormed black African villages in the south, shot all the men, and then dragged the women and children away to be sold. They also described how, in Mauritania, Muslim Berbers—members of the dominant light-skinned North African ethnic group—still enslaved black Africans who themselves were Muslims; and the horrific punishments meted out to slaves for the slightest offenses. They ended by calling out the media and politicians for their silence:

"Most distressing is the silence of the American media," they wrote, "whose reports counted for so much in the battle to end apartheid in South Africa, and of mainstream African-American organizations. The Congressional Black Caucus has yet to take a stand on the issue. Does freedom count for more in Johannesburg than in Nouakchotl and Khartoum?"

But according to Jacobs's "human rights complex" theory, the silence on the suffering in Sudan makes perfect sense. The oppressors in Johannesburg, after all, were Christian Europeans. In Nouakchotl and Khartoum, they were Muslim Arabs. And that made all the difference as far as indifference goes. It did not matter that slavery is even worse than apartheid. What seems to have mattered more to Western human rights activists has been the ability to use "human rights" as an indulgence against Western sin, to show the whole world that one—unlike so many others—is not a bad white person.

For the better part of the next decade, the American Anti-Slavery Group (AASG) worked on two fronts: political pressure within the United States and, guided by the Switzerland-based Christian Solidarity International, direct slave redemption actions in Sudan. In the United States, the AASG launched a campaign of awareness and coalition building that was to reach Capitol Hill and the White House on a wave of overwhelming bipartisan and popular support. The AASG allied with grassroots African American groups and white Evangelical churches to press the issue with their representatives in Congress. Both the Black Congressional Caucus and key congressional Republicans came to back the AASG's fight against slavery in Sudan. Even white East Coast liberals joined the cause. Charles likes to recount how how he was able to get Barney Frank, the ultra-liberal, openly gay Massachusetts congressman, and Pat Robertson, the arch-conservative televangelist, to join in support of his movement, though he still couldn't get them to sit in the same room.

There were some who opposed Charles's abolitionist work in Sudan. Jesse Jackson said the AASG sounded like it was "anti-Arab." The Sudanese government under Omar al-Bashir armed militiamen to storm black African villages in the south. They shot the men, and captured the women and children as slaves. Bashir is also under indictment in the International Criminal Court for the separate genocide in Darfur. However, the Muslim Brotherhood has historically dominated Bashir's regime; and Muslim Brotherhood–associated groups in the United States began to run interference for the regime with a campaign denying the existence of black slavery under Arab Muslim masters in Sudan. One of the Muslim Brotherhood's primary targets for proselytizing in the United States is the black community.

Charles soon saw that, the Nation of Islam leader Louis Farrakhan felt AASG's Sudan campaign to be an existential threat. Nation of Islam ideology portrays whites, especially Jews, as the number-one enemy of blacks, and promotes Islam as the path to black freedom and empowerment. Farrakhan's long-standing goal was to break the black/Jewish civil rights alliance forged by Dr. Martin Luther King. And yet here was Charles Jacobs, a Jewish white guy and a veteran of Dr. King's alliance, working to free black slaves from their Muslim masters and partnering with African American leaders to tell the black community that Muslim Arabs in Africa capture, buy, sell, and own blacks as chattel. Most damaging to Farrakhan, perhaps, was the fact, generally unknown in the American black community, that Muslim Berbers keep black African slaves. This fact, and it persists today, directly contradicts Farrakhan's pitch: at least in Mauritania, Islam is not the utopian path to freedom for blacks. Twenty years later, today, Arab Muslims have black slaves in five African nations: Libya, Algeria, Sudan, Nigeria, and Mauritania. Still, the West's human rights organizations mostly remain unmoved.

Farrakhan became an adamant denier of Sudanese slavery, which he termed a Zionist lie; and the Nation of Islam began to target the AASG, as well as African American community leaders who supported its work, with vitriol and harassment. Charles remembers that period of time as the only time he had been truly afraid for his safety. He had received serious threats from two separate but allied sources. The first was direct. Charles had been introduced to an escaped slave from Sudan, Francis Bok, who was captured as a child in a jihad raid on his Dinka ethnic group, which killed many villagers, including both his parents. Bok toured campuses and churches around the country telling his story, eloquently and powerfully. Bok's outreach to black churches, however, sparked death threats against Charles in phone calls to his office over a period of weeks. The calls were from Canada, the police said. The message was, "We don't care what else you do, Jacobs, but stay out of black churches or we will come and take care of you." The police investigated and soon the calls stopped. It was only years later that Jacobs came to understand the reason for the calls: Islamist extremists hope to convert African American to Islam on a vast scale. Francis Bok's story, told in black churches across the country, would surely make that more difficult. The second threat to Charles came from the Nation of Islam newspaper

The Final Call had published a caricature of him, stylized into a bizarre mix of an ideal German Nazi and a Nazi caricature of a Jew: a menacing figure with blond hair under a *kippah*, a Jewish nose and a Nordic chin, holding a black man and woman bondaged by a chain in one hand, and a newspaper ad in the other: "SLAVES FOUND IN SUDAN: Only $50. Cheaper than American slaves."

The only truth in that caricature was the price: Jacobs, guided by Christian Solidarity International, had indeed been flying illegally into Sudan, purchasing the freedom of slaves at about $50 per person, and offering Americans the chance to, with what to them was a relatively small donation, actually buy a human out of a lifetime of bondage. The AASG began partnering with Christian Solidarity International's "underground railroad program," run by human rights activist John Eibner. The two groups would raise hundreds of thousands of dollars to buy back thousands of Sudanese slaves from their Arab masters. When they reached their homeland, the freed slaves would be given clothes, food, medicine, and farming tools. Some would be reunited with their families—if any relatives had survived the Arab ethnic cleansing raids.

The black African Dinka tribes from southern Sudan lived on the border with the north. They were the primary targets of Khartoum's jihad and slave raids. But the Dinka had found unlikely allies in nomadic Arab herdsmen, who helped to redeem Dinka slaves in exchange for grazing rights in Dinka territory. These friendly Arabs would go north and buy or steal away Dinka slaves. AASG raised enough cash in the United States to free seventy thousand slaves. The pitch to Americans who cared was simple: for every fifty-dollar donation, you buy the life and freedom of a human being.

Charles has personally taken part in three slave-redemption missions. He and Christian Solidarity's John Eibner flew illegally on tiny planes, into the war zone in southern Sudan from Kenya, with suitcases filled with cash. They camped out with Dinka militia and awaited the latest rescued slave caravan. Then, the exchange of humans for dollars would happen and the redeemed would begin to celebrate their freedom. For his part in freeing tens of thousands of slaves, Charles Jacobs was given the first, and so far only, Boston Freedom Award in September 2000 by Boston mayor Thomas Menino and Martin Luther King's widow, Coretta Scott King. Jacobs insists that all the credit must go to John

Eibner, the brilliant and genuinely heroic leader of the Underground Railroad program.

The direct slave-redemption tactic was as successful as it was controversial. Establishment human rights organizations like Amnesty International and Human Rights Watch did not like the upstart group AASG, which showed them up and often criticized them for their inaction. In 1994, Jacobs won a debate at Amnesty International's national conference, convincing the gathered delegates to add fighting slavery to the group's mandate. But the Amnesty headquarters in London overturned the decision. The mainstream human rights groups came out against the AASG's tactic of directly purchasing slaves from their captors. Human Rights Watch issued a statement declaring that "Human Rights Watch opposes foreign-organized or funded buy-backs or purchases of freedom for slaves in southern Sudan." In response, Jacobs confronted one of the organization's spokesmen in a discussion on National Public Radio with Human Rights Watch's own buy-back program in India for parents to redeem their enslaved daughters.

Unlike Farrakhan's absurd lie that Jacobs was "selling slaves" by raising money for slave redemption, Human Rights Watch did have a legitimate argument against the AASG's tactics, based on a simple supply-demand principle. If there's more money out there to buy Dinka slaves, the Arabs slave raiders who sell those slaves are going to capture more slaves to get more money.

This argument does make sense on a superficially rational level. The same argument was made during the Holocaust, when Irgun activist Peter Bergson came to the United States to set up an effort to save European Jewry. When Romania offered to sell its remaining un-murdered Jews to the Allies, Bergson put out an ad in the *New York Times* to raise funds for the ransom, announcing: "For Sale to Humanity 70,000 Jews, Guaranteed Human Beings at $50 a Piece."

Like their heirs have tried to do to Charles Jacobs, mainstream Jewish leaders fought tooth and nail to discredit Bergson's effort, claiming that it was reckless and would cause the deaths of more Jews. Bergson was ultimately credited with saving two hundred thousand Jewish lives from the Holocaust.

Neither the AASG nor Peter Bergson's critics took into account one thing: war and genocide are not eternal, and the aggressor can be defeated.

This is exactly what happened, in large part because of the great success of Charles's political work back in the United States. The objections of Human Rights Watch and other left-wing human rights groups suddenly became moot. The slaves Charles freed in Sudan would remain free, and no new slaves would take their place. On October 21, 2002, Charles was welcomed at the White House by President George W. Bush for the signing of the Sudan Peace Act, which committed the United States to aggressively press forward negotiations between the Sudanese government and the Sudan People's Liberation Movement—the black African resistance fighters in the south. The act forced Khartoum to allow a plebiscite in the south, where southern Sudanese could vote on partition from the north. On July 9, 2011, South Sudan was established as an independent sovereign nation. The Arab slave raids stopped, but as many as thirty thousand South Sudanese nationals remain in bondage in Sudan. The emancipation struggle continues.

• • •

Back in Boston, as the twenty-first century began, Charles was once again drawn to a new cause. He told me that in 2002, he had gotten to thinking:

"I felt the need to help the Dinka tribes of South Sudan because to me, the Dinka were the Jews of our time, targeted by a fascist regime, the object of mass murder while the "civilized" world sits on its hands. And then, all of the sudden, I looked around at the forces aligning against Israel, treating it as the collective Jew, and I thought maybe it's the Jews that are the Jews of our time. Maybe there was a new threat against world Jewry, a new antisemitism filling the space left by older hatreds based on Jewish religion and Jewish race, which were, after the Holocaust, no longer socially acceptable—a new and fashionable hatred based on the Jewish state. I got worried."

With the outbreak of the Second Intifada in September 2000, the Oslo-era dreams of peace for Israel were shattered. In 2002, the Jewish State saw a crescendo of forty-seven suicide bombings. Externally, it was dealing with an equally ferociously sustained attack in the public opinion and diplomatic fronts. In the United States, nowhere was this truer than on college campuses.

In July 2002, Charles met Avi Goldwasser, then a high-tech executive and a board member of the American Jewish Committee in Boston, who was frustrated by the failure of the existing Jewish community groups to protect his daughter and future son-in-law from the hostile environment they faced as Jews while attending New England universities. Together, they formed the David Project to support Jewish students on college campuses. Charles and Avi were among the first Jewish leaders to raise the alarm about the threat to Jewish students from campus anti-Israel activity, which was increasingly metastasizing into outright anti-Semitism. They had hoped to enlist Jewish leaders in Boston in the effort.

The David Project was a startup with limited funds but with a core of dedicated activists and a strong combination of experience in activism, business, and education. It was originally born as a small counter to the campus anti-Israel goliath. Under Avi and Charles's leadership, the organization had several breakthrough achievements. The David Project developed an innovative approach to help college and high school students understand the Middle East conflict. It launched a successful campaign against Harvard Divinity School's acceptance of a two-million-dollar gift from the anti-Semitic United Arab Emirates ruler, Sheikh Zayed bin Sultan Al Nahyan. With the David Project's help, Rachel Fish, a divinity student at Harvard, succeeded in getting Harvard to return the tainted gift. But, in what was a harbinger of establishment Jewish leadership failure, Fish could not get any other Jewish organization to support her.

The David Project also exposed, in a widely publicized documentary produced by Avi Goldwasser and called *Columbia Unbecoming*, the abuse of Jewish students by anti-Israel and anti-Semitic professors at Columbia University. The documentary alerted the American Jewish community, for the first time and in a very public way, the extent of hostility to Jewish students on the twenty-first-century American college campus. This led to attacks on the David Project in media outlets from Cairo to Tehran.

After the documentary was released, Charles and Avi went to New York to meet with David Harris, the president of the American Jewish Committee, whom Shimon Peres once called the "foreign minister of the Jewish people." Harris agreed there was cause for concern, but told Charles and Avi that at AJC, "we don't do campus."

Another of Avi's documentaries for the David Project, called "Forgotten Refugees," was an award-winning film about the destruction of the two-thousand-year-old Jewish communities in Arab lands. Jews, who lived in the Middle East and North Africa under oppressive conditions for centuries, were mostly driven from their homes after Israel was established in 1948. These documentaries and many other materials comprised David Project training curricula, used in over one hundred Jewish day schools in America to prepare Jewish students to become activists for Israel and to survive the campus anti-Israel battlefield.

But even as the David Project was confronting the anti-Israel threat on campus, that threat was morphing into something more ominous. Until the 1990s, the main anti-Israel activists were campus radical leftists and Arab nationalist students of the PLO variety. But in the new Second Intifada and post-9/11 climate of the early twenty-first century, there was suddenly a shift. Increasingly, it was the religious Muslim students, many of them immigrants from countries steeped in anti-Semitic rhetoric, who began to lead the campus war against Israel. Most of them were connected with and supervised by area mosques. They were highly aggressive, they were extremely well organized, and they seemed to be flush with funding and training.

• • •

On September 11, 2001, Charles was on Capitol Hill, testifying before a congressional committee about his ongoing abolitionist efforts in Sudan. Suddenly, the place erupted in panic. As the smoke from the burning Pentagon rose in the distance, Capitol Police yelled for everyone to evacuate, afraid that the Capitol building could be hit next. If not for the passengers who fought off the hijackers of Flight 93, it very likely would have been.

By that day's evening, Charles knew that what he had previously feared had indeed happened: As he recalled the phoned-in death threats to the AASG office, he saw that the same jihadist forces he was fighting in Sudan had now come to America. Concern about the danger to America and Israel from the increasing radicalization of the historically moderate American Muslim community was why Charles positioned the David Project into a challenge against the ISB in 2003, just a year after he founded it. Now, in 2007, the fight with the ISB was over, or so we had thought. Instead, we would begin discovering what was in the ISB's internal documents.

PART TWO

CONNECTING
THE DOTS

CHAPTER 8

THE INVESTIGATION BEGINS

It was at first hard to believe how much civic and media leaders had underestimated the scope and the danger of the movement to which the ISB belonged. Throughout the second half of 2007, my colleague Sasha and I sorted through tens of thousands of pages of documents, discovering the inner workings of the radical Islamic movement in New England. Meanwhile, the Holy Land Foundation (HLF) trial in Dallas, Texas, which was going on at the same time, was providing an alarming big picture into which we could place our own discoveries. As the United States Court of Appeals for the Fifth Circuit wrote in its unanimous opinion upholding the convictions of five HLF leaders—and upholding their sentences of up to sixty-five years in federal prison:

> Established in the late 1980s, the Holy Land Foundation held itself out as the largest Muslim charitable organization in the United States. It raised millions of dollars over the course of its existence that were then funneled to Hamas through various charitable entities in the West Bank and Gaza. Although these entities performed some legitimate charitable functions, they were actually Hamas social institutions.

As we would discover, a legal case can be made that the ISB, along with many Boston-based Islamist activists had an intimate role to play in facilitating, causing, aiding and abetting, and/or conspiring to participate in that Hamas terrorist-financing scheme, as well as several other terrorist-financing enterprises.

• • •

On Friday, August 20, 2004, a carload of Baltimore County police officers returning from their training exercises saw a BMW sport-utility vehicle driving across the Chesapeake Bay Bridge, with a woman in the passenger's seat hanging out of the window and videotaping the bridge's structure. The cops radioed the Maryland Transportation Authority, whose officers stopped the BMW after it got off the bridge. They found Ismael Selim Elbarasse, a former assistant to Hamas political chief Mousa Abou Marzouk, behind the wheel. According to court documents, the video footage his wife was taking of the Chesapeake Bay Bridge included close-up shots of bridge parts that were "integral to the structural integrity of the bridge," including "the cables and upper supports of the main span." A search of the Elbarasse residence turned up a huge haul of incriminating evidence.

Inside his Annandale, Virginia, home, authorities discovered a library of the most intimate documents detailing the Muslim Brotherhood's operations in the United States: phone directories, implementation manuals, business plans for the group. These documents revealed the individual leaders of the Muslim Brotherhood in the United States and their intentions in the country. The documents would form the core of the prosecution's case against the Holy Land Foundation.

It was actually a particular document that had been fairly peripheral to the government's case, which held the most significance for researchers working to understand the American Muslim Brotherhood network and its goals. Entered into the docket as Government Exhibit 003-0085, the "Explanatory Memorandum on the General Strategic Goal of the [Muslim Brotherhood] Group in North America" was written in 1991 by Mohammed Akram, a member of the Executive Office of the Muslim Brotherhood's American branch and a senior Hamas leader.

The document outlined in systematic detail the steps needed to achieve the goal set in 1987 by the Muslim Brotherhood's highest deliberative body, called the Shura Council. This goal was to "establish an effective and a stable Islamic Movement [in America] led by the Muslim Brotherhood which...presents Islam as a civilization alternative, and supports the global Islamic State..." Here is how the Muslim Brotherhood's mission in the United States was explained, under the heading "Understanding the Role of the Muslim Brother in North America":

> The Ikhwan [Muslim Brotherhood] must understand that their work in America is a kind of grand Jihad in eliminating and destroying the Western civilization from within and "sabotaging" its miserable house by their hands and the hands of the believers so that it is eliminated and God's religion is made victorious over all other religions....It is a Muslim's destiny to perform Jihad and work wherever he is and wherever he lands until the final hour comes.

As we looked through the memorandum and the other HLF trial exhibits, we saw many familiar names. Top ISB/MAS leaders from Boston were turning up in the exhibits, listed at the highest level of the American Muslim Brotherhood's leadership. Other organizations with which the ISB had formal links, as well as other groups founded by ISB leaders, were there as well. At the back of the "Strategic Goal" memo was a list of what the document called "our organizations and the organizations of our friends"— the aboveground front groups run by or allied with the clandestine Muslim Brotherhood movement. At the top of the list was the Islamic Society of North America (ISNA), the largest national Muslim organization in America and ISB's parent group, which Steven Emerson had long argued was dominated by the Muslim Brotherhood. Prosecutors listed ISNA as an unindicted co-conspirator in the HLF's Hamas-fundraising efforts.

Until 2004, when the ISB scrubbed its controversial affiliations in the face of public scrutiny, its bylaws stated: "The organization shall be affiliated with the Islamic Society of North America (ISNA), the Muslim Arab Youth Association (MAYA), the North American Islamic Trust (NAIT) [the financial arm of ISNA], and the Muslim Student Association (MSA)." All of these organizations were on the U.S. Muslim Brotherhood's list of "our organizations and the organizations of our friends." Osama Kandil, the chairman of the ISB's board of trustees, founded, in particular, the Muslim Arab Youth Association. ISB founder Abdulrahman Alamoudi's name was frequently found throughout the HLF trial exhibits.

The ISB's newest trustee, Jamal Badawi, appointed in July 2007—a month after the ISB dropped the lawsuit against its critics—turned out to be one of the Muslim Brotherhood's top leaders. A secret 1992 Muslim Brotherhood leadership phone directory entered into evidence at the HLF trial listed Jamal Badawi as a member of the Executive Office of the American Muslim Brotherhood and a member of its Shura (Judicial) Council. A former professor of business management at Halifax University in Canada, Badawi has claimed that his biggest influence in life has been the Muslim Brotherhood's founder, Hassan al-Banna. As a top leader in the international Muslim Brotherhood, Badawi has led many Muslim Brotherhood organizational initiatives in the United States, Canada, and Europe on behalf of the Brotherhood's spiritual leader Yusuf Qaradawi. He was also one of the three founders in 1993 of the Muslim American Society—the Muslim Brotherhood front group that was now in charge of the ISBCC mosque in Roxbury. The newest ISB Trust member was also listed as an unindicted co-conspirator in HLF's Hamas-fundraising crimes. According to the prosecution, he was a frequent speaker at Hamas fundraisers, which featured open calls to murder Jews and destroy Israel. According to the appeals court that affirmed the HLF leaders' convictions, Badawi was a member of an HLF overseas speakers' bureau "that included numerous individuals who were identified through testimony as Hamas members."

The HLF documents also shed some light on an enigmatic figure on the ISB's Board of Trustees. Mohammed Attawia was always the least visible ISB trustee, rarely seen in public. But, he seemed to pull a lot of strings behind the scenes. It was Attawia who hashed out the ISB's first plans for the Roxbury mosque with Boston city official Muhammad Ali Salaam. As Ali Salaam has claimed in an interview for the ISB, he got involved with the mosque plans after he "was contacted by the Islamic Society of Boston in Cambridge—by one of their trustees, Mohammed Attawia, who is a physician, a research medical doctor….He was the first of the board members who understood what the project was about."

Government exhibit 003-0034 in the Holy Land Foundation trial is a 1991 Muslim Brotherhood leadership phone directory. It identifies Mohammed Attawia as the *masul*, or "regional leader," of the New England branch of the Muslim Brotherhood. As I later learned, this region-based *masul* hierarchy is a hallmark of the Muslim Brotherhood's organizational structure in Egypt and around the world. In October 2006, when the ISB began facing discovery subpoenas from the people it was suing, the other ISB trustees removed Mohammed Attawia from the Trust. The David Project's lawyers were perplexed by this move and took note, but dropped the investigative thread when the ISB dropped the lawsuit. Now, with the information coming out of the Holy Land Foundation trial documents, the picture started to come into focus.

There was little doubt over what the evidence from the ISB and HLF trials was showing. The Islamic Society of Boston *was* the Muslim Brotherhood's New England base. Its top leadership was deeply involved in a variety of terrorist-fundraising and -radicalization schemes all over the United States. And the Muslim Brotherhood's goals here were nothing less than, in its own words, "eliminating and destroying the Western civilization from within."

Unfortunately, this discovery was happening at a time when Boston's political, civic, and religious leaders were tripping all over each other to express their support for the ISB and its ISBCC mega-mosque project in Roxbury. Never before had we had a better case that the ISB was a dangerous and extremist organization; yet at the same time, we had less opportunity than ever to make that case. The ISB, with the help of Boston's media, had reframed the issue, and the David Project was accused of denying the Boston Muslim community a place of worship.

Charles was under intense pressure from the David Project's top donors to cease all efforts to confront the ISB. Their point of view was understandable. The fight with the ISB had cost the David Project somewhere in the neighborhood of a million dollars, and it distracted the organization from its primary mission—training Jewish high school and college students to make the case for Israel on campus. Other concerns were also at play. Many of the David Project's donors felt pressure from within their liberal social circles as a consequence of the very public battle between the David Project and the ISB.

After dealing with the David Project's attorney, Jeff Robbins, over the ISB lawsuit's litigation costs, Zurich dropped the David Project as an insurance client. Robbins, who had by then become a member of its board, demanded that Charles institute a "pre-publication review policy" for the organization. This was a choke collar on the David Project, controlled entirely by Robbins. Every little thing said publicly by every David Project employee, no matter how junior, including every single blog or Facebook post, would now go through this Kafkaesque process:

The blog post would be sent to the employee's "immediate supervisor for review. Once the supervisor has reviewed the material and approved its content, he/she shall send the material to the Executive Director with an accompanying memorandum identifying the material, the name of the supervisor who reviewed the material, and the date that it was reviewed."

Then, "[o]nce the Executive Director, or her/his designee, has reviewed and approved the material for publication, she/he shall create a memorandum documenting the name of the material and the date of the review by the Executive Director or her/his designee."

And then, the executive director "shall provide [the material] to the David Project's legal counsel for final review. No educational material may be published or disseminated without being reviewed and approved for publication by legal counsel."

Conveniently, that legal counsel was Jeff Robbins, and he charged a hefty fee for reviewing all those blog posts. It is my opinion that this began a bleeding of talent and initiative in the organization, which ultimately led to its gradual demise.

Whatever Robbins's motivation was for this coup d'état at the David Project, emails between him and Charles from that time show that Robbins had clearly developed an animosity to Charles. In response to a request to put a video clip on YouTube, Robbins wrote, "What a foolish 'joke' to make," and told Charles that he did not have time to review anything that day. Speaking as an attorney myself, I believe that this was entirely inappropriate behavior by a lawyer toward his client. And, the ability of the David Project to continue exposing the ISB was severely curtailed.

The situation proved untenable. One day in June 2008, Jacobs took me out to lunch, and told me that Robbins has swayed the David Project board against fighting Islamist extremism, a threat that Charles thought was the most serious threat Jews faced. "What's the point of teaching Jewish students on campus to make a better case for Israel if we let Hamas come to America?" Charles said that he has decided to leave the David Project and start a new organization. He wanted me to come with him. He wanted to move on from an organization he had founded and nurtured into a successful pro-Israel advocacy group. He thought that he had created a machine and a strategy that could be run without him, that he had invented a machine that worked. He was leaving behind excellent people to take over. It was the right thing to do. We needed the freedom and flexibility to educate the public about the Islamic Society of Boston and the threat it continues to represent to the Cradle of Liberty.

In late August 2008, Charles Jacobs, Avi Goldwasser, and I founded Americans for Peace and Tolerance. Our mission was to preserve American exceptionalism by promoting peaceful coexistence in an ethnically diverse, but integrated, American society. We felt that Islamist extremism was a threat to this mission, and to the people of Boston. Dennis Hale and Ahmed Mansour of Citizens for Peace and Tolerance agreed to serve as members of the board of directors, and Bill Sapers joined the board a bit later. The launch of the organization coincided with the 2008 "great recession" and funds were extremely hard to come by. Our goal was to educate the American people about the Islamic Society of Boston, and its connection to the Muslim Brotherhood's project to "destroy [Western civilization] from within."

It was an underdog effort, but by now we were used to that. Even getting started was hard: we had to spend a year in legal negotiations with the David Project and Jeff Robbins for the simple rights to use the material from the discovery process. For that entire year, the David Project held and refused to release much of my work related to the ISB investigation, while Robbins refused to let me see the ISB case file—the so-called forty boxes. When I finally got the file in hand, we began researching and putting together the facts behind the history of the Islamist movement in New England and the United States. We have continued those investigations ever since. Here is what we have learned.

CHAPTER 9

THE MUSLIM BROTHERHOOD COMES TO BOSTON

Muslims have been in New England for a long time. Toward the end of the nineteenth century, the first of several Lebanese Arab families fleeing conscription into the Ottoman army settled in the southern Boston suburb of Quincy. This first trickle of immigration, like the larger waves to follow, was driven by conflicts inside the Muslim world—in this case, Arab resistance against the brutal and corrupt Ottoman Turkish regime. Subsequent waves of migration would be driven by even greater upheavals in the Muslim world—with each wave bringing more of the dysfunctional ideology and culture that drove the migrations in the first place.

Earlier in the twentieth century, in a time of rising global nationalism, Islam was a much less important force for association than ethnic or national identity. Plus, some of the early migrants from the Middle East were not Muslim, but Christian, and some were not Arabs. The first specifically Muslim organization in Boston (Nation of Islam excluded), formed in 1937, was called the Arab American Banner Society, and its bylaws reflected both the Arab nationalism in vogue in the home countries, and a deep appreciation for American democratic values:

> The purpose of the Society shall be the preservation of the racial
> identity among the Arabs in the United States and its develop-
> ment in accordance with the highest principles and traditions
> of American life and education...The Society shall endeavor to

conduct a school to teach the Arabic language and to educate our
youths in the fundamentals of American Democracy.

For several decades, New England Muslims would pray privately or in
small groups in their homes. But by the 1960s, the leaders of the Arab-
American Banner Society had decided to build a mosque in order to make
their observance of the Islamic faith more formal. In 1962, according to
an academic paper by the granddaughter of some of these first Muslim
families of New England, Mary Lahaj, a group of the families combined
resources to purchase a property in Quincy. They incorporated the Islamic
Center of New England (ICNE) as a charitable organization to own that
property. The ICNE's stated purpose was "the establishment and maintenance of the public worship of God, in accordance with the principles and
doctrines of the Islamic faith." The ICNE would become New England's
first mosque, and it opened for services in 1963. Yet almost as soon as it was
built, the mosque became host to a conflict that was playing out across the
postcolonial Islamic world.

As it happened, the Muslim world of the 1960s was very different from
the one the original Muslim immigrants to New England had fled at the
turn of the century. For one thing, the Ottoman Turks were long gone,
replaced by a collection of Arab nation-states. Some of those states payed
lip service to democracy, but all were actually ruled by dictators, usually
from the upper ranks of the army, like Egypt's president, Gamal Nasser,
and sometimes from traditional royal families like in Morocco and Jordan.
The main political opponents to these Arab strongmen were followers of a
powerful religious and political ideology now known as Islamism, whose
goal has been the establishment of a worldwide Islamic theocracy under
Sharia law. That is, not an *Arab* state, and not a state in a regular sense,
but a global empire in which all Muslims, whether Arab or otherwise, are
subjects of a single Muslim *caliph*—a divinely sanctioned ruler. This ideology was increasingly at odds with secular Arab nationalism in many Arab
countries, as the Muslim Brotherhood gained a wide following throughout
the Arab world.

The Muslim Brotherhood is the oldest, largest, and, arguably, most
influential Islamist organization in the world. It was formed in Egypt in
1928, and since then it has expanded into a loose and secretive international
network. It has also spawned a number of terrorist organizations that

support or engage in terror. These include Hamas (which, according to its founding charter, is officially "The Muslim Brotherhood in Palestine"), Islamic Jihad, al-Qaeda, and the Islamic State (ISIS). The Brotherhood's goal is to create a single Islamic state governed by Islamic Sharia law on the territory of all Muslim countries, to reconquer formerly Muslim-ruled lands like Israel or Spain, and then, ultimately, to conquer the entire world and unite all mankind under a utopian global Islamic government.

Dennis Hale has studied the Muslim Brotherhood as a political scientist. "In order to understand the Muslim Brotherhood," he told me, "it's important to think about the particular political predicament that Muslims found themselves in, particularly in the Middle East, after the First World War. The Muslim Middle East was the heart of the Muslim empire, and that empire was, at one time, the biggest empire in history. It stretched from Spain to China. And now, lately, it had been reduced to the Ottoman Empire, and in 1924 the Ottoman Empire went extinct. So now the world of Islam, the *Dar al-Islam*—the world of submission—was reduced to this tiny little place in Arabia where it all started twelve centuries before, and the *Dar al-Harb*—the world of war—was everywhere else.

> Now imagine if liberal democracy suddenly disappeared from the face of the planet except for some little town in New England. That would be a catastrophe and it would require an explanation. We would want to know how could such a thing have happened. And I think this must be how it was with Muslims after the First World War. How could this catastrophe have happened? The Quran tells Muslims that they are the best of God's creatures, and now here they are at the bottom of the heap. Actually, they'd been at the bottom for quite some time. Hassan al-Banna had an explanation.

Hassan al-Banna was an obscure Egyptian Islamic scholar and schoolteacher when he founded the Muslim Brotherhood in 1928. The wrecked Muslim world that the first Muslim immigrants to New England had fled at the turn of the twentieth century was the opposite of Mohammad's prophecy about a worldwide Islamic utopia. This caused a lot of soul-searching for many Muslim theologians, including al-Banna. But according to Dennis Hale, al-Banna's explanation was most appealing because it was very simple:

"The Muslim empire had died because Islam was no longer the religion of Muslims," Hale claims.

> Muslims had backslid, to use an old Protestant term. They had abandoned the faith. They were not living as pious Muslims. Instead, they were chasing after these false gods of the West, parliamentary democracy, freedom of speech, religious freedom, abundance, wealth, power. These are false gods; these are the gods of the Jews and the colonialists, Al Banna said. Abandon them, reject them and we can have the empire back.

Al-Banna believed that the only way to regain Islam's rightful place as a world empire would be by returning Muslim society to its pure state, the way it existed at the time of Muhammad and his followers. Al-Banna's movement soon spread throughout the Arab world. After al-Banna, the most influential ideologue of the Muslim Brotherhood was Sayyid Qutb. Abu Mus'ab al-Suri, top al-Qaeda strategist and arguably "the architect of the extant Islamic State of Iraq and Syria (ISIS)," identified "the organizational program of Sayyid Qutb," as one of the main sources of militant Islamist ideology. According to current al-Qaeda leader Ayman Al Zawahiri: "Qutb's message…fanned the fire of Islamic revolution against the enemies of Islam at home and abroad. The chapters of his revolution are renewing one day after another."

In the 1950s, Sayyid Qutb developed al-Banna's original platform into a far-reaching attack on the religious practices of the vast majority of the world's Muslims. Qutb argued that true Islamic society and true Muslims went extinct many centuries prior—except, of course, for Qutb himself and those who agree with him. All Muslim countries in the world had regressed back to the state of pre-Islamic ignorance and persecution of Muslims known in Arabic as *jahilliya*. Today's world, according to Qutb, has ended up in the exact state of persecution against Muslims mentioned in the Quran. The powers of the world must therefore be fought until Islam prevails globally, as foretold by Muhammad: "And fight them until persecution is no more, and religion is all for Allah."

The reascendance of Islam, in fact the survival of humanity itself, depended, to Qutb, upon reviving the original pure Islamic society through a long and painful process of reeducation in the Muslim world and struggle against the Western world—seen as the major obstacle to Islamic revival—through proselytizing (*dawa*) and holy war (*jihad*). The end goal would be a pure Islamic society based on Sharia in every part of the world.

While al-Banna also blamed Western secularism for the majority of the corrupting influences on Islam, Qutb took this attack to the extreme with his Manichaean contrast of a pure Islam under constant threat from the corrupt but powerful West. And preaching was not enough in this cosmic struggle: Qutb also gave divine sanction for the Muslim Brotherhood movement to wage jihad against any institutions in the Muslim or Western world that were perceived to be standing in the way of the Islamic revival.

At the same time, Qutb's attitude toward the West was nevertheless a love/hate relationship. He despised Western culture and morals, but he recognized the immense gulf between Western scientific achievements and the Islamic world's backwardness. He believed it was vital for the Islamic world to catch up with Western scientific knowledge. Thus, Muslims could study Western "technology," but not Western philosophy and culture. This is how Qutb, with the help of the U.S. State Department, came to study at an American college. Muslim Brothers soon followed his example in large numbers. The Muslim Brotherhood was attracting young, idealistic, ambitious, and driven members, and its leaders were encouraging them to study hard sciences in the West, so as to eventually be able to compete with and overcome Western countries. And what better place to get a higher education than in New England?

Muslim Brotherhood members and other Islamists began coming to New England in large numbers to study at universities like Harvard and the Massachusetts Institute of Technology after the 1965 Immigration Act made immigration from the Middle East easier. But what these ardent Islamists found when they encountered the Islamic Center of New England—then the only Sunni mosque in the Boston area—infuriated them. After all, Islamists preach that the Muslim world suffers because it has abandoned orthodox Islam in favor of secular Western culture. And in New England, over the course of a generation, the Muslim founders of the ICNE had become thoroughly Americanized. They were practicing a very liberalized form of Islam, and this horrified the newcomers. Many ICNE members had married non-Muslims. The mosque's first Imam, Mohamed Omar Awad, was self-taught, and was married to a Protestant. The mosque leaders' children had names like Mary and Nathan. In a pattern that would continue as more and more immigrants arrived from the Middle East, the new arrivals saw the "Americanized" mosque as spiritually corrupted. It was financed in part with a mortgage, which is forbidden in orthodox Islam, and in part with fundraisers that included raffles and bingo nights, although gambling is also forbidden in orthodox Islam. The ICNE had even adopted a variety of liturgical and educational customs traditionally associated with churches, such as Sunday services and Sunday school for the children. Men and women mixed freely together, and the mosque even hosted belly-dancing demonstrations.

But, just as they were ignorant of orthodox Islamic practices, the ICNE's members knew next to nothing about the Islamist movements that had grown in their home countries since they or their parents had left. The new arrivals, for example, continued in America the same conspiratorial practices the Muslim Brotherhood had first devised in Egypt, among them secrecy of membership, leadership, and long-range intentions. As more and more Muslim Brotherhood members arrived to study in New England and in other regions of the United States in the late sixties, they began to make tentative contacts with each other and to reorganize their movement along American lines.

• • •

Several decades later, and shortly after the 9/11 attacks, businessman Marcial Peredo had just bought a new home in Falls Church, Virginia, and was sprucing up his backyard when his landscaping crew's Bobcat tractor stumbled on a cache of videotapes buried in the ground. Peredo bagged up the tapes for the dumpster, but then remembered hearing his new neighbors gossiping about how they thought the man from whom he bought the house, Fawaz Mushtaha, was under surveillance. Peredo turned over the tapes to the newly created Department of Homeland Security and they ended up figuring prominently at the Holy Land Foundation trial, as they chronicled the secret meetings of the Muslim Brotherhood in America.

One of the most revealing recordings among the many tapes entered as evidence in the trial was a lecture on the history of the Muslim Brotherhood in America by the head of the group's Executive Office, Zeid al-Noman. Addressing an audience of Muslim Brotherhood members at a gathering in Missouri, al-Noman described the group's origins.

According to al-Noman, Muslim Brotherhood activism in the United States was almost unintentional at first. It was still a time of nationalism and most Muslim foreign students would mainly socialize with other students from their own countries. A member of the Boston Muslim community who had studied at MIT in the 1960s told me that this was the norm with Muslim students in general. A Pakistani Muslim shared as much in common with an Egyptian as an Irish immigrant to America would have shared with a Polish one—a common religion, to be sure, but no common language, and a completely different culture. So the Brotherhood's activists were at first splintered along national lines. Still, as new Brotherhood members arriving to study joined these social circles, they would soon identify fellow members. They would also make contacts with non-Arab Islamist students and form alliances with them, especially with members of the Jamiat Islami movement from Pakistan, founded by the father of jihad on the Indian subcontinent, Maulana Maududi. Eventually, a loosely coordinated network developed in various regions, New England included.

According to Zeid al-Noman's history lesson, now in FBI hands, Muslim Brotherhood students began holding regular conferences, first on a regional, and then a national level. They began planning a more visible and systematic structure for their movement. Based on these plans, in 1963, at a national gathering of Muslim Brothers on the Champaign/Urbana campus of the University of Illinois, the Muslim Students Association was inaugurated as the beachhead organizational vehicle for the Brotherhood's overt activity in the United States. Muslim Brothers registered an official front group called "Islamic Society," or "Cultural Society," with the IRS in 1965, but it mostly existed on paper. The Muslim Students Association is where all the action happened.

There are now hundreds of MSA chapters on campuses across the United States and Canada, many of them independent from the national Muslim Brotherhood group. I even ran into one promoting the genocide of Jews and nuclear proliferation on my campus at Dartmouth College. But, I had no idea back then—and few know now—that the MSA was founded specifically as the Muslim Brotherhood's first front group in America; or that it was inseparable from the Brotherhood for a long time. Of course, the scope and ambitions of the Brotherhood movement were much bigger than could be contained within a student group. According to al-Noman, as the students graduated and then aged, they formed new groups and developed the core Muslim Brotherhood secret organization into a massive hidden guiding hand for the public MSA groups on campuses. In 1969, the still consolidating underground network began holding separate, more secretive, side meetings at the MSA's annual national conferences. In 1972, these councils became fully independent and concealed from the non-Muslim Brotherhood MSA members. But, essentially, until the 1970s, the MSA *was* the Muslim Brotherhood in America.

Universities in the New England area served as some of the earliest centers for MSA activities. Harvard's Muslim student group, the Harvard Islamic Society, was the first of its kind, founded in 1956. MSAs at MIT, Boston University, and other schools were soon formed and became centers of Muslim Brotherhood influence on the other Muslim students.

While most of the original Muslim Brothers in America had joined the Brotherhood back in their home countries, once the MSA was fully operational, it became much easier for the Brotherhood to recruit new members in the United States, which it did in large numbers. After all, even the late Mohammed Morsi, president of the short-lived Muslim Brotherhood government in Egypt during the so-called Arab Spring, did not join the Muslim Brotherhood in Egypt, the land of his—and the Muslim Brotherhood's—birth. He joined the Brotherhood on the campus of the University of Southern California, where he earned a PhD in materials science in 1982.

The more outreach Muslim Brothers were doing with unsuspecting Muslim students through the MSA, the more there was a need for secrecy and separation of Brotherhood activity from public MSA events. The Muslim MIT alumnus who talked to me about the MIT MSA, told me that most student members of the MSA were not initially aware of the MSA's hidden agenda, and were drawn to the group because of its universalist Muslim inclusiveness: "These students do not know that they are acting as fronts for the Qtubist ideology of Muslim Brotherhood," he said. "They are interested in being part of the Muslim Student Association because, if you come from different countries, it's a good way to gather together, and it takes a while to find out what's really happening."

The Muslim Brotherhood students in New England were especially eager to infiltrate the ICNE mosque and begin indoctrinating and recruiting from among its Americanized members. The original ICNE leaders, respectful of the newcomers' apparent learning, were willing to change their practices to become more spiritually correct. To ICNE members, the newcomers appeared to be pious and sincere young Muslims who were glad to reacquaint their assimilated co-religionists with the proper practices of Islam. ICNE members wanted their children to maintain links to Muslim traditions, so they saw nothing wrong with letting the Islamist young men, many of whom had formal religious education, mentor their own children. Many future Islamist leaders in New England—such as Nabeel Khudairi and Bilal Kaleem—were born in the United States or came here as young children. Yet they were radicalized and recruited by the Islamists at the ICNE or at universities like MIT.

A longtime member of the ICNE told me:

> There was a stealth organization that came into us, and it took a very long time for the people to really know what was happening around them. A group of people came into our community and wanted to help; and people didn't know that they had a hidden agenda.

By the 1950s, the various Muslim Brotherhood branches in the Middle East had developed a sophisticated organizational code of secrecy to survive repression by secular Arab dictators. And by the late 1960s, the Muslim Brotherhood had reproduced the major elements of that organization in America. Eric Trager of the Washington Institute for Near Eastern Policy is one of the foremost Western experts on the Muslim Brotherhood's "mothership" organization in Egypt, although he is not an expert on its American branch. "The [Egyptian] Brotherhood is structured like a pyramid," Trager told me in an interview.

"At the very lowest level, you have the *usras*, which literally means 'families.' These are typically five- to eight-person units. The *usra*, the 'cell,' is the most basic level of the Brotherhood structure. It's also an important component of what it means to be a Muslim brother. You meet with your family typically once a week for about three hours. You discuss the Qur'an. You review the Brotherhood's curriculum. You discuss politics. You discuss your personal lives. This becomes a very important part of what it means to be a Muslim Brother, and you're socially interacting with these people who become your best friends. That's one of the reasons why Muslim Brothers rarely leave the organization."

ICNE members, especially young ones, would be approached to participate in what Zeid al-Noman, in the recording recovered by the FBI, termed "open *usras.*" Within these, the recruit could be vetted, and then inducted into the Muslim Brotherhood with an oath of secrecy.

At the surface, these invitations to the "open *usras*" would appear to the potential recruits to be completely benign religious fellowships, much like church youth groups. But Dennis Hale warns that the Muslim Brotherhood is very far from your neighborhood church group:

"It is an organization designed to recruit people who can help overthrow modern governments, who can help overthrow modern states," he says.

> So it's constructed in circles. The outer circle is apparently a social
> welfare organization and most of the people who encounter the
> Brotherhood probably don't encounter anything more than that
> outer circle, and there they are also taught about the faith and what
> the faith requires of them. But the ones who are really suitable
> become inducted into the inner circle, and that's where they learn
> what the Brotherhood is all about. That's where they become full
> members of the Brotherhood.

The extremist and jihadist aspects of the Muslim Brotherhood's indoctrination training are not advertised—both for the sake of keeping this radical indoctrination from outside scrutiny and for the sake of keeping it, at first, even from the Muslim youths who are thinking about joining it.

Initially, potential recruits are involved in completely legitimate religious study. Participants read the Quran and other Islamic religious texts. They learn about the life of Muhammad, and they study the importance of the Five Pillars of Islam: the declaration of faith, prayer, charity, fasting, and pilgrimage. But soon, those participants who show a high level of dedication and zeal are told that simply praying and giving charity are not enough. At this next stage, they are introduced to the core Islamist idea that Muslims need to be more than pious; they need to rule over all mankind.

As Eric Trager told me:

> The Brotherhood, more than anything, is similar to a totalitar-
> ian party in the sense that it has a mechanism for indoctrinating

its members, a mechanism for unifying them ideologically and a mechanism for mobilizing them in a militia-like fashion. The process of educating Muslim Brotherhood youths and new recruits is called *Tarbiya*, which literally means upbringing or education. Based on my research, the Muslim Brotherhood uses the *Tarbiya* process as a vetting mechanism. Do they participate actively in Brotherhood activities? [Do] they follow orders when they're given? Because the Brotherhood aspires first and foremost to be a strong organization.

• • •

The Muslim Brotherhood in New England showed the strength of its organization at the Islamic Center of New England as it steadily gained recruits, both at the mosque and among Boston's students. Throughout the late 1960s and into the 1970s, the practices at the ICNE changed—gradually, but in a consistently radical direction. Under the leadership of Islamists like Muzammil Siddiqi, who later became the general secretary of the Islamic Society of North America, ICNE began to resemble an orthodox Middle Eastern mosque. Men and women were segregated at prayer. Gone were the bingo nights and the belly dancing. The mosque began to follow orthodox Sunni Islam, which resulted in some of the more assimilated members leaving the community. Yet throughout this period of increasing religiosity, the leadership of the ICNE resisted the Islamists' specifically *political* ambitions. The Islamist members did not yet have the numbers or the organizational experience to prevail ideologically, and the ICNE kept its traditional commitment to American democratic values, the separation of church and state, and patriotic devotion to the United States.

As a sign of its commitment to this combination of religious orthodoxy and political moderation, the ICNE's leadership took a major step in 1982, hiring Talal Eid, an orthodox Sunni cleric from Lebanon, to be its imam and religious director. Imam Eid came with impeccable credentials in theology, but also with a reputation for being resolutely nonpolitical. He immigrated to America with an advanced degree in Sharia from Al Azhar University in Cairo and, while at ICNE, earned a master's in Religion and a doctorate in Theology from the Harvard Divinity School. In Lebanon, Eid was a close disciple of former Lebanese Grand Mufti Hassan Khaled, one of the few religious voices calling for peace and sectarian moderation during Lebanon's civil war—a thought crime for which he was assassinated, most likely on the orders of Hafez Assad's secret police. Like his teacher, Talal Eid refused to use his pulpit to promote Sunni participation in the civil war as a religiously sanctioned jihad, and was glad for the chance to leave war-torn Lebanon for America.

Imam Eid was given the title of religious director, which came with exclusive responsibility for charting the ICNE's religious programming. All governance issues were vested with an elected Board of Directors, so even within the mosque's internal affairs there was a kind of a separation of the religious and the secular. Imam Eid was more than capable of challenging the Islamists' political agenda on theological grounds—something that the assimilated Muslim leadership of ICNE was not capable of doing. So, during the 1980s, a time when mosques across America were becoming more and more politicized due to Muslim Brotherhood penetration, the ICNE was an island of moderation.

Under the leadership of Imam Eid and ICNE presidents Abdul Kareem Khudairi and Dr. Mian Ashraf, the mosque membership grew fivefold in the 1980s, and the ICNE became a well-known and respected institution in the New England Muslim community, and among Muslims throughout America. But it was a jewel ready to be seized, and the Islamists, who had thus far not succeeded in making ICNE a base for their political activity, were only waiting for the right opportunity. It would come, soon enough, in the form of a competitor in Cambridge: the Islamic Society of Boston.

• • •

Throughout the 1970s, the Muslim Brotherhood's presence in the United States was undergoing a subtle evolution. The 1960s wave of Muslim Brotherhood students who came as members or were recruited to the group in the United States had now graduated. The very first Brotherhood members, like Sayyid Qutb, got their degrees, went back to their home countries, and rejoined the local movements there. Many of the new Muslim

Brothers, however, especially the ones recruited here, were increasingly deciding to stay in the United States.

As Muslim Brotherhood members graduated and began their careers in the United States, the organizational foundation of the Muslim Students Association was used to create a wave of Muslim Brotherhood professional organizations in the 1970s: the Association of Muslim Social Scientists (1971); the Association of Muslim Scientists and Engineers (1974); and the Islamic Medical Association (1976).

Osama Kandil, the Chairman of the ISB's board of trustees, cofounded the Muslim Arab Youth Association (MAYA) in 1976. The goals of MAYA were explicitly to absorb the new Muslim students for settlement in America. In New England and all over America, Muslim Brotherhood activists were now getting established in their adult professional and community lives; and the movement entered a new phase—transitioning from a movement of foreign students to a settled movement of permanent residents. The decision to focus its activism on settlement and recruitment within the United States was, for some time, a source of tension within the American Muslim Brotherhood movement. Many members shared Said Qutb's hatred for America, combined with a commitment to their native countries' own Muslim Brotherhood groups. Some felt that those who wanted to stay in America were betraying the movement back home, sacrificing their ideological purity by becoming residents of a spiritually depraved country. Others felt that those staying in America were wasting their time: How did they plan to build an Islamic society in a country that is overwhelmingly non-Muslim?

On the other hand, America, with its freedoms and opportunities, turned out to be a very welcoming place for an underground totalitarian movement like the Muslim Brotherhood. In the Middle East, membership in the Muslim Brotherhood came with a good likelihood of persecution, imprisonment, and even execution. Said Qutb was hanged in 1966 for conspiring to overthrow the Egyptian government, after Egyptian dictator Gamal Nasser cracked down on the Brotherhood. Qutb would not have faced the same fate if he had stayed in the America he hated, where Muslim Brothers enjoyed freedom of speech and association.

By the late 1970s, Muslim immigration to America was booming and a now-significant Muslim community became a fertile source of Muslim Brotherhood recruitment and funding. Compared to countries in the

Middle East, Muslims were a tiny fraction of the population—but this was a matter of quality over quantity. Muslim immigration to America before the 1990s was primarily composed of students and professionals, and the community was actually—and still remains, overall—far more affluent and educated than the American average. There was almost no hostility in America to Islam, which most Americans saw as just another funny-hat exotic culture within the American mosaic.

Those who wanted to plant permanent roots in America ended up getting the upper hand. With the movement's reorientation almost complete at the time that he gave it, Zeid al-Noman's 1982 talk describes what happened:

> The reality of the Movement is that it is a students' Movement. What the movement should be is to become a Movement for the residents....In the years '80 and '81, we started to work on a new kind of plans. The first change was moving the Ikhwans [Muslim Brothers] from working at the branches of the MSA and the [Muslim Arab Youth] Association, as branches whose activities are based on universities, to what is called at that time "The Muslim House," a house near the university with Ikhwans living in a part of it and the rest of it becoming a mosque. We notice that during the past two or three years that many of the students' gathering started to establish Islamic centers.

These changes were both centrally planned and major. At its 1979 annual convention, the American Muslim Brotherhood launched what it called the "ISNA concept." The idea was ambitious: the Muslim Brotherhood would found mosques all over the country that would serve as "centers" for the propagation of the Brotherhood's program. These centers would be places of prayer, but also schools, community centers, and recruitment places. The Muslim Brotherhood, through a new front group developed out of the MSA infrastructure—the Islamic Society of North America (ISNA)—would centrally direct the entire effort. The funding for the centers would be funneled from generous locals and the Brotherhood's new patrons in the Gulf through a central financial disbursement entity, the North American Islamic Trust (NAIT). The Muslim Brotherhood had decided to stay in America for good.

• • •

Researching what was essentially a complex conspiracy by religious millenarianists, part criminal and part fantastical, it's hard to avoid a certain nagging doubt. Was I becoming a conspiracy theorist? That seemed to have been the conclusion of David Cole, then a constitutional law professor at Georgetown University, which had just received the second-largest gift in its history from Saudi Prince Alwaleed Bin Talal. While researching for this book, I read a book review written by him in the *Washington Post* titled "When is Freedom of Speech Irresponsible?"—an absolutely amazing question to be made by a supposed constitutional law scholar who would go on, just one year later, to become the national legal director of the American Civil Liberties Union.

Cole's answer to that question was, essentially: "When it is the same kind of speech as you are now reading in this book, bigot!" Apparently, and here he was speaking of some of my friends and colleagues by name, our words "pose a real threat to the political freedoms of others, as they tar with unjustified suspicion Muslim civic organizations that are engaged in the promotion of civil liberties, religious freedom and Muslim identity, not terrorism." In reality, the suspicion that these "Muslim civic organizations" were engaged in a broad terrorism financing conspiracy was raised by federal prosecutors, resulted in a conviction by a federal jury, and upheld on appeal by a federal circuit court panel. The Supreme Court then declined twice to listen to any further appeals. The suspicion would appear to be well justified.

Nevertheless, professor Cole's 2015 *Washington Post* article explicitly dismissed researchers and national security experts like Frank Gaffney and John Guandolo, who were reporting on what they were learning from the HLF trial exhibits, as "conspiracy theorists." Addressing the "Strategic Goal Memorandum" that calls for "destroying Western civilization from within," Professor Cole huffed that "in fact the document is nothing more than a thought piece drafted by a single individual in the early 1990s, and that there is no evidence it was ever considered, much less adopted, by the Muslim Brotherhood or anyone else."

I have taken a deep look at the HLF trial history, the judicial opinions, and the massive evidentiary record in that trial and its appeals—a deep look that I now highly doubt Professor Cole took himself. It is clear to me that Professor Cole's attack on the Muslim Brotherhood Strategic Goals Memorandum's probity and relevance came from both ignorance and deceit. It was deceitful because, as a law professor, he was well aware of the federal rules of evidence and the federal rules of criminal procedure—laws that govern what a federal judge in a criminal case like the HLF trial will allow prosecutors to present to a jury. These rules are tough—circumscribed by the Constitution, statutory codification, and centuries of Anglo-Saxon common law doctrine. To be entered into evidence, the American Muslim Brotherhood's "Strategic Goals Memorandum" had to have met those rules. As a result, the document, and the hundreds of others, went through their own mini-trials in which the defendants could challenge the evidence. And, as the Fifth Circuit wrote in dismissing the HLF appeal: "The jury rejected the defense's theories and credited the Government's evidence by finding each defendant guilty of all applicable charges."

To be admitted into evidence, the "Strategic Goals Memorandum" document must have only been relevant to proving the specific elements of the criminal charges against the five HLF defendants, it must have been authenticated, and it could not include any hearsay. In this case, the charges were multiple counts of material support for a foreign terrorist organization, providing funds, goods, and services to a Specially Designated Terrorist, money laundering, and a count each of conspiracy to commit all three of the above. Even if the document was relevant to proving those charges, the court may exclude relevant evidence if its probative value is substantially outweighed by a danger of unfair prejudice, confusing the issues, or misleading the jury. All the evidence in the HLF trial was legitimately admitted, the appeals court ruled.

David Cole claims that the "Strategic Goals Memorandum" was the object of conspiracy theories by a "community of self-appointed guardians who make a business of issuing impassioned, McCarthy-like warnings about Islamist conspiracies to take over the United States." In truth, this document, and the hundreds of others entered into evidence at the HLF trial, was trial evidence of a very real conspiracy to support Islamist terrorism, with the Muslim Brotherhood at its center. The memorandum and the other documents in the Elbarasse search were admitted into the trial record as "co-conspirator statements" under the Federal Rules of Evidence. Under these rules and judicial precedent in the Fifth Circuit, such evidence was only admissible if the prosecution was able to prove by a preponderance of the evidence that (1) a conspiracy existed; (2) the statements in a document like the Memorandum were made by a co-conspirator of the defendants; (3) the statements were made during the course of the conspiracy; and (4) the statement was made in furtherance of the conspiracy.

As the Fifth Circuit concluded:

[A] preponderance of the evidence proved that the documents were created as part of a common enterprise. We also find that the Elbarasse and Ashqar documents were made "in furtherance" of the common goal, as the documents outlined and facilitated the [Muslim Brotherhood's Palestine] Committee's objectives....We conclude that the circumstantial evidence in this case made it "inescapable' that the declarants in the documents were joint venturers with the defendants in support of Hamas through the Palestine Committee....We are therefore satisfied that *the documents were drafted by insiders participating in the venture* and were designed to be in furtherance of the common goals of the Palestine Committee.

The Strategic Goals Memorandum was much "more than a thought piece drafted by a single individual in the early 1990s." As for Cole's claim that there is no evidence the memorandum was adopted by the Muslim Brotherhood; this part of his argument came from ignorance. Hundreds of other HLF trial exhibits belied his claim that the single exhibit he seemed to have actually seen was unique and unrepresentative of the Muslim Brotherhood's plans in the United States. For example, Government Exhibit 003-0092, "Implementation Manual for the Group's Plan for the year 1991-1992" contains meticulous instructions on how to implement the "thought piece" Cole claims was never "considered, much less adopted."

The Fifth Circuit wrote in its opinion:

The trial...produced a massive record on appeal. The Government produced voluminous evidence obtained from covert surveil-lance, searches, and testimony showing a web of complex rela-tionships connecting the defendants to Hamas and its various sub-groups....During the course of its investigation in this case, the Government intercepted tens of thousands of telephone calls and facsimile transmissions through 24-hour surveillance of the

defendants. . . The searches yielded numerous documents cor-
roborating the creation of the [American Muslim Brotherhood's]
Palestine Committee and its oversight of HLF as a fundraising arm
for Hamas. The documents included organizational flow charts,
bylaws, and meeting minutes.

Still, what if David Cole and the other detractors of research into the
American Muslim Brotherhood were right? Was there evidence of real-
world events that could show that the plans described in the Muslim
Brotherhood documents were actually implemented? Unlike Professor
Cole, I was interested in finding that evidence. If the Muslim Brotherhood
was really such a major force within the growing Muslim community from
the 1970s on, as the HLF documents seemed to suggest, would I be able to
quantify that influence based on concrete data?

Zeid al-Noman talked about the implementation of the "ISNA
Concept" developed by the Muslim Brotherhood in 1979: "The first change
was moving the Ikhwans [Muslim Brothers] from working at the branches
of the MSA...[.] We notice that during the past two or three years that
many of the students' gathering started to establish Islamic centers."

If the Muslim Brotherhood was anywhere near as influential in the
American Muslim community as the HLF documents suggested, there
ought to be a bump in new Muslim groups being founded around the time
that al-Noman said the Muslim Brothers began to establish Islamic centers.
The Internal Revenue Service keeps data on various categories of nonprofit
organizations and records the years these organizations were granted their
nonprofit status. I analyzed the rate of Islamic organizations gaining nonprofit status from the IRS from 1950 to 2008. I was looking for a bump
of a dozen or so groups that could be traced to a Muslim Brotherhood
origin that were founded shortly after 1979. It was more like an Everest
than a bump. Between 1978 and 1983, an average of only fourteen Islamic
organizations were granted IRS nonprofit status annually. In the five years
after 1983, the average was seventeen per year. But in 1983 alone, ninety-six
new Islamic nonprofit organizations were born, a sevenfold increase over
the previous five years. The vast majority of these ninety-six new organizations were named Islamic Society of [City Name], Islamic Center of [City
Name], or Islamic Association of [City Name]. They were scattered across
thirty-three states in all the regions of America.

What I was seeing was the real-world effect of the Muslim Brotherhood's 1979 "ISNA Concept." Four years after the Muslim Brotherhood issuing this central directive, a massive spike of mosque and center building occurred in eighty-seven cities across America—all within one year's time—and then subsided. The sharp pulse nature of this spike was evidence of a centrally coordinated effort. The timing indicated the effort was that of the Muslim Brotherhood. Sneers by critics like Professor Cole notwithstanding, I had my evidence and was convinced that my colleagues and I were not wrestling with an imaginary demon.

• • •

The Islamic Society of Boston was one of the ninety-six Islamic organizations that got their nonprofit status in 1983. Following the national Muslim Brotherhood's "ISNA Concept" of moving Brotherhood activism from the campus into the community, the Islamic Society of Boston was organized in 1981 and officially incorporated in Massachusetts in 1982 by members of the Muslim Students Associations of Harvard University, Boston University, MIT, Northeastern University, Wentworth Institute, Suffolk University, and Tufts University. The ISB's founding president, Abdulrahman Alamoudi, a foreign student from Eritrea who was recruited into the Muslim Brotherhood here in the United States, was by then a rising star within the movement.

ISB members first met in a reserved hall at MIT. In 1986, the ISB pooled funds and bought a four-bedroom residential building a few blocks from the MIT campus at—on Prospect Street in Cambridge. The mortgage for the building was listed under the name of Mohamed Akra, an MIT student who would soon become the head of al-Qaeda's largest fundraising front group in the United States. This was the ISB version of Zeid al-Noman's "Muslim House," "a house near the university with Ikhwans [Muslim Brothers] living in a part of it and the rest of it becoming a mosque." The ISB's Cambridge crash pad would serve throughout the 1980s as a growing Muslim Brotherhood organizing nucleus for Islamist students in the Boston area. Across the nation, in the 1980s, the American Muslim Brotherhood's clandestine underground organization grew into a sophisticated apparatus that would rival the Muslim Brotherhood movements in many Muslim countries.

By the 1990s, like many Muslim Brotherhood institutions around the country, the Islamic Society of Boston was undergoing increasing growth and diversification. As Walid Fitaihi's father was buying giant diamonds at auctions throughout the decade, Fitaihi the son appeared to be investing in real estate for the ISB instead. In 1993, the ISB purchased a former Boy Scout headquarters building on Prospect Street, a few houses over from the ISB's "Muslim House." That same year, Brotherhood leaders created the Islamic Society of Boston Trust to control the property and funds of the ISB. In 1994, the Trust repurchased the "Muslim House" property from Mohammed Akra, whose allegiances were at the time moving closer to al-Qaeda. In 1995, it bought two more properties on Prospect Street. The original ISB Trustees were almost entirely citizens of Middle Eastern countries, some residing in Massachusetts at the time. They were Mohammed Attawia, Osama Kandil, Walid Fitaihi, Soud Ahafi, and Ali Tobah, with Muslim Brotherhood spiritual leader Yusuf Qaradawi being named as an "additional trustee."

The old Boy Scout headquarters in Cambridge was retrofitted into a mosque and an Islamic Center that functioned according to the Muslim Brotherhood model. Meanwhile, as the Muslim Brotherhood's underground apparatus in the United States became more and more sophisticated, it was put to good use. The time had come to wage jihad. The Muslim Brothers of Boston would play a key role. Massachusetts law enforcement would play a key role in the cover-up.

CHAPTER 10

BOSTON JOINS THE GLOBAL JIHAD

In 1979, a Muslim Brotherhood cleric moved with his family to Pakistan. His name was Abdullah Azzam, and he would become known as the "Father of the Global Jihad." Azzam was born in Mandatory Palestine near the city of Jenin in 1941 and joined the Muslim Brotherhood in his teens. At age twenty-nine, he moved to Egypt to get his doctorate in Islamic law at Al Azhar University. While there he became close with the family of Muslim Brotherhood ideologue Sayyid Qutb, who had been executed by the Egyptian government just a few years earlier. Azzam not only wholeheartedly embraced Qutb's ideology; he developed it into an even more extremist form. The mainstream Muslim Brotherhood movement took a slow and gradual approach to the ultimate goal of a global Islamic State. For the Muslim Brotherhood, armed jihadist conquest should come later, only after a long phase of preparation, base building, and proselytism. Azzam, on the other hand, believed that jihad must be the first and foremost obligation for all Muslims, that jihad must be fought immediately and continuously to liberate all formerly Muslim lands, and that jihad must not stop until all the world is conquered under Islam.

Azzam came to Pakistan to fight the Soviets, who had invaded neighboring Afghanistan in December 1979 after traditionalist Muslims rebelled against the Soviet puppet government ruling the country. Up until then, Azzam had been living in Saudi Arabia, where he was a professor of Islamic jurisprudence at King Abdulaziz University. Saudi Arabia had become a refuge of sorts for Muslim Brotherhood activists, many of whom had to flee Egypt and other secular dictatorships in the 1960s and '70s. Saudi Arabia's radical Wahhabi clerics felt an affinity with the Muslim Brothers. Universities like Jeddah's King Abdul Aziz became hotspots of Islamic extremist agitation, with Muslim Brotherhood professors like Abdullah Azzam leading the way. When Soviet Union tanks rolled into Afghanistan, Azzam declared that no true Muslim could sit out the jihad, and left for Pakistan. Many of his students, including a young Osama bin Laden, followed. Azzam's oratorical, organizational, and military skills, combined with bin Laden's fortune, would help defeat one superpower and then train their sights on the other.

In 1984, Azzam took up residence in Peshawar, a city on Pakistan's border with Afghanistan near the strategic Khyber Pass. There, with bin Laden's cash and help from the Muslim Brotherhood's Jordanian branch, he founded the Mujahideen Services Bureau, also known as Al Kifah Refugee Center, which recruited and deployed foreign Muslim fighters for the Afghan Jihad. This organization would eventually develop into al-Qaeda. Following the mountain routes taken by the armies of Alexander the Great more than two thousand years earlier, Azzam's network of mujahideen holy warriors moved large amounts of weaponry and significant numbers of Muslim volunteers from around the world into Afghanistan.

Over the next five years, Azzam would travel the world to raise funds and recruit for his jihad efforts. Much of the funding came from bin Laden's personal fortune and many other wealthy Saudis. The American Muslim community also became one of his primary sponsors, often unwittingly, thanks to the Muslim Brotherhood's clandestine dominance of its mosques. Federal authorities did more than turn a blind eye to Azzam's activities in the United States, despite Azzam's rhetoric being as anti-American as it was anti-Soviet. Through the CIA, the United States covertly funded and supported Azzam's efforts. Between 1985 and 1989, when Soviet troops withdrew from Afghanistan for good, Azzam visited dozens of American cities and gathered enough recruits to be able to found branches of his Al Kifah organization in thirty of them. Boston was one of those cities, and would eventually become the main fundraising base in the United States for Azzam, for Al Kifah, and ultimately for al-Qaeda.

Many Muslims from the Boston area would get involved with Al Kifah, as it raised money and recruited throughout the 1980s at Boston area

Muslim Students Associations. Several Boston Muslims would die on the battlefields of Afghanistan, and later in Bosnia. One of Al Kifah's leaders in Boston was Mohammad Akra, the MIT student and ISB leader who briefly held title to the ISB's first off-campus Muslim House in Cambridge. The MIT Muslim Students Association, which was the ISB's main base in the 1980s, would also become Al Kifah's main base in the Boston area a decade later.

• • •

In 1988, Soviet forces were on the verge of defeat in Afghanistan. I was six years old then, growing up in the Siberian city of Tomsk. My uncle was nearing drafting age and I remember a vague feeling of dread in the hushed conversations about the war against the "ghosts" (*dukhi*), as the Afghani mujahedeen were called. Mothers of sons whose call-up dates were getting close quietly lost their minds. Then, some would lose touch with their drafted sons for months, only to receive them back in hermetically sealed zinc coffins for a hushed-up funeral. More than thirteen thousand would come back this way—six times as many as the American deaths in Afghanistan so far. Those who came back alive after hunting Azzam's ghosts were a lot crueler, more savage. The so-called limitlessness (*bespredel*) period of murder and extortion in the post-Soviet 1990s was probably intensified by the tainted psyches of these young men. Luckily for my uncle, my grandmother paid off the draft board to have him excused from service on medical grounds. Luckily for me, my family left Siberia for the American South in 1992—arriving exactly five hundred years after Christopher Columbus, to the very calendar day.

Last time Abdullah Azzam was in the American South was in 1988. In a speech at an Oklahoma mosque, with the Soviet withdrawal imminent, Azzam told the American Muslims gathered to hear him speak: "Oh brothers, after Afghanistan, nothing in the world is impossible for us anymore. There are no super powers or mini powers. What matters is the willpower that springs from our religious belief." As Azzam saw it, the coming mujahedeen victory was proof that nothing would be able to stand in the way of the divinely guided project to force the entire world to submit to an Islamic Caliphate.

Azzam was assassinated in November 1989, when still-unknown

culprits targeted his car with a roadside bomb in Peshawar, Pakistan. But his prophesy seemed to bear out. In 1991, just two years after being defeated in Afghanistan by the Islamic holy warriors, the Soviet Union collapsed. Islamists the world over felt that they were responsible for this collapse and that it was a sign from Allah that nothing could stand in their way. As Azzam told them, there are no longer any superpowers that can withstand the will of the Muslim mujahideen. Azzam's followers and Islamists in general now focused their jihadism on the United States, the last remaining world superpower.

The same year that the Soviet Union fell, the American Muslim Brotherhood's Executive Office issued its infamous memorandum, "General Strategic Goal for the Group in North America," calling for the "grand Jihad in eliminating and destroying the Western civilization from within." The Muslim Brotherhood itself did not officially call for violent attacks and terrorism against America yet, preferring subversion and sabotage to direct violence. Abdulrahman Alamoudi, the ISB's founder, for example, told a gathering of Hamas supporters in 1996:

> [T]his country will become a Muslim country. And if we are outside this country we can say "oh, Allah destroy America", but once we are here, our mission in this country is to change it....There is nowhere for Muslims to be violent in America, nowhere at all. We have other means to do it. You can be violent anywhere else but in America.

On the other hand, many Muslim Brothers, especially those influenced by Azzam, began to believe that jihad can only mean violent struggle, and that jihad must be fought everywhere and at all times until Islam is the only religion in the world. Any Muslim who did not participate in the jihad was, according to this belief, guilty of cowardice and religious hypocrisy. As Abdullah Azzam admonished his 1988 Oklahoma audience, contradicting Alamoudi's advice to refrain from violence within the United States:

> The Jihad, the fighting, is obligatory on you wherever you can perform it. And just as when you are in America you must fast [for Ramadan], unless you are ill or on a voyage, so too must you

wage Jihad. The word "Jihad" means fighting only, fighting with the sword.

Abdullah Azzam's main base in America was the Al Kifah central branch in Brooklyn, New York. After Azzam's death in 1989, Omar Abdel-Rahman, also known as the Blind Sheikh, who had met Azzam through the Qutb family while both were studying at Al Azhar University in Cairo, became its leader. Shortly after the end of the Afghan War, the Blind Sheikh came to Brooklyn, where he and his followers began putting Azzam's dreams of jihad against the United States into practice. Mass-scale Islamic terrorism had come to America.

• • •

Around lunchtime on February 26, 1993, a Ryder van packed with 1,400 pounds of explosives blew up in the basement parking garage of New York's World Trade Center. The plan was to topple the North Tower onto the South Tower, but luckily both towers survived the explosion. Six people did not. The bombing was carried out by a terrorist cell operating through Al Kifah's New York branch and organized by the Blind Sheikh, who had issued a religious fatwa calling for attacks on American skyscrapers. Three months later he was arrested together with nine of his followers, who actually carried out the plot.

Andrew McCarthy was the U.S. attorney who prosecuted the Blind Sheikh and his co-conspirators. In an interview, he described to me the convictions he was able to obtain against Abdel-Rahman: "Ultimately, he and a number of people who were affiliated with his cell were convicted of a Civil War era criminal statute called the seditious conspiracy statute," McCarthy said. He continued:

The specific charge was conspiring to wage a war of urban terrorism against the United States. It included the bombing of the World Trade Center in 1993, a subsequent plot to bomb New York City landmarks, including the Lincoln and Holland tunnels and the UN Complex on the East Side, as well as the FBI's lower Manhattan headquarters. And there were also other charges including the murder of Meir Kahane, who had been the founder of the [Jewish

Defense League] and also a conspiracy to kill Hosni Mubarak, the then president of Egypt.

After his conviction, the Blind Sheikh had become a cause célèbre within both the Muslim Brotherhood and al-Qaeda movements. Multiple terrorists attempted to exchange hostages for his release. After the Muslim Brotherhood came to power in Egypt in 2012, the government of president Mohammed Morsi engaged in intense diplomacy with the State Department seeking Abdel-Rahman's transfer to Egyptian custody. But, the Blind Sheikh stayed in jail until his death in 2017 and Al Kifah's New York branch had stopped functioning after its leaders were arrested. However, it was never officially shut down by the U.S. government and its other branches were allowed to keep operating, which Andrew McCarthy says was a major mistake:

> After the case was over, the government did not follow up with prosecutions against the organizations that had been shown to be complicit in the conspiracy and those organizations continue to operate as if nothing had happened, as if they hadn't been shown in court to have facilitated the terrorist activities of an organization that's actually designated as a terrorist under American law.

As a result of the government's reticence to go after it, Al Kifah remained relatively unscathed, and it was the network's Boston branch that would eventually pick up the slack and take over the American operations of Al Kifah as it morphed into the al-Qaeda we know today. Less than two months after the World Trade Center bombing—even before the Blind Sheikh was arrested—Al Kifah leaders in Boston incorporated a new organization, Care International, as a front group for their activities. Mohammed Akra, the legal owner of the ISB's "Muslim House" property in Cambridge at the time, was listed as one of the group's founding directors. A Care International leader would later admit to the FBI that they formed this new organization to conceal their connection to Al Kifah in New York. Al Kifah's Boston branch took over the duties of coordinating all the other branches, collecting the funds raised for al-Qaeda and other terrorist groups by supporters around the country, and publishing Al Kifah's propaganda magazine: *Al Hussam* (*The Sword*).

ISB leader Mohammed Akra became this new front group's president in 1998. He was an MIT alumnus, and the MIT Muslim Students Association would become Care International's main base of operations. Many MIT Muslim students would get involved with Care fundraising through the MSA, and through events at Mohammed Akra's ISB "Muslim House" not far from campus.

In 1990, shortly after Care International was incorporated, a new transfer student arrived on the MIT campus, Suheil Laher. An Indian Muslim raised in Zimbabwe, Laher was extremely pious. His family was from the Deobandi movement—an extremist strain of Islam common in India and closely linked with the Saudi Wahhabi ideology. Laher had memorized the Quran as a child and had studied with a variety of extremist clerics, receiving several *ijazahs*, or certifications as an Islamic scholar who earned the right to transmit his religious knowledge to others. Laher quickly became active in the MIT MSA and joined Care International, ultimately succeeding Mohammed Akra as its president in 2000. After graduating from MIT, Laher went on to become MIT's Muslim Chaplain in 1998, a position that he held until 2014. He has been and continues to be a frequent preacher at the ISB.

As a religious scholar and an engineer, Laher was both the spiritual and technological leader of Care International. He pioneered the use of the new Internet medium to fundraise and recruit for al-Qaeda causes online. Laher's personal website prominently featured a quote from Abdullah Azzam's notorious call to Jihad, a tract called "Join the Caravan": "Beloved brother! Draw your sword, climb onto the back of your horse, and wipe the blemish off your ummah. If you do not take the responsibility, who then will?"

Laher's website contained a large collection of his writings and of sermons he gave in the Boston area. These sermons are replete with calls for Jihad, such as this passage:

When the Muslim lands are being attacked, and the Muslims are being raped and killed, the only solution prescribed by Allah is jihad. Jihad is for all times....Jihad does not stop. Those of us who have not yet managed to go and physically help our brothers and sisters should support...our mujahidin brethren with prayer, with money, with clothes, by taking care of their families, and at some point in person. Otherwise, we must face the wrath of Allah.

While Laher's sermons preached the general Islamic obligation to go on jihad, or at the very least to support it financially, Care International's website, along with its newsletter *The Sword*, fulfilled that responsibility. In the late 1990s, Care International focused its fundraising activity on the Russian breakaway republic of Chechnya. Specifically, Care International backed the al-Qaeda–affiliated terrorists under the leadership of Chechen warlord Shamil Basayev, describing him as "a Muslim hero" and praising his suicide bomber squads.

Basayev can arguably be described as one of the cruelest Islamic terrorists in modern jihadist history, due to his role in the Beslan School massacre. On September 1, 2004, during a ceremony marking the first day of school, Basayev's men surrounded the school in the town of Beslan in southern Russia and took over 1,100 people hostage, nearly 800 of them children. They murdered several people on the spot in front of the children and herded everyone into a sweltering gymnasium, where the hostages were kept without food or water for three days as bombs were hung up from the rafters and basketball hoops above them. On the third day, the terrorists started setting off the bombs and Russian security forces stormed the school as shell-shocked children ran the other way and were shot in the back by the terrorists. Three hundred and eighty-five people were murdered, among them 186 children. Subsequently, Shamil Basayev bragged about his "success" at Beslan and the fact that the attack only cost him eight thousand euros to launch. Russian security forces killed Basayev in 2006. How much of the money for the Beslan massacre had been gathered by Laher and Care International in Boston?

One of the MIT students who answered Laher's call to join the jihad in person was a bright young biology major named Aafia Siddiqui. Siddiqui also came to MIT as a transfer student, arriving in 1995. Her family was also Deobandi, and had some connections with the jihadist movements on the Indian subcontinent. Siddiqui had initially seemed to be a normal, if fairly religious, student. But after getting involved with the Muslim Student Association at MIT, Siddiqi became increasingly militant. She became a prolific fundraiser for Care International, and would give impassioned speeches inciting and fundraising for jihadist causes like Bosnia and Chechnya at MIT, at MSAs on campuses around Boston, and in mosques like the ISB. Laher, Siddiqui, and their fellow activists at Care International raised large amounts of money for jihad around Boston, $1.7

million according to federal authorities. Some of Care's money went back to the community. In March 2001, Care wrote a $10,000 check toward the construction of the ISBCC Roxbury mosque, although the money was returned in 2003, after the FBI first questioned Care International leaders about the nature of their fundraising.

There were also other means by which al-Qaeda–affiliated funds were being moved around Boston. In 1994, Oussama Ziade, a young Lebanese immigrant fresh out of Harvard Business School, started a computer software company named PTech in the Boston suburb of Quincy—not too far from the ICNE mosque. PTech's biggest investor was Yassin Al Qadi, an accused al-Qaeda financier who knew Osama bin Laden personally and who was declared a Specially Designated Global Terrorist by the Treasury Department one month after the 9/11 attacks. Qadi was the director of a Saudi al-Qaeda charity that moved millions of dollars to Bin Laden's operations.

Many Care International and ISB leaders were employed by or invested in PTech. ISB founder Abdulrahman Alamoudi was a founding investor. Suheil Laher, the MIT Muslim chaplain and Care International president, was PTech's chief software architect. Another software engineer at PTech was Hossam Al Jabri, the MAS Boston president whom I confronted about his donation to the Holy Land Foundation at the meeting with Jewish leaders in 2007. Care International's treasurer, Muhamed Mubayyid, served as the customer service manager at PTech. A PTech board member, Soliman Biheiri, who happened to be close personal friends with Yusuf Qaradawi, would ultimately serve time for his business dealings with Hamas leader Mousa Abu Marzook. And PTech's network administrator was Saladin Ali-Salaam, the son of none other than Muhammad Ali Salaam—the Boston Redevelopment Authority official who got the ISB that sweet piece of land in Roxbury, for its ISBCC mosque, at more than 90 percent off.

Despite PTech's connections to terrorist movements seeking to attack the United States, the Massachusetts company received a security clearance from the U.S. government in 1997, and subsequently was awarded contracts to service the software needs of various government agencies in collaboration with the secretive Defense Advanced Research Projects Agency (DARPA). According to the *Wall Street Journal*: "Among other projects, Ptech helped build the Military Information Architecture Framework, a software tool used by the Department of Defense to link data networks from various military computer systems and databases." PTech also provided its software to the Department of Justice, the Department of Energy, Customs and Border Control, the Air Force, the Federal Aviation Administration, the White House, NATO, the House of Representatives, and the FBI.

Although it was willing to help bin Laden's organizations move money through its groups and activists, the Muslim Brotherhood in America never officially affiliated itself with the nascent al-Qaeda movement. Although they shared the same goal, they disagreed on the tactics: jihad on America now versus jihad on America later. However, there was no disagreement over violent jihad on Israel—at all times; and the Muslim Brotherhood threw in the weight of its entire clandestine apparatus behind another terror group that Abdullah Azzam had co-founded: Hamas.

CHAPTER 11

FOREIGN CONFLICTS
ON BOSTON TURF

The Muslim Brotherhood is a rabidly anti-Semitic movement. Anti-Semitism has always been a historical reality within the Islamic world, even though some Islamic polities and eras were more tolerant of Jews than others. The Muslim Brotherhood, whose leaders admired and even allied themselves with Nazi Germany, added modern European anti-Semitic theories to its religious hatred of the Jews. Sayyid Qutb wrote in "Milestones" that the purpose of "world Jewry" is "to eliminate all limitations, especially the limitations imposed by faith and religion, so that the Jews may penetrate into the body politic of the whole world and then may be free to perpetuate their evil designs." In a 1988 speech to Al Kifah supporters in Kansas, Abdullah Azzam told the audience that "humanity is being ruled by Jews and Christians. The Americans, the British and others. And behind them, the fingers of world Jewry, with their wealth, their women and their media."

From its birth in 1928, the Muslim Brotherhood adopted jihad against the Jews of Palestine as one of its primary objectives and rallying causes. In 1947, an Armenian American author and anti-fascist activist, writing under the pen name John Roy Carlson, traveled to the Middle East disguised as a Nazi and Arab sympathizer to chronicle the looming Arab-Israeli War. In 1951 he published *From Cairo to Damascus*, an account of his travels. While in Cairo, he met Hassan al-Banna, who told him, "We aim to smash modernism in government and society. In Palestine our first duty as Moslems is to crush Zionism, which is Jewish modernism. It is our patriotic duty. The Koran commands it."

By 1947, Al-Banna's followers were already well trained in what Dennis Hale describes as the arts of political terror, extortion, and assassination. Carlson colorfully paints the men he encountered on his visit to al-Banna's Muslim Brotherhood headquarters in Cairo:

> I was surrounded by what were undoubtedly some of Egypt's most vicious thugs, who were studying me with as much grim interest as I was them. Here were zealots of every description—ultra-nationalist, ultrareligionist, ultra-fanatic Moslems who had vowed to make every day a day of Jehad against nonbelievers. From every Arab country, from North Africa to Pakistan, they were flowing into the Cairo headquarters: Arab trigger-men carrying daggers and pistols; men from the Sudan with their cheeks slashed; fighters from the Sinai desert; recruiters from Palestine; gun-runners; spies; lice-ridden Bedouins from everywhere. Greasy, bearded men with diseased eyes and mutilated faces, crude and barbaric, all sat sullenly, sizing up the Amrikani. The fires of fanaticism had consumed them deeply, and the flames had burned out all warmth and humanity from their faces. They said nothing—only sat there in sullen silence in my presence. The most antiforeign, murderous crew in Egypt, to whom nothing counted but the Koran, the sword of Islam, and the dictates of their Moorshid [al-Banna].

Carlson talked to some of these Muslim Brotherhood members, and one thing was on their mind first and foremost: killing Jews. A "fearlessly mustachioed" Bedouin from the Negev showed off his automatic rifle and said: "Allah! I paid £20 for this, and I won't have my money's worth until I have killed twenty Jews. One pound, one Jew." Another Muslim Brother also showed off his gun: "This is for the Jew in battle. But this"—pointing to a dagger—"is for the Jew in Cairo." While the Jews of Israel won that battle, the thousands of Jews of Cairo were forced to flee. In 2017, six elderly Jewish ladies were the only ones left.

By 1947, al-Banna was organizing his thugs into paramilitary Muslim Brotherhood battalions and sending them off to fight the Jews in Palestine. They would be the first organized fighting forces of modern Islamism, to be emulated by his successors, from Azzam to ISIS. Carlson's book reprints an article from a Brotherhood newspaper about the latest battalion's departure for the Palestinian border:

> Last Sunday was one of Allah's days in Port Said, for at one o'clock in the morning there arrived the Cairo train filled with people going to fight in the Holy War of Palestine. These faithful believers jumped on to the platform in Port Said, each carrying his own belongings, and marched in line to the Moslem Brothers' House as compact as the stones of a building. They were enthusiastically and energetically prepared to go on their way to the field of action and to fight for Allah. It was lovely to hear them singing: "Struggle is our way, and to die for Allah our highest ideal."

Neither the Muslim Brothers nor the five Arab armies that attacked Israel in 1948 were able to defeat the Jews, but the dream remains. Although the Muslim Brotherhood was temporarily suppressed by Israel's martial laws within the Green Line, it thrived in the Palestinian territories occupied by Jordan throughout the 1950s and '60s. It was at this time that Abdullah Azzam joined the Muslim Brotherhood near Jenin in the West Bank.

After Israel conquered the Palestinian territories in the Six-Day War, the Muslim Brotherhood apparatus in the territories, aided by the Muslim Brotherhood movements of Jordan, Syria, Lebanon, and Egypt, became active in inciting Muslims around the world against Israel and Jews through the International Organization of the Muslim Brotherhood. In 1987, the First Intifada broke out in the Palestinian Territories and the Muslim Brotherhood swung into action.

Locally, within the Palestinian territories, the Muslim Brotherhood response to the 1987 First Intifada was to form the Islamic Resistance Movement in Palestine, also known as Hamas. Muslim Brotherhood apologists have tried to minimize the link between Hamas and the Muslim Brotherhood, insisting that first, the Muslim Brotherhood had foresworn violence in the 1970s and, second, that Hamas is an independent movement. These claims are contrary to the Hamas founding charter, which, in a section titled "The Islamic Resistance Movement's Relation with the Moslem Brotherhood Group," states: "The Islamic Resistance Movement is one of the wings of Moslem Brotherhood in

Palestine." Likewise another internal American Muslim Brotherhood memo from 1992 found in Ismail Elbarasse's basement and entered into evidence at the Holy Land Foundation trial, states the same point in clear language:

> [T]he Islamic Resistance Movement (Hamas)...was bred in the bosom of the mother movement, 'The Muslim Brotherhood' [and] restored hope and life to the Muslim nation and the notion that the flare of Jihad has not died out and that the banner of Islamic Jihad is still raised.

As the HLF trial evidence indicates, by 1989, after two years of Hamas jihadist terrorism and Israeli counterterrorism operations, the IDF and Shin Bet had killed or imprisoned a large portion of the local Palestinian leadership of Hamas. In order to make sure Hamas survived and continued its jihad against the Jews, the International Organization of the Muslim Brotherhood stepped in and began directly running Hamas operations. According to the 1992 memo:

> Due to the successive strikes and continuous arrests in the ranks of the leaders in particular, the General Apparatus for Palestine became the acting central leadership for the Islamic Resistance Movement (Hamas) in the inside and the outside.

This central leadership then directed all the daughter movements in multiple countries in both the Muslim world and in Western countries to form Palestine Committees within their organizations. The American Muslim Brotherhood obliged. Its 1992 memo explained why American Muslims must join the Brotherhood's Jihad against the Jews of Israel:

> Palestine is the one for which Muslim Brotherhood prepared armies—made up from the children of Islam in the Arab and Islamic nations—to liberate its land from the abomination and the defilement of the children of the Jews....The struggle is with the Jews who do not constitute a danger to Palestine alone, but a danger to Arabs and Muslims in their homelands, resources, religion, traditions, influence and political entity.

By 1991, the American Muslim Brotherhood's clandestine Palestine Section had become a complex underground apparatus that managed three front groups: the Islamic Association for Palestine, the United Association for Studies and Research, and the Occupied Land Fund—soon to be renamed the Holy Land Foundation. Ruling over this as the head of the Palestine Section was Mousa Abu Marzook.

These days, Mousa Abu Marzook is the second in command within the Hamas Political Bureau and lives in Qatar. But in 1977, Marzook was a twenty-six-year-old engineering graduate student at Colorado State University. He was also an active Muslim Brotherhood member. By 1991, he was elected chairman of the Hamas Political Bureau and was aggressively fundraising and propagandizing in the United States on behalf of Hamas. Through the Islamic Association of Palestine, Marzook would raise hundreds of thousands of dollars in appeals to mosques across America. The HLF trial featured one such missive, sent to Marzook's hometown Falls Church mosque, Dar Al Hijra, titled "Soliciting donations on appropriate occasions to support Jihad in Palestine," which told the mosque's leaders that "Dar al-Hijrah's supportive stand to Jihad in Palestine and other Muslim causes will strengthen its position in the eyes of Muslims in general which will increase Muslims' affiliation with the Dar."

Mousa Abu Marzook moved to Jordan in 1992, but he left a major Hamas infrastructure in the United States. The Muslim Brotherhood in Boston participated in that infrastructure and was also involved in fundraising for Jihad in Palestine in the 1990s. HLF trial documents reveal that Mousa Abu Marzook made phone calls to Massachusetts numbers in Salem, Waltham, East Boston, and especially frequently to a particular phone number in Quincy during the year 1992. In 1997, ISB founder Abdulrahman Alamoudi became the secretary of one of the Palestine Committee's front groups, The United Association for Studies and Research. In 1998, ISB trustee Mohammed Attawia became a national director of Islamic Relief, an alleged Hamas charity, and served as its chairman of the board in 2006. At least eight Massachusetts Muslims, including future MAS Boston president Hossam Al Jabri, were listed among the major donors to HLF in trial exhibits.

•   •   •

The American Muslim Brotherhood's obsession with the Israeli-Palestinian conflict reached a fever pitch in 1993. The reason: Oslo. Under the Oslo peace process, the United States was leading an unprecedented diplomatic effort to end the First Palestinian Intifada and pave the way for a two-state solution to the Arab-Israeli Conflict. Within the HLF trial evidence, American Muslim Brotherhood documents from the period show a complete rejection of the peace effort, whose success would put an end to a dream that the Brotherhood has carried since its founding: the complete destruction of the Jewish State, as well as the final annihilation of the Jews.

Internal Muslim Brotherhood documents from this period reveal an obsessive loathing of the peace process, and the concerted efforts by American Islamists to derail it. At the same time, the Holy Land Foundation began a broad and massive fundraising campaign that would eventually see it funnel $12 million dollars to Hamas in the 1990s, concurrently with a wave of Hamas suicide bombings and other terrorist action calculated to prevent peace.

The American Muslim Brotherhood decided to also fight the Oslo Accords on the battlefield of American politics. On October 2, 1993, a group of twenty-five men met in a Philadelphia hotel for a conference organized by the Palestine Committee. According to the FBI, which wiretapped the conference, "all attendees at this meeting [were] Hamas members" or sympathizers. The goal of the meeting was "determining the strategies, policies, and frames of Islamic activism for Palestine in North America."

It was decided at the meeting to found a new organization that would promote the goals of Hamas in the United States through a roundabout manner. HLF CEO Shukri Abu Baker, speaking at the meeting, said that "war is deception." The Muslim Brotherhood and Hamas must "[d] eceive, camouflage. . . Deceive your enemy." Therefore "we should start right now...[and] begin thinking about establishing alternative organizations...whose Islamic*hue is not very conspicuous."

The organization that Abu Baker was conceptualizing in 1993 was founded in 1994 by Palestine Committee members and Philadelphia meeting participants Nihad Awad and Omar Ahmad. It was called the Council on American Islamic Relations (CAIR). The stated mission of CAIR was "to enhance understanding of Islam, encourage dialogue, protect civil liberties, empower American Muslims, and build coalitions that promote justice." In reality, CAIR was, and remains, a Hamas front. The deception, however, has apparently worked. CAIR is frequently described as "America's largest Muslim civil rights group" and its claims of promoting justice are taken at face value by top media outlets and high-level government officials. The group would eventually show up in Boston.

. . .

As most American Jewish communities expressed their support for a peaceful two-state solution to the Arab-Israeli conflict, the American Muslim Brotherhood was drafting plans to push back *specifically* against the Jews. The Palestine Committee's meeting notes from July 1994 have a section titled "Confronting the Zionist infiltration to normalize relations with the Muslims in America," in which it outlines its position on the peace process:

> The Islamic and Arabic world is being overrun by a vigorous campaign to normalize the relations between the Muslims and the Arabs from one side, and the Zionist entity from another side. Hardly a day passes without us hearing that some Arab or Muslim country has established diplomatic or commercial relation with the Zionist entity. This campaign is not limited to countries only but also extends to Arab and Muslim organizations....Dr. Edward Sa'id, one of the participants in these dialogues, says that the Zionist organizations were planning this type of dialogues in order to break the psychological barrier that the Arabs and Palestinians have so that they accept the Jews and their country... And now the Muslim's turn has come! The normalization attempts have started to reach the Islamic organizations and personalities in America... The Jews' objective from these meetings is clear: The approval of the peace process by the Muslims and the recognition of Israel....[T]his is a formidable danger that does not serve the Islamic aspect of the Palestinian cause.

The Muslim Brotherhood appointed the Muslim American Society to lead what it termed the "confrontation work plan" and "educate the brothers in all work centers, mosques, and organizations on the necessity of stopping any contacts with the Zionist organizations and the rejection of any future contacts." The Muslim American Society in Boston would go one step further—it would co-opt unwitting local Jews to the Muslim Brotherhood's genocidal cause.

• • •

By the time the Oslo Accords were signed in 1993, the Islamic Society of Boston was a growing Muslim Brotherhood organizing nucleus for Islamist students in Boston—and a major competitor of the moderate Islamic Center of New England (ICNE). That competition was not a friendly one, as ISB members began a gradual infiltration of the ICNE mosque in Quincy, some of them managing to secure spots on the ICNE's governing board, where they waited for an opportunity to expand their influence. That opportunity would come very soon.

By the early 1990s, the ICNE had outgrown its Quincy mosque building, and its leaders began a search for a site where the congregation could continue to grow. In late 1991, ICNE bought fifty-four acres of farmland in Sharon, Massachusetts, a southern suburb of Boston, and began plans for building a large new mosque. Sharon was a town with a large Jewish community, including many Orthodox Jews. In an ironic case of misplaced prejudice, the seller of the property, a Jewish resident, was so angry at the town for refusing to let him rezone his farmland for development that he decided to retaliate by selling the land to Muslims, expecting that this would deeply alarm the town's leaders.

But Imam Talal Eid and ICNE president Dr. Mian Ashraf were not the kind of Muslims that some Sharon Jewish residents feared. Dr. Ashraf was married to a Jewish woman; and the leaders of ICNE reached out to their new Jewish neighbors with sincere love and respect. In a historically unprecedented and highly symbolic move, they invited a rabbi from Sharon to be the first person to break ground on the new mosque's construction. This was the first of the "unforgivable sins" of the ICNE leaders, and Boston's Islamists were incensed. It was bad enough that the original ICNE mosque was spiritually tainted by gambling, belly dancing, and interest-based debt. The second ICNE mosque had now been spiritually defiled at its inception by a cleric from another religion.

That the cleric was also a Jew only doubled the affront to Islamist ideology, in part because of the geopolitics of the 1990s. The ICNE's outreach to the Jewish Community of Sharon was a direct threat to the Islamist campaign to derail the Oslo peace process within the American Muslim community. Raising even more ire among the New England Islamists, U.S. president Bill Clinton's appointed the ICNE's Dr. Ashraf to represent the American Muslim community at the Oslo Accords ceremonies.

The time was ripe to act, and the motivation to act had become intense. In the early 1990s, Islamist activists affiliated with the Muslim Brotherhood and South Asian Islamist movements, empowered by their leadership roles in the growing Islamic Society of Boston, began joining the ICNE and acquiring leadership positions on its board of directors by manipulating the results of ICNE's elections. By 1997, the ICNE board was dominated by Islamist leaders; and one of them, Abdul-Badi Abou-Samra, was elected president. Yet the Islamists still had one powerful force standing in their way: the religious authority of Imam Talal Eid. Even though Islamists dominated the management decisions of the ICNE, as its two mosques' religious director, Imam Eid controlled all religious programming—and thereby could guard against extremist ideas being taught to young people. The Islamists had to find a way to counter his influence. They found it in Hafiz Muhammed Masood.

Hafiz Masood had come to the United States from Pakistan in 1987 on a USAID scholarship to pursue a master's degree in economics at Vanderbilt University in my adopted hometown of Nashville, Tennessee. In 1988, he transferred to Boston University. By 1991, despite having received $85,800 in taxpayer-funded USAID assistance, he took a leave of absence from classes. Masood's wife gave birth to their seventh child in 1992, and in 1995, with the time limit to earn his degree having expired, Massod was expelled from Boston University. Nevertheless, he continued to misrepresent himself as a BU student in order to continue living in subsidized graduate student housing. At this point, he was in the United States illegally, having failed to satisfy the requirements of his J1 exchange visa. He worked odd jobs as a parking attendant and a security guard, but his main activity during this time was promoting radical Islamist causes through local university Muslim Students Associations and in local mosques.

What few knew at the time is that Masood was the brother of Hafiz Muhammad Saeed, a notorious Pakistani terrorist leader, whose militant group, Lashkar-e-Taiba, co-founded with Abdullah Azzam, was designated as a terrorist organization shortly after 9/11. As of this writing, Saeed has a

$10 million FBI bounty on his head and Masood is back in Pakistan serving as his terrorist brother's communications director.

Masood became a sort of celebrity within Boston's jihadist circles in the 1990s. According to a local Muslim source, he would brag about going on jihad missions into Indian-controlled Kashmir to kill Indian soldiers. He recruited local Muslims into Lashkar-e-Taiba cells and raised money for his brother's terrorist group in the Boston area. But by 1998, the good life had run out for Masood. There had been complaints from his neighbors about the filth and refuse on the landing outside his apartment in BU's graduate housing. The apartment was meant for a single graduate student, but had, for several years, been housing a family with seven children. BU authorities finally realized that Masood had been ineligible for student housing for years and began eviction proceedings against the family.

With his housing now gone, and with a lack of steady income due to his illegal immigrant status, Masood faced the very real possibility of having to leave Massachusetts and go back to Pakistan. Given the respect for Masood within the radical Islamist network in Boston, it is likely not a coincidence that at that exact moment, he got a great new job that solved all of his problems. In 1998, Masood was hired as an imam at the Islamic Center of New England's Sharon mosque. His employment contract, signed by Abdulbadi Abousamra, leader of the Islamist contingent now in control at ICNE, stipulated both a good salary and the provision of a large residence on the sprawling grounds of the new mosque in Sharon. Masood's hiring had killed two birds with one stone: a top Islamist activist in Boston got to stay in the city and continue his efforts for the cause, and Imam Eid's religious authority would now be diluted by the presence of another imam on ICNE's staff.

In order to set Masood up in his new job and his new digs, the ICNE's new Islamist leaders filed a fraudulent religious worker visa with the help of a scam organized by Brooklyn-based radical imam Muhammad Khalil. Khalil had a long track record in this line of work, bringing in hundreds of individuals from the Muslim world, many with radical ties, by falsely claiming them to be religious workers. The scam worked like this: A cooperating mosque or religious school in the United States would file an R1 religious worker visa for the beneficiary of the fraud, claiming him as the "most qualified" and desired person for the job of leading the mosque. A cooperating mosque back in the country of origin—in Masood's case, the *Jamia*

Masjid Muqqaddas Ahl-e-Hadith in Pakistan—would then certify that the visa candidate is a bona fide religious scholar who has the credentials and the matching denomination to lead the mosque in America. Even though in Masood's case both of these statements were false, with verification being next to impossible, the visa was granted. Masood got to stay in Boston. In 1999, Abdulbadi Abousamra founded a new religious school, the Islamic Academy of New England, with ICNE resources, but incorporated it as a separate organization, completely outside of Imam Talal Eid's control. The private elementary school would radicalize many Boston Muslim children, with both Hafiz Masood and ISB's imam, Basyouni Nehela, teaching there. With total control of the mosque in Cambridge, and partial control of the mosques in Sharon and Quincy, the Muslim Brotherhood was well on its way to becoming the dominant force in the lives of New England's historically moderate Muslim community.

CHAPTER 12

THE INFILTRATION OF BOSTON'S AFRICAN AMERICAN MUSLIM COMMUNITY

There was one other Muslim community whose radicalization was vital to the Muslim Brotherhood's dominance in New England. As I discovered in the ISB case files, the ISBCC plot of land in Boston's Roxbury neighborhood was actually offered to an entirely different group of Boston's Muslims back in 1989. At the time, the neighborhood was in bad shape. Urban blight caused by Boston's period of economic decay in the 1960s and '70s resulted in large numbers of vacant buildings, which had been foreclosed and seized by the city for failure to pay real estate taxes. A massive construction project for the proposed I-695 highway that was to have run through Roxbury had begun in 1955; but it was aborted in 1971, leaving a huge swath of clear-cut empty lots across what are now parts of the Southwest Corridor, Melnea Cass Boulevard, and Columbus Avenue.

There was a small but significant community of African American "indigenous" Muslims in the Roxbury and Dorchester neighborhoods. Among the majority black residents who populated these neighborhoods after the Great Migrations of the mid-twentieth century, the Nation of Islam had gained a large number of followers. The Nation of Islam was a religious sect founded in Detroit in 1934 as a sort of nationalist African American mutual aid association loosely informed by Islamic principles that its founder, Wallace Fard Muhammad, molded into a theology. Malcolm X, a top Nation of Islam leader at first, preached in the Boston neighborhood of Dorchester on Intervale Street, where he established Temple 11 in 1953. By 1964, however, Malcolm X had become disillusioned with the Nation of Islam, whose then-leader, Elijah Muhammad, was—stereotypically for the leader of a cult—sleeping around with large numbers of his followers. Malcolm X converted to Sunni Islam during a pilgrimage to Mecca, and large numbers of Boston's Nation of Islam members followed him. Elijah Muhammad's men assassinated Malcolm X in 1966, but Malcolm's followers remained Sunni. By the 1980s Temple 11 in Dorchester was a Sunni African American mosque called Masjid al-Quran, under the leadership of Imam Taalib Mahdee.

Elijah Muhammad's son, Warith Deen, also became Sunni after his father's death. Warith Deen Mohammed, went on to lead about two million members out of the Nation of Islam. His followers in Boston were organized around another mosque in the Roxbury neighborhood, called the Mosque for the Praising of Allah, which was led by a Jamaican convert to Islam, Imam Abdullah Faaruuq. This mosque is still there, just a few blocks from where the ISBCC would one day stand. Back in the 1980s, Imam Faaruuq's congregation was looking to expand.

As it turned out, Muhammad Ali Salaam—the Boston Redevelopment Agency official who arranged the ISB's sweetheart land deal for the ISBCC—was originally a member of the Mosque for the Praising of Allah and had mentioned to his imams the city's plans to redevelop the blighted parcel near Roxbury Community College. Perhaps the mosque could expand there—virtually next door. In 1988, leaders from the Mosque for the Praising of Allah, including Imam Abdullah Faaruuq, incorporated the Muslim Council of Boston (MCB), with the purpose of "the acquisition, owning, maintenance, improvement and operation (including the provision of a space for the holding of regular religious services on the real estate situated in Roxbury."

In 1989, Muhammad Ali Salaam got tentative approval to sell the plot of land to the MCB for $1. But by 1992, the MCB's mosque project was in jeopardy. Faaruuq's Mosque for the Praising of Allah didn't have the resources to keep its own building well maintained. It certainly did not have the money to build the planned new $5–7 million mosque. Other Muslim groups, including the ICNE under Dr. Mian Ashraf, stepped in to help, almost too late. The BRA had a new director, Paul Barrett, who felt that giving away the land to the MCB for free was unfair, and that there should be a competitive bidding process for the land. But Muhammad Ali Salaam pulled many strings and saved the project.

Unfortunately, Dr. Ashraf had his hands full building the ICNE's new suburban mosque in Sharon, and the expected contributions from the ICNE's relatively affluent membership were tied up in that construction project as well. Over the next four years, the cash-strapped MCB project stagnated. But, Muhammad Ali Salaam, however, would not abandon his dream of a new mosque in Roxbury and there were other Muslim groups who wanted that land for themselves. They reached out to Muhammad Ali Salaam and offered a way out of the impasse. In 1996, Ali Salaam wrote to the MCB's board of directors with the news:

"I initiated conversations with a local Islamic organization based at MIT," Ali Salaam announced to the MCB leaders. "These Brothers have incorporated under the name Jamaa Masjid of Boston, Inc., and are prepared to raise the funds necessary to complete the project."

The MIT "Brothers" were none other than the leaders of Care International, the al-Qaeda–fundraising front group. The president of Jamaa Masjid was Suheil Laher, the MIT chaplain, and one of the directors was Muhammad Akra, founding member of the ISB and founder of Care International. Over the next year, the moderate leaders of the Muslim Council of Boston would battle for the ideological soul of the project with the al-Qaeda sympathizers. As a condition for raising the required funds to build the Roxbury mosque, Laher and his comrades demanded that the mosque promote a militantly extremist ideology. Dr. Ashraf and the African American Muslim leaders would have none of it. Eventually, even Muhammad Ali Salaam had had enough. He wrote to Suheil Laher on June 2, 1997:

I have concluded that an effective alliance between the Jami' Masjid of Boston and the Muslim Council of Boston is not forthcoming. Consequently, I want to encourage you to pursue the development of the Jami' Masjid at a site other than BRA Parcel R-14, located in Roxbury.

But the damage was done. Laher had so poisoned the moderate Muslim alliance that the Muslim Council of Boston was no longer able to function as a cohesive group. He did so by radicalizing the leaders who had formed the MCB in the first place—the leaders of the Mosque for the Praising of Allah. The mosque's imam, Abdullah Faaruuq, formed a close bond with the Care International activists and bought into their cause. His closest relationship was with Aafia Siddiqui, the bright-eyed biology major who had by then graduated MIT, entered a PhD program at Brandeis University, and moved to Roxbury with her new husband. Siddiqui began attending the Mosque for the Praising of Allah and Faaruuq helped her with her efforts to indoctrinate local Muslims with radical Islamic ideology. Faaruuq had a chaplain's position with the Massachusetts Bureau of Prisons and he used his position to proselytize to a captive audience.

According to Deborah Scroggins, author of a book on Siddiqui: "Aafia ordered hundreds of Islamic books in English, usually from Saudi Arabia, and Faaruuq distributed them to the prisoners he visited. Faaruuq said the books included works by the famous Egyptian Islamist Sayyid Qutb." Luckily, according to law enforcement sources, Faaruuq was later removed from his chaplaincy position for smuggling cell phones to inmates.

With Faaruuq having switched sides, the Muslim Council of Boston fell apart and the stage was set for the ISB to enter. By 1999, the ISB got tentative approval for building the Islamic Society of Boston Cultural Center instead of MCB and the rest is history.

CHAPTER 13

OVERREACH AND UNDER ATTACK

At 7:59 on the morning of September 11, 2001, an American Airlines Boeing 767 carrying Mohammed Atta and four Saudi nationals took off from Boston's Logan Airport. Exactly fifteen minutes later, another Boeing 767 flew out of Boston, this one carrying three Saudis and two Emiratis. Within forty-five minutes, both would be flown into the World Trade Center's Twin Towers in New York.

Boston-based al-Qaeda supporters, in conversations intercepted by the FBI, would later speculate about whether they might have spotted Mohammed Atta praying at the ISB. They very well could have. As the 9/11 hijackers boarded their planes at Boston Logan, they were leaving behind a city whose growing Muslim population was dominated by a thriving Islamist movement. The ISB mosque in Cambridge was a central head-quarters for a powerful Muslim Brotherhood network controlling several Muslim K-12 schools, the Muslim Students Associations at all of the major Boston area universities, the Islamic Center of New England mosques in Sharon and Quincy suburbs, and the African American Muslim Mosque for the Praising of Allah in Roxbury. Boston's mayor, Thomas Menino, had just given the ISB the proverbial key to the city, as the ISB trustees embarked on building the largest mosque in New England on city land, which they got "virtually free of charge."

The Hamas campaign of terror raged, as the Second Intifada was in full bloody swing and the Muslim Brotherhood in New England was raising large amounts of money to keep the suicide bombs coming through the Holy Land Foundation and other charities identified in the ISB's bank records as recipients of ISB funds. The al-Qaeda contingent that revolved around MIT's Muslim Students Association and Care International was just as active in raising money for Shamil Basayev's murder campaign against Russian schoolkids and theatergoers. PTech, the software company these MIT al-Qaeda supporters founded with Saudi terror financier Yassin Al Qadi's money, had secured some very lucrative top-secret government and military contracts. At the ICNE, Hafiz Masood was recruiting and raising money for the Pakistani jihad against India in Kashmir. ISB founder Abdulrahman Alamoudi was in Washington, raising money for George W. Bush's first presidential campaign by day—and for an al-Qaeda assassination plot against Saudi crown prince Abdullah by night.

The radical Islamist project in the United States in general, and in New England in particular, was proceeding with full immunity. But everything changed on the morning of September 11, 2001, when big parts of the Islamist movement's infrastructure, carefully constructed over decades of patient growth and infiltration, came crashing down with the Twin Towers. As with the histories of many other ideological movements from the Zealots to the Jacobins to the Khmer Rouge, the more extreme elements of the Islamist movement came to dominate, and then jumped the gun. Abdullah Azzam's impatience with the Muslim Brotherhood's slower approach of proselytism, infiltration, and subversion of non-Islamist societies led his disciple Osama bin Laden to carry out an act of terrorism against the American homeland so brazen and destructive that it jolted the U.S. government into action.

In short order, the Muslim Brotherhood and al-Qaeda institutions established within America felt the blowback. On September 23, 2001, President George W. Bush issued Executive Order 13224, authorizing the U.S. Treasury Department to designate terrorist-affiliated entities and seize their assets. The very first group to be put on the terrorist designation list was Al Kifah—the global al-Qaeda–funding network established by Abdullah Azzam, whose Boston branch was the main al-Qaeda–fundraising organ in the United States. On December 4, 2001, the new executive order was used to take down the Holy Land Foundation—the primary vehicle used by the American Muslim Brotherhood to finance Hamas terrorism. Supporting it now, like the ISB had done until HLF was designated, was now a serious federal crime. Over the next year, U.S. authorities neutralized many other Islamic terrorist charities to which the ISB contributed large sums of money. The Global Relief Foundation was designated as a terrorist entity on October 18, 2002. The Benevolence International Foundation was designated November 19 of that year.

Although Al Kifah, the original al-Qaeda charity in the United States, was the first terrorist group designated after the September 11, 2001, attacks, the federal government somehow missed its Boston branch, doing business as Care International, as well as the for-profit company PTech, which staffed with many of the same al-Qaeda and Muslim Brotherhood supporters and funded by an alleged Saudi al-Qaeda financier. For its part, the FBI was caught completely flatfooted by a senior risk management investigator at J.P. Morgan, Indira Singh, who was given the job of doing customer due diligence research on PTech ahead of a potential business deal. It was she who ultimately took the lid off PTech's operations by feeding the story to Boston's CBS outlet. Right up until then, the various government agencies had no idea that their critical systems software was being provided by a company affiliated with al-Qaeda. Amazingly, federal agents then proceeded to tip off PTech's executives by calling their office and asking them nicely if they have ties to money laundering.

The tipoff happened in late November 2002, so—whoever was involved in whatever at PTech—they had almost two weeks to prepare when, at midnight on December 6, 2002, PTech's office in Quincy was raided by several federal agencies as part of Operation Green Quest—a Treasury and Commerce departments investigation into a far-reaching Muslim Brotherhood money-laundering operation within the United States. ISB chairman Osama Kandil was also named in Operation Green Quest documents. Shortly thereafter, Boston's Fleet Bank, later bought by Bank of America, closed down the bank accounts of fifteen local ISB-affiliated Islamists, including MAS Boston president Hossam Al Jabri, MIT Muslim chaplain Suheil Laher, and Care International activist Aafia Siddiqui. Probably spooked, Siddiqui left Roxbury for Pakistan on January 2, 2003, and fell off the radar entirely. When the mastermind of 9/11, Khalid Sheikh Mohammed, was captured in March 2003, he identified Siddiqui, who was married to his nephew, as a top al-Qaeda "sleeper agent" and "fixer" for al-Qaeda activists coming to the United States. In 2004, then–FBI director Robert Mueller announced that the

U.S. government now considered Siddiqui to be among the ten most wanted al-Qaeda terrorists in the world.

Fleet Bank claimed that the bank accounts of Hossam Al Jabri, Aafia Siddiqui, and the other Boston-area Islamists were closed because of "patterns of account activity that triggered money-laundering suspicions." Other than that, the bank was extremely tight-lipped. Many years later, I would find out why.

The raids continued, as the feds continued following the trail of al-Qaeda fundraising in the Boston area. In April 2003, the FBI searched offices and storage units around Boston that held Care International's records. Although the organization was designated as a terrorist entity, its leaders were not prosecuted under terrorism laws. The evidence against them was too top secret to be presented at trial, and some of their activities, such as supporting the Chechen mujahideen, were not illegal before 9/11. Three Care International leaders were ultimately convicted using the same legal hook that put Al Capone behind bars: indictments for tax evasion. Care International leaders didn't just want to raise money for terrorism; they didn't want to pay taxes on it, either. In filing for tax-exempt 501(c)(3) status, Care International's leaders lied about its true activities and were prosecuted for defrauding the U.S. government. Their sentences, however, were small. Suheil Laher was never prosecuted because he never signed the organization's tax forms.

• • •

Law enforcement and military action by the U.S. government wasn't the only pushback to the Islamist project in the United States. Millions of ordinary Americans were now jolted into awareness. Despite the first attack against the World Trade Center and the rash of al-Qaeda attacks against U.S. embassies in the 1990s, most Americans knew nothing about the existence of a radical Islamic movement that saw America as its number one enemy. But, in the aftermath of 9/11, many Americans woke up. Even the left-leaning media reported truthfully on Islamic extremism for a period of time after the attacks. With the dawn of online blogging, many citizen researchers and journalists, such as Robert Spencer of *Jihad Watch* and Pamela Geller of *Atlas Shrugs*, began studying and reporting on Islamist ideology and its depredations around the world. Citizen organizations that monitored and countered Islamic extremists in local communities, such as ACT! for America, founded by Lebanese Christian activist Brigitte Gabrielle, proliferated around the country. Individuals like Bill Sapers began looking with much more scrutiny at the Muslim Brotherhood mosques and institutions that grew up around them in cities over the previous couple of decades.

To a certain extent, the initial reaction of American Muslim Brotherhood activists was to lie low for a while. The data on new Islamic nonprofits being founded show a significant drop in new Muslim groups in 2001. But the shock was very temporary, as the finest minds of the Muslim Brotherhood began to undo the damage to the movement done by the 9/11 attacks. Violence within America was not in the Muslim Brotherhood's interests. Infiltration, subversion, deception, and intimidation were far more effective. The year 2002 saw a significant spike in new Muslim groups, with many focused on public relations with the non-Muslim American population. Mosques like the Islamic Society of Boston threw large amounts of resources into newly formed outreach and interfaith committees. It was the ISB's outreach director, Salma Kazmi, who got the Boston Globe to kill its 2002 story about the ISB's ties to terror. And it was Walid Fitaihi, in his role as the interfaith director, who formed the exploitative relationship with the ADL and with Temple Israel's Rabbi Ronne Friedman.

As Friedman became the ISB's leading cheerleader and toughest defensive lineman, Fitaihi gloated in Arabic newspapers about how the ISB took advantage of leftists like Friedman and the increased interest in Islam after the 9/11 attacks to proselytize and promote Muslim Brotherhood goals, especially vis-à-vis the Jews. Writing in the Egyptian weekly newspaper *Al-Ahram Al-Arabi* just eleven days after 9/11, Fitaihi described the media coup he was able to pull off on the Jews of Boston:

> From the first day, the media began to insinuate that Muslim Arab hands were behind this incident. At noon, the directors and administration of the Islamic [Society] of Boston held an emergency meeting, and I stayed on the line with them from my clinic. We decided to hold a blood drive, and we set up a committee to contact the Red Cross and organize it for us. We invited the media to cover the event...

On Saturday, September 15, I went with my wife and children to the biggest church in Boston, [Trinity Church in] Copley Square, by official invitation of the Islamic Society of Boston, to represent Islam by special invitation of the senators of Boston. Present were the mayor of Boston, his wife, and the heads of the universities. There were more than 1,000 people there, with media coverage by one of Boston's main television stations. We were received like ambassadors. I sat with my wife and children in the front row, next to the mayor's wife. In his sermon, the priest defended Islam as a monotheistic religion, telling the audience that I represented the Islamic Society of Boston...

These are only some of the examples of what happened and is happening in the city of Boston, and in many other American cities, during these days. Proselytizing in the name of Allah has not been undermined, and has not been set back 50 years, as we thought in the first days after September 11. On the contrary, the 11 days that have passed are like 11 years in the history of proselytizing in the name of Allah. I write to you today with the absolute confidence that over the next few years, Islam will spread in America and in the entire world, Allah willing, much more quickly than it has spread in the past, because the entire world is asking, "What is Islam!"

• • •

By the time we founded Americans for Peace and Tolerance in 2008, the American Muslim Brotherhood was back on top in terms of public relations, especially in New England, after having achieved almost total victory in the court of public opinion in the wake of the ISB's legal battle with the David Project and Citizens for Peace and Tolerance, our predecessor group. However, the American branch of the Muslim Brotherhood was having much less success in the U.S. criminal courts. On July 23, 2007, the trial of five Holy Land Foundation leaders on a forty-two-count indictment for providing material support for Hamas began in the Federal Court for the Northern District of Texas. Despite the reams of evidence showing a Muslim Brotherhood conspiracy, the judge was forced to declare a mistrial because of a hung jury. Apparently, a left-wing activist among the jurors who somehow slipped past *voir dire*, graphic artist William Neal, intimidated and bullied fellow jury members. According to Steve Emerson's Investigative Project on Terrorism, whose researchers interviewed the jurors, "arguments for conviction [were] met with immediate scorn and ridicule" by Neal.

William Neal was sympathetic to Hamas, telling the *Dallas Morning News* that "part of it does terrorist acts, but it's a political movement. It's an uprising." He had a lot less sympathy for his fellow jurors' opinions, telling a local radio show that

> [a] lot of the jurors couldn't even say words that had four sylla-
> bles...A lot of these people are blue collar, you know, working UPS,
> working food, cafeteria cashier. You had people [from] secluded
> lifestyles. They had no idea of the Palestinian-Israeli conflict. They
> had no idea about worldly affairs.

Despite the setback, the prosecution moved for a new trial and on November 24, 2008, an uncompromised jury returned guilty verdicts on every single count against the five HLF defendants. Two got fifteen years in prison; one got twenty; and two others got sixty-five. It was a major blow to the American Muslim Brotherhood, and not just because of the heavy prison sentences handed to its top leaders.

During the trial the prosecution released a list of unindicted co-conspirators who were in on the plot to raise millions for Hamas, but whom the government, for various reasons, chose not to indict. Among the 246 individuals and organizations on the list were the largest Muslim organizations in America, many with direct connections to Islamic extremists in New England affiliated with the Islamic Society of Boston. Listed as "members of the US Muslim Brotherhood" were the Islamic Society of North America, the North American Islamic Trust, and the Muslim Arab Youth Association. All were officially listed as affiliate organizations in the ISB's original constitution. The ISB's board chairman, Osama Kandil, was one of the Muslim Arab Youth Association's founders. The ISB's founder, Abdulrahman Alamoudi, was also on the list of co-conspirators as a Muslim Brotherhood member involved with HLF's crimes.

Abdullah Azzam, the infamous "Father of the Global Jihad," whose followers founded Boston's Care International, was listed as a leader in the

Palestine Committee of the International Organization of the Muslim Brotherhood. Azzam had in fact been one of the founders of Hamas. According to the list, Azzam also actively contributed to HLF's fundraising activities on behalf of Hamas. So did another unindicted co-conspirator, Jamal Badawi, the ISB's newest trustee, appointed just days before the first HLF trial in July 2007. The ISB's original trustee, Yusuf Qaradawi, joined Azzam and Badawi on the list as yet another ISB-affiliated Hamas fundraiser.

These designations hurt the Muslim Brotherhood, and they were especially damaging to CAIR. The Holy Land Foundation trial evidence exposed CAIR as the American political arm of Hamas. When CAIR tried in 2009 to challenge its designation as an unindicted co-conspirator, U.S. district judge Jorge Solis denied the challenge in a sealed order. CAIR and NAIT appealed the ruling to the U.S. Court of Appeals for the Fifth Circuit, but the only part of Judge Solis's order overruled on appeal was his decision to keep the order secret under seal. This backfired spectacularly on CAIR because Solis's unsealed order stated that the HLF trial exhibits "do create at least a prima facie case as to CAIR's involvement in a conspiracy to support Hamas." In denying CAIR's demand to expunge its name from the co-conspirator list, Solis concluded that "the Government has produced ample evidence to establish the associations of CAIR, ISNA and NAIT with HLF, the Islamic Association for Palestine ('IAP'), and with Hamas."

After Judge Solis's ruling, the FBI cut all ties with CAIR. In an April 28, 2009, letter to several U.S. senators explaining the FBI's reasons for shunning CAIR, the FBI assistant director for Congressional Affairs, Richard Powers, cited the HLF trial evidence and said that it "demonstrated a relationship among CAIR, individual CAIR founders (including its current president Emeritus and its executive director) and the Palestine Committee. Evidence was also introduced that demonstrated a relationship between the Palestine Committee and HAMAS, which was designated as a terrorist organization in 1995. In light of that evidence, the FBI suspended all formal contacts between CAIR and the FBI." Powers added that "until we can resolve whether there continues to be a connection between CAIR or its executives and HAMAS, the FBI does not view CAIR as an appropriate liaison partner." The ban on contact was reaffirmed once again as a Department of Justice–wide policy in 2013.

These hits to CAIR's reputation happened just two years after it had opened its branch in Massachusetts, at a time when the ISB controversy was in its climax. It was probably CAIR's intention to aid the embattled ISB/MAS, but the last thing the ISB needed at that moment was more connections to terrorist causes. CAIR's Massachusetts branch died in its infancy, but would be resurrected later into a formidable force.

Others among the Brotherhood's American terrorist fronts took major hits under the Bush administration's counterterrorism policies. The largest terror financing conduits in America—the Holy Land Foundation, the Global Relief Foundation, the Benevolence International Foundation, Care International, and several others—had been shut down. A sword hung over the 246 unindicted co-conspirators in the HLF trial, among them the largest Muslim organizations and top Muslim leaders in the United States and Canada, including ISB trustee Jamal Badawi. The federal prosecutors in Dallas were also ready to bring cases against CAIR founder Omar Ahmad, and against CAIR, NAIT, and ISNA.

Unfortunately, by the time the government was ready to move on the rest of the American Muslim Brotherhood, there was a new occupant in the White House. The Obama administration would not only stop the ongoing law enforcement efforts against the Islamist project in the United States, it would also greatly roll back new investigations. President Obama would take advice on dealing with Islamic extremism from the very same Islamic extremists who were responsible for radicalizing members of the American Muslim community in the first place. Under President Obama, American law enforcement capabilities had been dangerously curtailed, though it appears that President Trump is restoring much of what President Obama destroyed. But in Massachusetts, subversion of the Commonwealth's law enforcement agencies started immediately after the September 11, 2001, attacks and has continued to this very day.

CHAPTER 14

DID TOP MASS. COP MAURA HEALEY FACILITATE TERRORIST FINANCING AND MONEY LAUNDERING?

Some efforts to subvert American anti-Islamist law enforcement actions began shortly after 9/11, before President Obama was even a U.S. senator. As with many prior Islamist operations in the United States, Boston was again a major proving ground for new strategies being developed in the years after 9/11 to undermine counterterrorism and law enforcement efforts to deal with the Islamist threat. For example, while Walid Fitaihi jumped into action on the public relations front within days of 9/11, Boston City official Muhammad Ali Salaam took command of the ISB's government relations, using his connections and official status to lobby leaders of city, state, and federal law enforcement agencies. In 2002, Ali Salaam organized the BRIDGES (Building Respect in Diverse Groups to Enhance Sensitivity) Forums. The stated goal of the BRIDGES Forums is to create a space where representatives of law enforcement agencies, especially those from the U.S. Department of Justice and the Massachusetts Attorney General's office, could meet with "ordinary Muslims"—in order to engage in "outreach" and "dialogue." In reality those "ordinary Muslims" have been Islamists affiliated primarily with the ISB and MAS Boston, and BRIDGES is a useful tool for them to pressure and mislead law enforcement officials, while exploiting their relationship with law enforcement to gain legitimacy among the general public. Every time APT researchers found a new terrorism connection, the ISB/MAS would have a ready answer: But we work closely with the FBI. Why would the FBI work with us if we were extremists?

In return for the public legitimacy they granted to the ISB and MAS, the state and federal law enforcement agencies recruited into BRIDGES by Ali Salaam expected cooperation and support during their counterterrorism efforts. Yet as soon as the Bush administration's post-9/11 crackdown reached Boston, leaders of the ISB and MAS did just the opposite. Operation Green Quest was the first post-9/11 counterterrorism operation to reach Massachusetts. The FBI raided PTech and Care International. Many prominent Boston Islamists who were associated with the software company and the charity, including Aafia Siddiqui and MAS Boston president Hossam Al Jabri, had their bank accounts shut down by Fleet Bank on suspicion of money laundering.

MAS and ISB leaders retaliated against law enforcement with a campaign of incitement among Boston-area Muslims. The same law enforcement agents who continued to meet with MAS and ISB at Ali Salaam's BRIDGES Forums now did so while being smeared by Ali Salaam's spiritual leaders in mosques around Massachusetts as hateful Islamophobes whose aggression must be resisted by all true Muslims. In December 2002, just twenty days after the PTech raid, ISB Imam Basyouni Nehela gave a sermon at the ISB in Cambridge, posted on the ISB's website, titled "Stand out firmly for justice on the issue of Ptech Inc."

"The people who are running and working in this company are well known within the Muslim community, and are respected among this community," Imam Nehela complained. He addressed the authorities directly: "For our government and elected officials: All of us love this country and love to see it in peace and prosperity. And all of us are working hard to contribute in achieving this goal, but we do not like to see oppression, nor do we like to see families and children crying because of oppression." And, according to Imam Nehela, Muslims are "obligated to stand with the oppressed ones."

• • •

As early as 2007, when we first started looking through them, I could vaguely sense that there was something fishy wrapped up within the ISB's bank records. But, I couldn't quite see what it was. For that, I would have to go back to school and get a law degree. In 2015, I entered the J.D. program at Boston University Law School, where I focused on international trade and national security law. In law school, I studied banking secrecy, anti–money laundering, and counterterrorism-financing (AML/CTF) laws. Only after that would the discoveries Sasha and I made in the tens of thousands of pages of ISB bank records make full sense.

So would a very strange collaboration between the ISB and the Massachusetts Attorney General's Civil Rights Division. Knowing what I do now, the ISB's financial records tend to show that the ISB and several of its leaders might have been part of a money-laundering "layering" and "placement" chain that moved Saudi money to terrorist causes around the world. When Fleet Bank discovered this money-laundering chain and disrupted it, several officials at the Civil Rights Division, among them current Massachusetts attorney general Maura Healey, pressured the bank to modify its federally required anti–money laundering compliance programs and reinstate the bank accounts of terrorist-financier Islamists like Hossam Al Jabri, essentially exempting them from the very counterterrorist financing laws that were intended to stop them. The pretext? Fighting Islamophobia.

In testimony before the Senate banking committee shortly after PTech was raided, former counterterrorism tsar Richard Clarke pointed out how terrorist networks were able to obscure their Saudi sources of funds. According to Clarke, the Saudi authorities actually keep very close watch over wealthy Saudi citizens who are suspected of supporting terrorism. As result, these individuals are prohibited from sending money to terrorists via direct bank transfers from Saudi Arabian accounts. Instead, the money must be laundered by funneling it through externally based intermediaries, including those in the U.S.

"From magazines to mosques and charities, the agents of terrorism are well rooted in the United States, exploiting the strengths and weaknesses of our financial backbone," Clarke told the Senate committee. This initial step of the money-laundering process, called "placement," is how the money earmarked for terrorism is placed into the financial system.

In his testimony to the Senate, Mr. Clarke went on to name top PTech investor Yasin Qadi as "allegedly the financier behind several U.S. organizations which have been tied to terrorist support." According to Clarke, once Saudi money from terror financiers is in the United

States, it is moved around so as to conceal its source and ultimate use." This essential part of the money-laundering process is called "layering," and this layering was, according to Clarke, carried out by terrorist supporters in the United States "us[ing] a variety of means to move funds, including charities [like mosques and aid groups], private companies, offshore accounts, U.S. accounts, real estate transactions, blank checks and bulk cash couriers." Boston's Care International, for example, moved its charitable funds to Chechnya through multiple middlemen in Turkey and Azerbaijan.

Once the layering conceals the source of the funds is concealed, the funds move to terrorist organizations in "conflict zones such as Chechnya, Bosnia, Kashmir or Israel." This last stage of the money-laundering process, called "integration," is how the funds are made available for terrorist use. This is usually accomplished through Muslim Brotherhood or al-Qaeda charities operating in the conflict zone, like the "zakat [alms] committees" in the West Bank and Gaza that distributed the U.S.-raised HLF funds to Hamas. According to Clarke, "Terrorist operatives then withdraw large sums of money in cash and provide phony receipts for medical supplies, food or disaster relief. The cash and its ultimate use become virtually untraceable."

Finally, another general technique of money laundering, which has itself been criminalized, is called "structuring," and it involves getting around bank regulatory reporting requirements. Under the Bank Secrecy Act of 1970, banks must file "currency transaction reports" (CTRs) when any cash transaction of $10,000 or more is made. Under what's known as the Annunzio-Wylie Anti-Money Laundering Act of 1992 (AMLA) and Treasury Department regulations, banks are also required to file "suspicious activity reports" (SARs) on any transactions over $5,000 that the bank finds suspicious and "relevant to a possible violation of law or regulation." Criminal structuring, also known as "smurfing," happens when a money launderer tries to avoid detection while moving large sums by breaking up the sums into many smaller transactions.

I saw several variations on these money-laundering techniques in the ISB's bank records. The records subpoenaed during the ISB's lawsuit only went back to the year 2000. Still, within two years' worth of deposited checks and wire transfers, made between the beginning of the records and the federal raid on PTech's offices, there was a lot to learn. The suspicious activity related to PTech that I found in the ISB records seems to have been part of a scheme that went something like this:

Wealthy Saudi invests in an American private for-profit company. The for-profit company's employees, officers, and directors, or at least the ones in the know, then steer the money in donations to mosques and other Islamic nonprofits. Mosques donate this money to Islamic charities, or to other Islamic nonprofits that, in an additional layer of concealment, then donate it to Islamic charities. The charities then move the money into overseas accounts, ostensibly to aid humanitarian relief efforts in conflict zones. In reality, the money is placed into the hands of terrorist groups.

As with Care International, there was a financial relationship between the ISB and PTech; and the money seemed to be flowing in the expected direction of a Saudi terrorist money-laundering chain originating with PTech investor Yasin Qadi. The cash flow was being layered and structured through for-profit businesses, individuals, and nonprofits. In 2000, for example, PTech CEO Oussama Ziade gave the ISBCC $5,000. After PTech's executives were tipped off by the feds in late November, the ISB covered its bases by returning the money to Ziade on November 26, 2002— well ahead of the feds' raid on PTech. In 2003, when the dust from the raid settled a bit, Ziade gave the money back to ISB again, except that this time he structured the transaction, splitting it into two checks of $3,000 and $2,000, dated a month apart. He might have been trying to evade the $5,000 cut-off for the suspicious activity–reporting requirement.

In 2005, Oussama Ziade was indicted for dealing in the property of a Specially Designated Global Terrorist, Yasin Qadi, and defrauding the Small Business Administration. The indictment, however, was not unsealed until 2009, when President Obama took office. Ziade had fled the country long before then.

While Ziade was the one ultimately indicted for dealing in terrorist property, the primary cash conduit between PTech and the ISB was Hossam Al Jabri, the MAS Boston president, whom I had confronted in 2007 about his donation to the Holy Land Foundation. Even to a layperson like me at that point, Al Jabri's financial relationship with the ISB seemed out of the ordinary. Between the beginning of the ISB's bank records in 2000 and late November 2002, when the feds tipped off PTech that they were investigating its involvement in money laundering, Al Jabri wrote seventeen checks totaling over $30,000 to the ISB—a rather large sum for a young professional with no known resources other than his salary. Among small sums of a hundred dollars here and there were very large round number checks: repeated sums of $2,000, $4,000, and even $6,000 at a time. It looked like a steady step pattern on a graph—regularly spread out large-sum transfers.

The memo lines in Jabri's checks were mostly either empty or had "donation" written in them. One check, however, written shortly after the start of the Second Intifada in Israel, says "brothers in need" on the memo line—a phrase that has been used as code for support of armed jihad, presumably since fighting usually involves "brothers" and not "sisters." Certain patterns in Al Jabri's payments seemed to suggest that Al Jabri might have been smurfing his checks to the ISB in order to avoid suspicious activity reports (SARs) being sent by his bank to the feds: For example, Al Jabri split a $5,000 sum between two checks less than a month apart in early 2000—much like Oussama Ziade did when he returned his $5,000 donation to the ISB. Another suspicious maneuver occurred in late 2000, when Al Jabri wrote a $4,000 check and, two days later, wrote three checks on the same day: one for $2,000, one for $300, and one for $56.

But the most suspicious transactions happened on November 22, 2002—right around the time the feds tipped off PTech about their money-laundering investigation. Al Jabri wrote two $6,000 checks, one after another, on that same day. It seemed like he was trying to unload, and that he was less careful than usual—the checks exceeded the maximum for a SAR filing and the ISB deposited them together, using a single deposit slip. It just didn't make sense that Al Jabri would write two checks without any apparent reason, when only one check would do. And then, Al Jabri's large round number donations to the ISB stopped immediately and permanently after the PTech raid. PTech continued functioning as a business for a while after the raid. Al Jabri got a new job and continued to do well for himself. But the big sum donations flow to the ISB had dried up at its source for good.

The ISB was not the only recipient of Al Jabri's suspicion-arousing largesse before PTech was raided. The Holy Land Foundation, which mostly funded Hamas, got at least $900 from him in 1999 or 2000. Al Jabri also sent $5,150 to the Global Relief Foundation at some point before it was designated as a terrorist organization in 2002 for funding al-Qaeda and the Taliban.

There was another long-term funds-transfer chain in the ISB's bank records that dried up immediately and permanently right before PTech was raided. At the same time that Al Jabri was writing checks to the ISB, the ISB was writing checks to the national office of the Muslim American Society in the tens of thousands of dollars. The amount of money flowing out of the ISB's accounts to MAS National fluxed exponentially after the beginning of the Second Intifada in September 2000, mostly due to three large checks totaling almost $50,000, with "Palestine" or "relief for Palestine" written in the memo line. And, like Al Jabri's large round sum payments to the ISB, the ISB's large round sum payments to MAS National stopped on November 22, 2002, right after the feds tipped off PTech about their money-laundering investigation.

This money-laundering typology matches the pattern described in Richard Clarke's 2003 Senate testimony describing the Muslim Brotherhood money-laundering network: A Saudi terrorist financier, Yassin Kadi, invests in a private American company, PTech, set up by Muslim Brotherhood members or sympathizers like Soliman Biheiri, Muhamed Mubayyid, Suheil Laher, Abdulrahman Alamoudi, and Hossam Al Jabri. The Muslim Brotherhood members or sympathizers at that private company then donate large amounts from their salaries to a mosque like the ISB. Their private company writes off the salaries as a business expense, the employees get to write off the donation as a charitable expense, and the mosque doesn't have to pay taxes because it is a 501(c)(3) nonprofit. The money then goes to another nonprofit like MAS National and from there—perhaps through another nonprofit charity like the Holy Land Foundation or Islamic Relief—to a conflict zone like Basayev's Chechnya or the West Bank and Gaza at the start of the Second Intifada.

There was other shady business in the ISB's bank records. Until very recently, money transfer companies like Western Union and MoneyGram—the two largest money transfer companies in the world—kept a willfully blind eye to abuse of their services by money launderers to conceal the origin and destination of laundered funds. For its part in making it easier for scammers, drug dealers, and terrorist financiers to move money around the world, Western Union was fined $586 million by the federal government in 2017, and $60 million by the State of New York in 2018. MoneyGram got away relatively more easily after admitting to criminally aiding and abetting wire fraud and failing to maintain an effective anti–money laundering program. Its deferred prosecution agreement with the Department of Justice obligated it to create a $100 million compensation fund and invest $84 million into anti-fraud and anti–money laundering programs in 2012. MoneyGram also reached a $13 million settlement with forty-nine states' attorneys general and the District of Columbia in 2016 and, in 2017, its former chief compliance officer ponied up $250,000 of his own money in the largest such fine against an individual executive.

The ISB has received money from abroad through large numbers of small-scale and anonymous international MoneyGram transfers. For example, in June of 2003, someone outside of the United States bought $9,327 worth of MoneyGram international money orders—which function similarly to travelers' checks. A total of twenty separate money orders denominated in $500, or smaller, amounts were purchased over the space of three weeks. This person would buy a batch of money orders, wait exactly seven days, then buy another batch—doing this twice. The MoneyGram international money orders were then sent to the ISB, where the money orders were shuffled randomly and split into two separate batches, both of sums less than $5,000, which were deposited three days apart.

Off the bat, when I picked up the ISB's bank records again after studying financial compliance law at Boston University, I could see evidence of several potential violations of U.S. anti–money laundering and counterterrorist-financing laws. The chain of funds transfers from Yasin Qadi to PTech to Al Jabri to the ISB to the MAS to "Palestine" has all the hallmarks of the "concealment" category of money laundering crimes.

The money-laundering crime of concealment in financial transactions would occur if the ISB and its leaders engaged in financial transactions using the proceeds of a predicate crime like terrorist financing in order to conceal the nature, source, or ownership of these proceeds, in violation of 18 U.S.C. § 1956(a)(1)(B)(i). The pattern of behavior related to this fund transfer chain exhibits substantive evidence of intent to conceal, as articulated by several federal courts of appeals, including "careful structuring of transactions to avoid attention, folding or otherwise depositing illegal profits into the bank account or receipts of a legitimate business, use of third parties to conceal the real owner, or engaging in unusual financial moves culminating in a transaction." Courts will also look to "expert testimony on practices of criminals," like the testimony Richard Clarke gave to the Senate in 2003.

In addition to concealment in financial transactions, the ISB and some of its leaders could have been on the hook for concealment in international transmission of funds under 18 U.S.C. § 1956(a)(2)(B)(i)—directly or as accomplices or co-conspirators—due to the original Yasin Qadi seed money for PTech being moved from Saudi Arabia to the United States. Because the ISB and its leaders would have engaged in this money-laundering crime of concealment in order to promote further predicate crimes—money laundering, terrorism financing, and all sorts of crimes of violence committed by the terrorist groups that ultimately received the money—there is evidence that the ISB and its leaders could also be liable for money-laundering "promotion" crimes in financial transactions and international transmissions under 18 U.S.C. §§ 1956(a)(1)(A)(i) and 1956(a)(2)(A), respectively.

Since many of the transactions in the PTech funds transfer chain look like they were structured to avoid a state or federal-transaction-reporting requirement, the ISB and its leaders could be liable for violation of the financial transactions anti-smurfing statute, 18 U.S.C. § 1956(a)(1)(B)(ii). They didn't even have to know their conduct was criminal—only that they knew of the reporting requirement and that the structuring was intended to avoid compliance with this requirement. If prosecutors can prove that the ISB and its leaders knew that structuring was illegal, they could be on the hook for violating 18 U.S.C. § 5324, which forbids causing financial institutions like Fleet Bank to fail to file required reports.

If prosecutors can prove that Hossam Al Jabri knew his donations to the ISB were being used to finance terrorism, and yet that he had written them off as tax-deductible, he would also be liable for money laundering involving financial transactions in proceeds of predicate crimes like terrorist financing, made with the intent to evade taxes, under 18 U.S.C. 1956(a)(1)(A)(ii). So would the ISB as a nonprofit entity channeling terrorist funds. Federal prosecutors are not required to prove that a defendant against money-laundering tax evasion charges knew he was violating tax laws.

Many participants in this scheme can be indicted as co-conspirators, which are each liable for the foreseeable crimes of the others committed in furtherance of the conspiracy. Unlike with standard federal conspiracy charges, under an 18 U.S.C. § 1956(h) money-laundering conspiracy charge, no overt act to further the conspiracy is required. All that had to happen was that two or more persons agreed to a plan to launder some money together in violation of the law. This applied to any person that knew of the unlawful purpose of the agreement and joined in it with the intention to further that purpose.

Even those participants in the funds transfer chain who were completely unaware of the possible underlying criminal conspiracy could also be liable under U.S. anti–money laundering laws if they engaged in transactions that involved proceeds of a predicate crime like terrorist financing aggregating to $10,000 or more. And that gets us to Fleet Bank.

Long before the USA PATRIOT Act, federal banking secrecy and money-laundering laws and their enforcement were already strict. Since the 1970 Bank Secrecy Act, banks have been required, as, essentially, deputized private-citizen financial law enforcement officers, to report patterns of activity that trigger money-laundering suspicions—or other suspicions of illegality—to the federal Financial Crime Enforcement Network (FinCEN). These obligations are no joke. The Annunzio-Wylie Anti-Money Laundering Act of 1992 requires banks to establish a proactive Anti-Money Laundering Program to constantly monitor their money flows for suspicious activity and report it to FinCEN. Not doing so is criminal.

Another anti–money laundering law, the Money Laundering Control Act of 1986 (MLCA), was passed three years after *Scarface*—the Al Pacino film about the Miami cocaine trade—came out. There is a scene in *Scarface*, in which Pacino's Tony Montana and his boys pull up in a van and haul duffel bags of cash into the glass-walled offices of a legitimate banker. The MCLA's blind eye provisions were specifically aimed at legitimate bankers, lawyers, and other financial professionals who engaged in willful blindness to launder the legendary proceeds of the late 1970s and early 1980s, cocaine trade. The MCLA criminalizes knowingly engaging in transactions over $10,000, where the source of the funds is derived from specified unlawful activity—a long list of crimes that includes material support for terrorism and terrorist financing. A financial institution doesn't even have to know that the funds are derived from unlawful activity. It just has to know that the transaction occurred, which is not much to prove at trial.

It is no surprise that bankers like making money, and that everything has a price. In *Scarface*, Tony gets mad when his banker raises his laundering rates to 10 percent. These days, the pressure of the MLCA criminal sanctions for turning a blind eye to dirty money, as well as many other such laws, have significantly driven down the supply of money-laundering services by unscrupulous U.S. banks. So, the rate for laundering money on the international market is up to a solid 20 percent and, with American banks mostly leashed by FinCEN, it's the European banks like Deutsche Bank and HSBC that launder both Mexican cocaine cartel profits and Islamist terrorist funding.

The USA PATRIOT Act significantly tightened the screws of U.S. government counterterrorist-financing and anti–money laundering enforcement. The legislation added money transfer companies like MoneyGram, informal money transfer services like the Islamic *hawalas*, and even check cashing businesses to the list of financial institutions required to file suspicious activity reports (SARs) and maintain anti–money laundering programs. There is no longer any specific situation—like a suspicious transaction over $5,000—that triggers a SAR. Rather, the banks must use their best judgment, and will get hit with a criminal penalty if that judgment turns out to be wrong. Federal regulations simply say that a bank or another financial institution must file a SAR when it "knows, suspects, or has reason to suspect that," essentially, one or an aggregate of transactions totaling $5,000 or more involves funds derived from illegal activity, is meant to disguise those funds and evade banking laws, or has no business or apparent lawful purpose. "Has reason to suspect" is a killer legal term of art. Criminal law is full of "woulda, shoulda, coulda," and "has reason to suspect" is one such catchall legal phrase. It does not matter what the bank knew or suspected. If the government can prove that the bank should have known or suspected, it's on the hook for the same crime as if the bank knew exactly what was happening.

Even worse, where the bank even "feels" that it is being used to facilitate illicit transactions aggregating to $25,000 or more, even if it cannot identify the suspect behind the transaction, it must file a SAR. Finally, along with the already then-existing requirement to maintain anti–money laundering programs, the USA PATRIOT Act required banks and financial institutions to institute Know Your Customer programs. Every customer must now be screened and due diligence research must be done to make sure that a customer will not pose a risk of abusing the financial institution's services to commit financial crimes. If such a customer or abuse is identified, even after he becomes a customer, the federal government requires financial institutions to file an SAR and, in some situations, shut down the customer's accounts.

After the September 11, 2001, attacks, the USA PATRIOT Act, along with multiple federal financial investigations like Operation Green Quest, debilitated many terrorist-financing and money-laundering schemes. The closing of Aafia Siddiqui's bank account, as well as the accounts of at least five PTech employees like Hossam Al Jabri, were part of this counterterrorist-financing counteroffensive.

The newly mandated know-your-customer (KYC) screening and due diligence process was likely what Indira Singh was doing for J.P. Morgan when she discovered PTech's terrorism connections. It is also likely that Fleet Bank closed down the bank accounts of Hossam Al Jabri, Aafia Siddiqui, and thirteen other Boston-area Islamists after implementing such a KYC program and learning about their connections to entities that were then being raided one after the other by financial crimes investigators. As Bank of America, which bought Fleet Bank in 2004, insisted all along in response to the Islamist account closures: "In this instance, as in any case of this nature, Fleet followed standard industry practices dictated by federal regulations and guidelines designed to protect institutions and individuals against money laundering, including terrorism."

Bank of America was entirely justified in being tight-lipped about what happened beyond that perfunctory statement. The Annunzio-Wylie Anti-Money Laundering Act made it illegal to notify the subject of a suspicious activity report (SAR) that he had been reported. If the flatfooted feds who tipped off PTech employees and officers were private citizens, they would have been liable for a crime—and for good reason. As a federal court ruled in 2004, tipping off the subject of a financial crimes investigation that a suspicious activity report had been filed against him could "compromise an ongoing law enforcement investigation, provide information to a criminal wishing to evade detection, or reveal the methods by which banks are able to detect suspicious activity." Recently, one large-scale Turkish money launderer who helped Iran to convert its oil receipts into dollars was busted by surprise when he came to the United States to visit Disney World—something he would have never done if he knew he was under investigation. Secrecy and the element of surprise are extremely important in these types of investigations against sophisticated and highly intelligent operatives like MIT graduates Hossam Al Jabri, Suheil Laher, and Aafia Siddiqui.

American, and now European, banks are under tremendous pressure from the U.S. federal government to interdict money laundering and terrorism financing—and for good reason. Shamil Basayev was able to pull off his school massacre in Beslan, Russia for eight thousand euros. Every penny counts toward the commission of unspeakably evil acts. In a fungible sense, some of those euros came to Basayev through the Fleet Bank accounts of people like Suheil Laher and Aafia Siddiqui.

Nothing works without money. The September 11, 2001, attacks cost less than half a million, but that half million still needed to be laundered in order to pay for the flight school lessons and the box cutters. The Islamic State would have had a much tougher time burning people alive on high-production-value video without the cash that bought the fancy video equipment, the cage, and the gasoline. Iran wouldn't have been able to fund its nuclear weapons program and Hezbollah's rockets without a way to launder its oil profits. The Russian *Vory v Zakone* mafia, the Mexican *Sinaloa*, and the Columbian *Norte del Valle* cartels—all have been able to use legitimate banks like the United Kingdom's HSBC to launder their proceeds and to reinvest them back into their murderous trade.

Fleet Bank did a major service to the American people and to the officials fighting the war on terror when it shut down what was likely a significant terror-financing money-laundering scheme in Boston. If the bank hadn't, it might have been in serious legal trouble because of the heavy federal statutory and regulatory reporting, due diligence, and know-your-customer duties that banks are forbidden to breach. Its executives and the employees responsible could have been held criminally liable and faced prison time. Its license to operate could have been pulled. And, most importantly, if Fleet Bank allowed this terrorist-financing money-laundering scheme to operate, more children in the United States and overseas could have been murdered by the terrorists whom the scheme was set up to support. More Muslim children's minds could have been poisoned by the propaganda that the scheme subsidized. From all the evidence I have seen and considered, Fleet Bank seems to have acted exactly as it should have, both in terms of doing the right and moral thing, and in terms of following the law with due diligence and good faith.

On June 13, 2003, the ISB, through its new MAS Boston front group, threatened to sue Fleet Bank. To lead the shakedown effort against the bank, MAS Boston brought in Mahdi Bray, then the head of the MAS Freedom Foundation, based out of the MAS National office in Washington, D.C. The ISB trustees were financing this operation. The

ISB's bank records reveal that the ISB Trust paid Bray thousands of dollars for his services.

A close friend of Louis Farrakhan who converted to Islam in the 1970s, Bray continued to rack up drugs and fraud felonies throughout the 1980s. Leaving prison in 1991, Bray became a close associate of Abdulrahman Alamoudi in the late 1990s. When Alamoudi was yelling at a Washington, D.C., rally, held shortly after the outbreak of the Second Intifada:

> "Hear that Bill Clinton! We are all supporters of Hamas!," Bray was
> by Alamoudi's side on the stage pumping his fist in the air. Later
> on in the rally, Bray bangs on a tambourine while the crowd chants
> in Arabic: "Al-Aqsa is calling us, let's all go into jihad, and throw
> stones at the face of the Jews."

Bray was no stranger to defending Islamist criminals. Along with aggressive public support for Abdulrahman Alamoudi, the five HLF defendants, and Sami Al Arian during their trials, Bray was the National Mobilization Chairman of the defense fund for Jamil Al Amin, aka H. Rap Brown, a violent Islamist extremist and cop killer from Atlanta, who is serving life in a Georgia prison and was then on trial.

On June 19, 2003, Bray's MAS Freedom Foundation issued a press release announcing its "plans to file discrimination suit against Fleet Bank" and advertising a nationwide search for plaintiffs to participate in the suit. In the press release, MAS Freedom Foundation complained:

> Several Muslim Fleet account holders, found that their accounts
> were closed without any explanation by the bank. In an effort to
> resolve the situation, coalition members have held meetings with
> Fleet executives demanding an explanation as to the bank's actions,
> citing the institution's history of discrimination, predatory lending
> and other unfair banking practices.

Banking laws make the bank legally obligated, under penalty of criminal law, not to provide any explanation for its actions if that explanation reveals to the subject of a suspicious activity report that one has been filed against him. The press release went on:

MAS Freedom has developed a brochure on how to recognize unfair banking practices, including refusal to open a new account or to accept deposits into existing accounts, or complete an electronic transfer of funds, unexplained account closings, and employment discrimination, and is calling on all Muslim organizations, mosques, and community members to report to its office any complaints involving unfair practices by any financial institution.

Far from unfair, all of these banking practices are mandated by federal law in situations where a financial institution suspects that its services are being used for money laundering, whether by Muslims or not. Nevertheless, Mahdi Bray launched an incitement campaign aimed to persuade Boston Muslims to boycott Fleet. The ISB trustees took the lead, moving their own bank accounts from Fleet to the rival Citizens Bank, and to the out-of-state Southern Bank of New Hampshire, although probably more out of precaution than protest.

In their fight against Fleet Bank, Boston's Islamists deployed some powerful new allies—the law enforcement officials whose eagerness for Muslim outreach had led them directly into the arms of the Islamists themselves. In June 2003, they met "with members of the Massachusetts Attorney General's Office (AGO) to discuss how the AGO may be able to help" in the campaign against Fleet Bank. Muhammad Ali Salaam helped Hossam Al Jabri file a discrimination complaint with the Civil Rights Division at the AGO. Thus started a long and friendly collaboration — some would say collusion—between the AGO and ISB/MAS, documented in a stack of records I requested under Massachusetts Public Records Law and obtained only after a long period of bureaucratic obstruction.

At the time, the assistant attorney general heading up the Civil Rights Division was Richard Cole, who is now a civil rights attorney specializing in school bullying and discrimination. Mr. Cole failed to find any discrimination in Fleet Bank's actions whatsoever. Nevertheless, in early 2006, he pressured Bank of America, which had acquired Fleet in 2004, into satisfying several demands made by ISB/MAS.

"[I]n response to the adverse community perceptions that may have resulted," Bank of America promised to reinstate some of the accounts closed by Fleet Bank on money-laundering suspicions. The bank also appointed a special liaison to the Muslim community who would respond to complaints about account closings and other enforcement actions, although the bank hedged its promises in a footnote that read: "Account closings for terrorism or money[-]laundering-related concerns are made after due consideration of available information by Bank of America, although we are unable to describe the account closing criteria or practices publicly." The bank also agreed to pay the Attorney General's Office $50,000 to fund financial education brochures and a video geared toward "the Arab-American and Muslim communities." Lastly, the bank agreed to let the AGO subject its Boston-based employees to Muslim sensitivity training, "especially pertaining to banking, lending and financial practices relevant to Arab-Americans and Muslims."

Among the documents produced by the Attorney General's Office in response to my public records request was the PowerPoint presentation that was used to train Bank of America employees in Muslim sensitivity. The PowerPoint was put together by MAS Boston, but was being represented as coming from the Attorney General's Office. MAS officials, who, it seems from the records, were paid for their time from the $50,000 Bank of America payout, did the training. It started with some pabulum about Islam being a religion of submission and peace; how Muslim cultural values include "a strong sense of destiny and fate" (whatever that means); and how, to Muslims, "family and relationships are important." (Aren't they to us all?)

But the training seemed to have two primary purposes. The first was to hard sell the bank's employees on the idea of *Sharia* financing by, essentially, implying that the bank would be accused of discriminating against Muslims if it doesn't start offering *Sharia*-compliant financial products. The Attorney General's involvement in pushing Islamic investment products onto banks seems to have gone uncomfortably close to the boundaries of the Establishment Clause of the First Amendment.

The second purpose of the Attorney General's training was to discourage Bank of America employees from their federally mandated screening, due diligence, and reporting duties. The training presentation reminded the bank's workers that Bank of America "provided assurances that it will only close accounts after extensive scrutiny and consideration." According to the presentation slides: "The primary concerns that led to the collaboration between the Attorney General's Office and Bank of America" were that the "bank closed accounts on the suspicion that the account holders were engaging in unlawful activities" and "without any reason." "Bank officials were not forthcoming about why the accounts were closed and were limited in how much information they could provide about closures," the AGO complained in the presentation.

Indeed, that is exactly what the bank was supposed to have done. Federal regulations require banks to subject all customers to a strict customer due diligence process and assign each customer a risk rating for how likely the customer is to abuse their services for money laundering, terrorist financing, fraud, or other crimes. If a customer's risk rating outweighs the benefits of continuing to business with him, federal regulations require the bank to close that customer's account. In many cases, this account closing would be accompanied by a suspicious activity report. It is a crime to notify the subject of a suspicious activity report to the feds or to disclose any information that would reveal the existence of a suspicious activity report—information like why Al Jabri's accounts were closed.

But, the Massachusetts Attorney General's training for Bank of America's employees ended with this direct threat on the final PowerPoint slide: "If customers feel that they are victims of discrimination, they can file a complaint with your bank, with their state's attorney general, with a private attorney, or the U.S. Justice Department. They may seek compensatory and punitive damages."

Actually, various money-laundering laws give banks broad immunity from civil suits for many of the things that banks do in connection with anti–money laundering and counterterrorist-financing reporting and enforcement. Plus, the percentage of Muslim accounts among all Fleet Bank accounts that had been closed on suspicions of money laundering—5 percent—was the same as the percentage of Muslim accounts among all accounts that were being opened. There was no statistical disparity that would indicate the bank factored religion or ethnic origin into its methodology for closing accounts. Al Jabri looked like he pulling some shady tricks with his bank accounts—that was all.

The Massachusetts Attorney General's Office had no business interfering with federal enforcement of financial criminal laws, like it did with the MAS-created and AGO-administered training for Bank of America employees. The Attorney General's Office did not seem to be concerned about any possible chilling effect that railroading Bank of America might have had on the willingness of it and other banks to monitor and report suspicious financial activities by Islamic extremists.

In fact, an argument can be made that the Attorney General's Office broke several federal laws, and that some of its officials could have been prosecuted under conspiracy or accomplice liability theories. That argument depends on whether Richard Cole, and later Maura Healey, acted with the knowledge that their pressure would cause Fleet, Bank of America, or any other bank to do any one of three things: First, modify its anti–money laundering programs and make them less effective—as Mahdi Bray's MAS brochures urged. Second, fail to file a required report with the federal government due to the fear of being sued for discrimination—as the Attorney General's training threatened. Third, allow money laundering to continue, as possibly might have happened with three closed banking accounts that the Attorney General's Office forced Bank of America to reopen. But this knowledge doesn't have to be actual knowledge. In legal terms, constructive knowledge, the "woulda, shoulda, coulda," come in. And that "should have known" standard is flexible, depending on individual circumstances. For assistant attorneys general like Cole and current attorney general Healey were at the time, of a major state like Massachusetts, this standard should be very high. As the top cops of Massachusetts, they knew—or should have known—that Fleet Bank had an obligation under federal law to do what it did; and that their pressure made Bank of America employees' adherence to federal law less likely.

Richard Cole might have started this mess, but the current Massachusetts attorney general, Maura Healey, made it worse. In 2007, Healey took over at the Massachusetts attorney general's Civil Rights division. According to the records I got from the Attorney General's office, Healey worked closely with newly minted MAS executive director Bilal Kaleem, to invest the $50,000 extorted from Bank of America into law enforcement "Muslim sensitivity" training seminars run, of course, by the Muslim American Society. In 2010, Kaleem, the epitome of charm and warmth, wrote to Maura Healey:

> Dear Maura, Hello! Bilal here. How are you? I have not had the pleasure of meeting you in several months now. I pray all is well with yourself, family, and work.
>
> Each time we run into each other, we often mention that we need to get together to discuss the usage of the $50,000 from the Bank of America case that was put aside to address discrimination/ cultural competency related needs.

Thus I and couple of other organizers have spent some time studying that with community leaders from over 24 different Muslim institutions and we would like to schedule a meeting to discuss it with you. Are you [going to] be available in the coming week for a meeting with myself, Muhammad Ali-Salaam, and a couple of other colleagues?

Warmly and thank you in advance,
Bilal

Along with Bilal Kaleem and Muhammad Ali-Salaam, Maura Healey met with several Muslim leaders on April 8, 2010. Among them were Aafia "Lady Al Qaeda" Siddiqui's friend Imam Abdullah Faaruuq, and a new name I hadn't heard of before, Yusufi Vali, one of "the organizers who work with us." Vali, who had only recently graduated Princeton, worked on President Obama's campaign in 2008 and was, in 2010, an organizer with the Greater Boston Interfaith Organization. Unbeknownst to us, the ISB was grooming him for much bigger things.

The ISB was preparing a major event. Massachusetts governor Deval Patrick was coming to the ISBCC mosque in Roxbury for a "Muslim Community Action" in an unprecedented endorsement of the radical institution. Could the collaboration between the ISB/MAS and the Attorney General's Office on $50,000 worth of trainings, to be called the Diversity Training Fund, be announced there? Perhaps Ms. Healey herself would like to attend and make the announcement in person. That is exactly what ended up happening. Healey asked that the check from Bank of America, which was supposed to go to the Attorney General's Office as per original agreement, be instead sent to the Boston Foundation, which would disburse the funds to MAS law enforcement "trainers." Bank of America asked that the funds be treated as an anonymous donation.

APT publicized this highly improper and possibly illegal collaboration between ISB/MAS and Maura Healey. In response, Healey dissimulated. As Bilal Kaleem wrote to the Boston Foundation:

There is some misinformation that is being spread about this $50k fund by a group that dedicates itself to undercutting whatever work Muslim organizations try to do to get involved in the civic process and engage with public officials. The AG's office knows about this and have fielded questions about that already clarifying the facts.

Maura Healey falsely claimed to the media she had nothing to do with either funding the Diversity Training Fund or with its disbursement. The records I got from her office told a different story. The Attorney General's Office is listed as the only donor on the paperwork establishing the fund, which was signed by Maura Healey. The fund's explicit purpose was: "To be used at the direction of the Office of the Attorney General of Massachusetts through the Diversity Training Fund."

MAS police sensitivity training had already been going on in New England since the September 11, 2001, attacks, spearheaded by Muhammad Ali Salaam. By the end of 2008, ISB/MAS had trained over twelve hundred federal, state, and local law enforcement officers in "Muslim sensitivity." Not surprisingly, given their source, these training exercises downplay the role that Islamist ideology plays in Islamic terrorism, making effective intelligence gathering difficult. Law enforcement officers are taught that they are guilty of racism if they connect a suspect's extreme religiosity to his potential for terrorist violence. After Maura Healey helped ISB/MAS steer the $50,000 Bank of America shakedown into law enforcement trainings, the ISB/MAS could get paid at the behest of the Massachusetts state government for doing these trainings, adding to their perceived legitimacy. With each training capped at $500, as many as a hundred ISB/MAS trainings of fifty to two hundred law enforcement officers at a time would have been funded by Healey's efforts.

Maura Healey went on to be elected as the Massachusetts attorney general in 2014, and the ISB/MAS subversion of New England law enforcement agencies continues, now with the support of the Commonwealth's chief law enforcement officer. One day the MAS might host a law enforcement career fair at the ISBCC mosque in Roxbury. Another day, the mosque might be host to an event featuring the families of convicted terrorists bashing law enforcement and the American government. ISB spokesmen might in one forum denounce terrorism, and in another forum denounce "the American system of justice" for prosecuting terrorism. After the Boston Marathon bombing, the MAS touted its collaboration with law enforcement authorities. Yet privately it sent an email to its members telling them not to talk to the FBI without contacting the MAS first. Meanwhile, the top law enforcers, makers, and interpreters of the law, continue to embrace the ISB and MAS. Maura Healey, Massachusetts senator Elizabeth Warren, Boston mayor Martin Walsh, various top brass from the

Boston Police Department, the chief justice of the Massachusetts Supreme Judicial Court Ralph Gants, and even the David Project's old lawyer Jeff Robbins, all have made their pilgrimage to the ISBCC Roxbury mosque.

CHAPTER 15

BATTLE FOR THE SOUL
OF A MOSQUE

There were *some* Boston Muslims who *were* willing to talk to the FBI and some FBI agents who were willing to listen. The moderate-extremist civil war at the ICNE mosques in Quincy and Sharon was coming to a head. In 2003, Hafiz Masood, the Sharon mosque's new imam, invited a delegation from Pakistan's Tablighi Jamaat to visit the mosque for several days. The "Tablighis," as they are known, are a group of itinerant Islamist fundamentalists who travel to Muslim communities around the world and proselytize an extremist version of Islam. The U.S. Institute of Peace has called Tablighi Jamaat a "gateway to terrorism" because of its potential role in terrorist recruiting. The Obama administration kept a jihadist detainee locked up in Guantanamo, and the courts allowed President Obama to do so, simply because there was evidence that the Guantanamo detainee had stayed at a Tablighi guesthouse in Pakistan, and not much else. The earliest American and British converts to Islam who went on to plot terrorist activity—the "American Taliban," John Walker Reid; the Shoe Bomber, Richard Reid; and Jose Padilla, who plotted to detonate a dirty bomb in New York—all got their start with the Tablighis. In early 2016, the Pakistani government took the extraordinary step of banning Tablighi chapters or events from any educational facility in the country due to concerns about extremist proselytizing.

Masood's brother's terror group, Lashkar-e-Taiba, is considered especially close with Tablighi Jamaat, embedding its terrorist operatives into

Tablighi missionary groups in order to avoid scrutiny. Masood would often travel with the group around the world when he still had a valid visa as a student at Boston University—often leaving Boston for weeks at a time. The moderate ICNE leaders were concerned that the Tablighi group was up to no good, and they took pictures of the group's members as they were sleeping in the ICNE's hallway one night.

It was because of these concerns about Masood's foreign friends that the moderate Muslims at the ICNE were able to uncover his terrorist background. They learned that Hafiz Masood was in fact a brother of Lashkar-e-Taiba's founder, Hafiz Muhammed Saeed, and that he was in the United States illegally. They demanded answers from Abdulbadi Abousamra, the ICNE president who was responsible for hiring Masood. Abousamra dismissed their concerns, insisting that everything was fine, that Masood's papers were all in order, and that he had no connection to Lashkar-e-Taiba. So, they reached out to law enforcement agencies for help and began providing them with information on Masood and the Islamist activists who had taken over the ICNE.

Meanwhile, the situation at the ICNE mosques in Sharon and Quincy was deteriorating rapidly. Imam Talal Eid was completely barred by the extremist directors of the organization from preaching at the Sharon mosque. Then the ICNE directors hired another extremist imam to lead prayers at the Quincy mosque as well. Imam Eid's English-language sermons began to be replaced by Arabic preaching at Quincy and Urdu preaching at Sharon. The community became "balkanized" along ethnic and linguistic lines. Imam Eid's event calendars were ripped off the walls so that no one came to his talks. Confrontations became more physical, with one of Imam Eid's supporters beaten in a mosque parking lot and Abousamra's enforcer—jail convert Bilal McLeod—stalking the mosques' hallways looking for moderates to intimidate. Exasperated and fearing for his safety due to concerns over attempts on his life, Imam Eid resigned in early 2005, followed by the five remaining moderate ICNE board members. Half of the ICNE's membership left with them.

The moderates tried to fight back, unsuccessfully. They circulated a flyer at the Sharon mosque sarcastically offering $90,000 to "anyone who could show a degree from B.U." for Masood, who had falsely claimed that he earned a Masters in Economics there, though he was actually expelled. They also reached out to the media to tell their own version of the story of why the longest-serving and most well-credentialed imam in New England had been pushed out of the mosque that he had led for twenty-three years, and replaced by a charlatan with multiple connections to terrorism. The local *Sharon Advocate* and *Quincy Patriot Ledger* newspapers ran stories about the Sharon and Quincy mosques' takeover by Pakistani Lashkar-e-Taiba and Arab Muslim Brotherhood members. The moderate ICNE Muslims also tipped off the media about Masood's connections to Lashkar-e-Taiba and multiple articles in national and international articles brought this secret out into the open.

The reaction from the ICNE Islamists was quick and ruthless. An email written to one of the moderate ICNE directors by Nabeel Khudairi—the same man who first suggested that the ISB should sue its critics in order to shut them up, and who had spread anti-Semitic conspiracy theories among the leaders of Boston's Muslim community—shows the rage that ICNE Islamists activists felt in reaction to being exposed:

"How is it you consider yourself a member of the Board [of] Directors, or a member or the Islamic Center, or even a decent Muslim for that matter," Khudairi wrote. "I have never witnessed anywhere in all my years a 'brother' as blatantly enthusiastic to cause trouble for the entire Umma [Muslim community] as yourself. You have the audacity to go and complain to the Sharon Police and give a story full of lies and slander to the Sharon Advocate newspaper without trying to get a single shred of evidence for your allegations. Only a totally irresponsible Munaffiq [religious hypocrite who is not a true Muslim] would go on the record about there being fundamentalists in the masjid…"

Khudairi lambasted the moderate ICNE director for holding his American patriotism in higher regard than his religion, invoking the memory of the poor guy's recently deceased mother and issuing an explicit threat:

First of all what would your mother have to say about your behavior if she were still alive today and knew what actions you have been committing against your fellow Muslims? Secondly, you better not get too used to the idea of being a member of the BOD [Board of Directors] or even the ICNE general membership for that matter. There is no way you will be allowed to et foot again in the same place that other decent Muslims go to for worship.

In 2015, when President Barack Obama named Boston as one of the three pilot cities for his Countering Violent Extremism project, he invited Nabeel Khudairi (but no moderates) to the inaugural Countering Violent Extremism Summit at the White House. Indeed, Khudairi had long been a member of Muhammad Ali Salaam's BRIDGES law enforcement outreach program. By the time Khudairi was invited to the Obama White House, Ali Salaam had become a paid consultant to the U.S. Department of Justice. It was not the last time that the federal government had hired a fox to guard the henhouse.

But Khudairi would soon have more than moderate imams to be angry about. Talal Eid may have been expelled from his mosque, but Hafiz Masood was about to be expelled from the country. Tipped off by moderate Muslims, the FBI and the DHS began investigating Masood. In the process, the agencies discovered the massive fraudulent religion visa scheme being run out of a basement mosque in Brooklyn, through which Masood got his visa to come to the States. In November 2006, federal agents arrested thirty individuals who had been involved in the scheme across eight states and Washington, D.C. As it turned out, Hafiz Masood was not the only illegal alien relative of Hafiz Saeed heading up Massachusetts Muslim institutions. Arrested along with Masood and his son Hassan was Hafiz Hanaan, who was both a cousin and a brother-in-law of Saeed. Hafiz Hannan was in charge at the Islamic Society of Greater Lowell, an old factory town north of Boston. Another blood brother, Hafiz Hamid, was the imam at the Islamic Society of Greater Worcester in central Massachusetts. He was deported in 2007 and started a new life running a Lashkar-e-Taiba safe house in Lahore, Pakistan. According to what moderate ICNE Muslims told the FBI at the time, in an email I obtained from my contacts at the ICNE, it was Abdulbadi Abousamra who was responsible for getting Hamid the post in Worcester, as part of his effort to set up "Lashkar extensions in different mosques." All of the terrorist mastermind's relatives in the United States were living illegally on fraudulent religious worker visas.

The criminal complaint against Masood should have been devastating to his image as a learned and respectable religious leader. The complaint alleged that Masood "[l]ied repeatedly both orally and in writing," including about being an imam in Pakistan. He "repeatedly told under oath a facially implausible story (with shifting details) of the circumstances under which he claimed to have returned to the United States." He had committed Medicaid fraud by lying about "his salary, his employer(s), his family's immigration status, and provid[ing] false social security numbers for some of his children" when applying for the Medicaid benefits. He had been arrested for shoplifting by switching price tags on store items in Norwood in 2000 and had fraudulently obtained a New Hampshire driver's license by giving a false address.

Masood's Muslim Brotherhood allies were quick to rally to his defense, declaring a PR war on the FBI and DHS, even while keeping up "dialogue" with law enforcement through the BRIDGES program. MAS Boston and ISBCC executive director, Bilal Kaleem, who had been so charming to Massachusetts assistant attorney general Maura Healey when setting up law enforcement Muslim sensitivity trainings, was now leading a protest in front of Boston's federal courthouse. In front of the assembled crowd of Masood's supporters, Kaleem accused federal law enforcement agencies of "an apparent witch hunt." He used the BRIDGES program as blackmail, telling the credulous *Boston Globe* that "the arrest of Masood on criminal charges damages an initiative [BRIDGES] launched two years ago to bring law enforcement officials and the members of the Muslim, Arab and Sikh communities together."

Almost fifteen hundred Islamic extremists from the Boston area, including almost all the prominent ISB, MAS Boston, and extremist ICNE leaders, signed a petition started online by former PTech employee and MAS Boston president Hossam Al Jabri, swearing support for Masood and slamming law enforcement. The extremists complained in the petition that "[t]he Muslim community in Boston is deeply concerned and outraged due to the recent arrests of Imam Hafiz Masood and Imam Abdul Hannan....They have always been voices of peace and wisdom and remain vital leaders for their respective communities." The supposed bridge-builder between law enforcement and the Muslim community, Muhammad Ali Salaam, also signed the petition.

MAS Boston collected and published on its website letters to Hafiz Masood from forty of his elementary and middle school students at the Islamic Academy of New England in Sharon, many of them children of Muslim Brotherhood members.

A first-grader wrote, "Dear Sheik Masoud. I know that you went to Jail. I love you. You are the best religion teacher."

A fourth-grader wrote,

> I love you SH. Masood. I want you to come out of Jail soon. I know
> you will come out Insha Allah. We all love you. You are our religion
> teacher. When you got into this horrible immense mess, I did not
> believe it. Insha Allah, it is a test from Allah. Remember, Allah tests
> those he loves. So [I]nsha Allah you will win this test.

A fifth-grader wrote,

> Dear Imam Masood, you are one of the best role models in my
> life. You have taught me so much in my religion class through your
> knowledge & wisdom. You are the best teacher because you teach
> us and befriend us at the same time.

In what had become a distressingly familiar pattern, members of Boston's
interfaith liberal community bought into this "peace and wisdom" propaganda without hesitation—despite the abundance of evidence on the
other side. The education director of the Massachusetts ACLU, Nancy
Murray, was at the head of the line of Masood's defenders. Amazingly, so
were two Jewish rabbis from Sharon. Barry Starr was the head rabbi at
the Conservative Temple Israel of Sharon, and Rabbi Meir Sendor was
the leader of the Orthodox Young Israel of Sharon synagogue. Having
participated with Hafiz Masood in interfaith dialogue, the rabbis were
convinced that Masood was indeed a voice of peace and wisdom. Rabbi
Starr even raised money for Masood's defense.

In 2008, I asked one of the moderate Muslim leaders at ICNE what
he thought about the support Masood was receiving from Boston's civic
and religious leaders. This was right around the time when Democratic
New York governor Eliot Spitzer got busted the same way that Hossam
Al Jabri was, except for a different reason. Spitzer's bank reported suspicious transactions by Spitzer to the feds. Spitzer, however, wasn't moving
al-Qaeda financier money—he was buying hookers. My friend from ICNE
had this to say:

"I mean, we are as Muslims appalled that you are condoning, in a
country where even Eliot Spitzer doesn't get any special treatment, you are
giving this man so much leeway that he is some descendant from heaven?

I mean, he has been a criminal and he has admitted to being a criminal and they're still saying he is a reverent imam."

In early 2008, Masood pled guilty to immigration fraud and left the United States for Pakistan the next day. He rejoined his terrorist brother Hafiz Saeed in Lahore and has since become the Secretary for Information for his brother's terrorist group.

• • •

On the evening of November 26, 2008, a few months after Masood returned to Pakistan, ten Lashkar-e-Taiba terrorists arrived by boat from Pakistan in the Indian city of Mumbai. They were heavily armed with explosives, grenades, and machine guns. Splitting up into teams of two, they fanned out across the city, beginning a four-day massacre at the city's major landmarks. They hit a major train station, Mumbai's iconic Taj Mahal hotel, another hotel, a café, a hospital, and an out of the way target that was likely to yield very few victims—but which Hafiz Saeed was adamant must be hit.

This target was Mumbai's Chabad center, opened in 2003 by Rabbi Gavriel Holtzberg and his wife Rivkah. Chabad is an Orthodox Jewish movement whose rabbis run centers across the world in order to provide religious and hospitality services to Jews wherever their travels might take them. The Mumbai Chabad center, called Nariman House, was popular with Israeli backpackers, India being a prime destination for the traditional post-army global trips many young Israelis take. Around 9:45 in the evening, two of Hafiz Saeed's Lashkar terrorists burst into Nariman House and took several people hostage. Over the next day and a half, they tortured, raped, and ultimately murdered the Holtzbergs. Rivkah was five months pregnant when she was killed. Two other rabbis, Bentzion Chroman and Leibish Teitelbaum, were also murdered. So were two women visiting the center as guests: Nora Schwartzblatt-Rabinowitz and Yocheved Orpaz. The Holtzbergs' two-year-old son, Moishele, miraculously survived and was rescued by his Indian nanny. In all, 179 people were murdered in the 2008 Mumbai Massacre.

The whole world was shocked by the viciousness and brutality of Hafiz Saeed's plot. But despite the fact that Saeed specifically targeted Jewish rabbis for painful death, and despite the fact that Hafiz Masood was now officially working for Saeed as his propaganda chief, Sharon's Jewish rabbis continued to support him. In 2015, long after Masood's true nature was well known, I gave a presentation to members of Rabbi Meir Sendor's Orthodox congregation and showed evidence of Masood's involvement in his brother's terror group. The rabbi interrupted me and insisted that I move on past that topic: The rabbi was adamant that Masood was innocent. As for Conservative rabbi Starr, four years after the Mumbai Massacre, he told the *Washington Post*: "He was a positive influence on the community, and I didn't think it made a whole lot of sense to deport him. I found him to be a gentleman, a gentle person, a person of peace."

In 2016, Rabbi Starr avoided a fifteen-year prison sentence for larceny and embezzlement from his synagogue after state prosecutors dropped the charges because the synagogue leadership did not want him to go to prison. Apparently, in 2011, a young Quincy man answered a Craigslist ad for sex with an older woman, only to find Rabbi Starr dressed in a wig when he showed up at what turned out to be Rabbi Starr's house. The man blackmailed Rabbi Starr out of almost half a million. Unlike Imam Masood, Rabbi Starr had no terrorist mastermind brother to turn to after his fall from grace. He is now driving a cab somewhere near Cleveland, hopefully not in a wig.

CHAPTER 16

THE TRIUMPH OF THE RADICALS

On June 26, 2009, the ISB held a grand opening ceremony for the Islamic Society of Boston Cultural Center, which had managed to survive the years of controversy, litigation, and federal investigations. It was a triumphal affair, with Boston mayor Thomas Menino in attendance, and Massachusetts governor Deval Patrick sending a video message congratulating the ISB and promising to visit soon. But, there was a fly in the ointment.

Despite ISB's attempt to silence us, Americans for Peace and Tolerance had succeeded in placing the issue of Islamic extremism and Saudi money on the public agenda—with a press conference, protests, and extensive behind-the-scenes legwork. As a result, even those who relied on the *Boston Globe* or Boston's NPR station, or who watched the TV news reports on the grand opening, would have understood that there was a problem with the new Islamic Society of Boston Cultural Center (ISBCC) mosque in Roxbury.

In particular, APT had been sharing its findings from the forty-one boxes of documents obtained during the lawsuit's discovery process. We shared this information with Boston's Jewish leaders, with various politicians, with FBI and DHS officials, and with local law enforcement teams. We presented our findings to the Anti-Defamation League of Boston, to the Combined Jewish Philanthropies of Boston, to then–city councilman and council president Mike Ross, and to many more religious, political, and civic leaders in Massachusetts.

Just a couple of weeks before the ISBCC's grand opening, Charles Jacobs and I gave a two-hour presentation to the *Boston Globe*'s Spotlight team on what we had discovered about the ISB's ties to Islamic extremists. Despite agreeing with us that our evidence was substantial, *Globe* editors refused to publish or mention it. The editors apparently believed that Boston citizens are bigots and that the Muslim community—a "vulnerable minority"—must be protected against xenophobia. But we had always been clear that we were not talking about, or indicting, the entire Muslim community. We even introduced the editors to moderates in the Muslim community who told them exactly what we had been telling them, and who urged the paper to be more vigorous in its reporting. But, unlike with the Catholic Church and its pedophile priests, the *Globe* seemed to believe that it had a higher responsibility toward communal peace than toward telling the truth. From our point of view, the *Globe* editors and reporters have sought to obscure from their readers any information that may reflect poorly on the official leadership of the Boston Muslim community. The newspaper bent over backward to describe Muslim leaders with exquisite sensitivity, while giving the back of the hand to anyone rude enough to raise questions about radical Muslims.

Nevertheless, even the *Globe* couldn't avoid the fact that the old problems at the ISB had not been put to rest. Its report on the ISBCC opening acknowledged the issue, even in the story's title: "Dissent Greets Mosque Opening." In another report, "Muslim Community to Celebrate Mosque's Ceremonial Opening," the *Globe* acknowledged that our outreach to the JCRC, the CJP, the ADL, and the AJC had borne fruit, noting: "Conspicuously absent will be leaders of most of the city's major Jewish organizations, who have been made uneasy by critics' assertions."

The Jewish leaders were made more uneasy still by events surrounding the grand opening ceremonies. Outside the center, Charles and Ahmed Mansour led an Americans for Peace and Tolerance protest against the mosque opening with the theme "Prayer Yes, Extremism No." Imam Abdullah Faaruuq, the al-Qaeda terrorist supporter and friend of Aafia Siddiqui, was picked to give the ISBCC's inaugural sermon, and Bilal Kaleem had come up with a brilliant way to use him in a PR stunt for the cameras.

Faaruuq came out of the mosque, leading a procession of congregants and left-wing "allies," each carrying a single white rose. They got into a single file and approached Charles. After they all demonstratively put their roses, one by one, in Faaruuq's outstretched hands, he presented them to Charles as a gesture of peace. But to give gestures of peace, one must be a man of peace, and Faaruuq couldn't keep up the façade. Faaruuq got mad when Charles raised the problem of modern slavery in the Islamic world. Faaruuq insisted that there are no black slaves with Arab masters in Sudan, then insulted Ahmed Mansour, claiming that he was not a real sheikh and not even a real Muslim. Instead of a gesture of peace, the media ended up reporting it as a confrontation provoked by Faaruuq.

During the confrontation, Bilal Kaleem's young assistant approached some of the protesters, one of whom was videotaping. Without any urging, he told the cameraman: "Jews tried to assassinate the prophet, and they were kicked out of Medina for betraying the prophet." Among other interesting views the young man shared before Kaleem sheepishly whisked him away: Synagogues should not be allowed in Mecca because Mecca was a holy place; a mosque had stood on the Temple Mount before the Jews built their Temple there; and, modern Jews have no connection to the ancient Hebrews.

JCRC executive director Nancy Kaufman, who had just a year before joined Bilal Kaleem at the head of the Greater Boston Interfaith Organization's Tenth Anniversary Gala, was now much more suspicious of the young and charismatic figurehead, in part because of what she was learning about the ISBCC's programming. A couple of months after the mosque's grand opening, for example, the MAS announced that a radical cleric, Sheikh Yasir Qadhi, would be leading a four-day seminar at the ISBCC mosque in Roxbury. We had let Kaufman know about this, and about Qadhi's multiple hateful statements. Several years before his planned ISBCC visit, Qadhi had given a sermon where he claimed that Jews study Islam because "they want to destroy us." Then, he denied the Holocaust, telling his students:

Hitler never intended to mass-destroy the Jews. There are a number of books out there written by Christians on this, you should read them. *The Hoax of the Holocaust* – I advise you to read this book, you want to write this down – *The Hoax of the Holocaust*, it's a very good book. All of this is false propaganda.

Yasir Qadhi had also given sermons calling Jews and Christians "polytheists," comparing them to "a filthy, impure, dirty substance," and insisting that their "life and property holds no value in a state of Jihad." In a lecture on the very same topic that he had planned to give at the ISBCC, Qadhi blasted democracy as against Allah's will:

> It is not my right to legislate or your right to legislate. No supreme court, no system of government, no democracy where they vote. Can you believe it – a group of people coming together and voting? And the majority vote will then be the law of the land? What gives you the right to prohibit something or allow something? Who gave you this right? Are you creators? Are you all-knowledgeable? Do you understand the repercussions and the implications of the laws that you're going to pass? Do they wish to follow the laws of ignorance? Verily, Allah is our judge, he knows what's best for us.

Nancy Kaufman felt betrayed by Bilal Kaleem and wrote him a letter, which read, in part:

> It recently came to my attention that Sheikh Yasir Qadhi will be teaching at the Islamic Society of Boston Cultural Center and that he is being sponsored by the Al Maghrib Institute....[T]he statements credited to Sheikh Qadhi appear to reflect a worldview that is hostile to Jews, Christians and other faith communities. It is difficult to reconcile this kind of teaching with the kind of interfaith engagement that we have all participated in here in Boston....This is, as I know you understand, a matter of serious concern. In considering the most constructive way to approach this letter, I have discussed my concerns privately with a select group of Jewish leaders whose good judgment I trust....I appreciate the seriousness with which you will treat my/our concerns.

Kaleem blew off Kaufman's concerns, and she would never again appear publicly with him at any interfaith event. She would soon leave Boston and be replaced by an even more doctrinaire leftist. Meanwhile, Dennis Hale's prophetic question made at the very first Citizens for Peace and Tolerance press conference in 2004—"Will this Islamic Center become a jihad academy?"—would soon receive a terrible answer.

PART THREE

THE DIRTY DOZEN

CHAPTER 17

MAKE MARTYRDOM
WHAT YOU SEEK

These are the Hoorees with round and firm chests
Pure untouched virgins, they're better than the best,
Seventy-two in all, with large eyes of dark hue
Each one created especially for you . . .

— ISB AND ICNE WORSHIPPER TAREK MEHANNA

On December 14, 2006, my friend from the Islamic Center of New England, who had been cooperating with the FBI, sent an email to his FBI contact, which he later shared with me. It read:

> It appears that there is a farewell get together for [Abou]Samra by the brotherhood very soon. Could be this Sunday night. There are many groups leaving for Haj [Muslim pilgrimage to Mecca] in the next two weeks. He may leave with one of them. It appeared there was urgency that he leave. It appeared that it could be within a week.

Something had really spooked the local Islamist activists.

The FBI already knew what this exchange was about, and why ICNE president and ISBCC vice president Abdulbadi Abousamra was in such a hurry to skip town. Just two days before, FBI agents had questioned his son, Ahmad Abousamra, about a trip to Yemen in 2004, where, the FBI had learned, Ahmad tried "to find a terrorist training camp to learn how to conduct, and to subsequently engage in, jihad." Ahmad lied to the agents and told them that he went to Yemen to study Arabic and Islamic theology. On December 26, 2006, he fled the United States for Syria while his father, Abdulbadi, moved to Detroit with the rest of the family.

The answer to why Abousamra had fled was revealed publicly on October 21, 2009, when the FBI arrested one of Imam Masood's brightest students, Tarek Mehanna. The son of Egyptian immigrants and one of Ahmad Abousamra's closest friends, Mehanna was also, according to the FBI, a co-conspirator in Ahmad's terror activity, traveling to Yemen with him in 2004 in order to train for jihad. But unlike Ahmad, after being questioned by the FBI late in 2006, Tarek had elected to stay put, taking his chances in America because he wanted to finish his doctor of pharmacy degree at the Massachusetts College of Pharmacy and Health Sciences, where his father was a professor. By the time he was ready to flee, the FBI was on to him. Agents arrested him at Logan Airport in 2008 when he tried to board a plane for Saudi Arabia. A false statements charge was the only thing they could pin on Mehanna back then, but it was enough to keep him under house arrest and in the United States while the Department of Justice built its case.

The FBI seized Mehanna's computer several days before his arrest, looking for information on his involvement with al-Qaeda and Lashkar-e-Taiba. Indictments against him and Ahmad Abousamra soon followed, charging the pair with providing and conspiring to provide material support to terrorists, conspiracy to kill in a foreign country, conspiracy to provide false information to law enforcement, and a number of false statements counts.

The indictments were a shock. These were the sons of distinguished members of the Muslim community—of a doctor and a pharmacist. Why would they want to get involved in terrorism? The answer appears to have been the imam brothers of Pakistani terrorist Hafiz Saeed, whom Abdulbadi Abousamra had been setting up in mosques all over the state. Tarek Mehanna studied under both Imam Masood and Imam Hamid—Masood's Worcester-based brother. According to federal prosecutors, Mehanna asked both of them for recommendations to the same jihadist schools in Saudi Arabia where Hafiz Saeed, their terrorist brother, once studied.

Tarek Mehanna and Ahmad Abousamra had also studied with Imam Abdullah Faaruuq and both had often given fiery speeches at the Islamic Society of Northeastern University. Faaruuq was Northeastern University's chaplain, and Abousamra a Muslim student leader there. Between 2000 and 2006, the ISB had given the Islamic Society of Northeastern close to

$10,000 in funds, and this student group was very much within the ISB's orbit. While Faaruuq would become Mehanna's most prominent defendant in Boston, it was, ironically, Faaruuq's prison convert, Bilal McLeod, who ended up dropping the dime on Mehanna and becoming an informant against him. Imam Masood's son, Hassan Masood, who was a part of the same jihadist circles as Mehanna and Abousamra, had also turned informant when he was arrested with his father back in 2006. Another cooperating witness was Ali Aboubakr, the son of Abdulbadi Abousamra's deputy at ICNE, Rajab Aboubakr. Mehanna, it seems, was the only schmuck in on the plot who didn't talk and, accordingly, became the patsy.

The court documents submitted by federal prosecutors ahead of Mehanna's trial detail the lengths to which Mehanna and Abousamra went to take part in violent jihad. In 2002, Abousamra traveled with Imam Masood's son, Hassan, to Pakistan to join Lashkar-e-Taiba. He was rejected because he was Arab and not Pakistani. A local Jihadist named Abdul Majid told Abousamra and Masood Jr. to go back to America and to try to carry out a jihadist attack there.

After coming back from Pakistan, Abousamra, Masood Jr., and Mehanna discussed potential targets. In late 2003, they hatched a plot to carry out a Mumbai-like machine-gun massacre at the Emerald Square Mall in Attleboro, Massachusetts. In their initial planning stages, they reached out for help to their friend Daniel Maldonado, a former gang member who had then recently converted to Islam. Mehanna held a secret meeting with Maldonado at the Islamic Society of Greater Lowell. What Abousamra and Mehanna wanted from Maldonado was access to automatic rifles, which they apparently believed Maldonado could acquire through his criminal contacts. But Maldonado told them that he could only get them handguns and had no access to fully automatic weapons. According to the Justice Department: "Because of the logistical problems of executing the operation with just handguns, the plan was abandoned."

Not long after, Mehanna and Abousamra traveled to Yemen and tried to join al-Qaeda there. Again, they were unsuccessful. Mehanna went back to the United States, while Abousamra traveled on to Syria and Iraq. It is unknown whom he saw there. Maldonado would go on to join the Somali terror group Al Shabaab and get captured by Kenyan forces, which transferred him to American custody. In 2007, he was sentenced to a ten-year prison sentence for training and fighting with Al Shabaab. Having failed to personally take part in jihadist fighting, Mehanna refocused his efforts into the areas where he would become a truly dangerous terrorist—the rapidly growing cyberspace battlefield, the so-called electronic jihad.

As the FBI pointed out in its court filings in the Mehanna trial,

> almost all terrorist organizations have an internet presence which is a critical component of their strategies to engage in propaganda, recruit, raise funds, operationally communicate, in essence, to perform the necessary support functions of terror. Al Qa'ida and Lashkar e Tayyiba specifically have recognized the priority of these functions and maintain robust networks on the internet.

By the middle of the 2000s, the rudimentary fundraising and recruiting websites pioneered in the 1990s by al-Qaeda supporters like MIT Muslim chaplain Suheil Laher had grown into a burgeoning cyber-jihadist network. Mehanna and Abousamra found online places where they could chat with like-minded Islamic extremists, read propaganda by jihadist Islamic religious scholars, publish their own calls to jihad, and—something that brought them immense pleasure—watch jihadi murder videos, especially where American soldiers were being killed. Mehanna in particular became a sort of mini-celebrity in online social circles after penning a poem titled "Make Martyrdom What You Seek." Here's a passage:

> *The bullets hit your hearts like the stings of a bee*
> *You fall on your face as all you can see,*
> *Are the Gardens so wide when you're put in the ground*
> *You've been searching for years and now you have found,*
> *The Ultimate Prize, so sacred, so sweet*
> *Your bargain with your Lord is finally complete,*
> *Because you are all martyrs without fear or grief*
> *Who gave all you had for your precious belief,*
> *You promised Him your souls and He promised you much more*
> *Now you can enjoy what He's kept in store . . .*

> *. . .*

> *You turn and behold! The voices are singing*
> *Coming from Maidens so fair and enchanting,*

These are the Hoorees with round and firm chests
Pure untouched virgins, they're better than the best,
Seventy-two in all, with large eyes of dark hue
Each one created especially for you…

So what if it was painfully insipid? The poem went viral and soon thereafter, individuals associated with al-Qaeda in Iraq, the forerunner of ISIS, began contacting Mehanna with requests for his help. According to the FBI, "Mehanna translated and distributed materials which promoted jihad, such as Al Qa'ida propaganda. Mehanna translated these materials from Arabic to English for purposes of wider distribution, primarily over the internet."

One of the documents Mehanna translated for al-Qaeda in Iraq was a pamphlet called "39 Ways to Serve and Participate in Jihad." After his English translation proved enormously popular, Mehanna began boasting that he is a member of the "media wing" of al-Qaeda in Iraq. According to the FBI, the translation became an important recruiting asset for jihadist causes. In court documents, the FBI makes clear that Mehanna was a serious threat:

"Mehanna is not an inept, 'wanna be' jihadi—particularly in connection with 'electronic jihad,' he was very important and successful," the FBI agent investigating Mehanna wrote. "The only failure in Mehanna's mind was in failing to fulfill his desire to participate personally in crimes of violence directed at U.S. personnel and interests."

In law school, I met one of the assistant U.S. attorneys who prosecuted Mehanna—and, later, Dzhokhar Tsarnaev. He told me that he had no doubt that Mehanna was the more dangerous of the two, despite Dzhokhar and his brother murdering four people and maiming hundreds more, while Mehanna's only tool of mayhem was his keyboard. But, as the prosecutor told me, Mehanna was dangerous because he was able to inspire hundreds of others, who could themselves kill hundreds.

Just as they were doing online, Mehanna and Abousamra were actively recruiting young men within the Boston Muslim community to join them in the jihad. The FBI intercepted Mehanna's communications, in which he described his "one-on-one efforts like, befriend a person slip stuff in here and there," in order to, as he put it, "recruit, brainwash," Muslim youths in Massachusetts. In recruiting new "acolytes," Mehanna used the Muslim

Brotherhood's *Tarbiya* methodology of slowly bringing the person around to jihadist ideology by starting out with benign Muslim beliefs and slowly progressing into more radical material. As he told one of his co-conspirators over AOL Instant Messenger:

> "u don't have to come out with everything at once"
> "not everyone is ready for everything"
> "like, start with stuff"
> "that people can easily accept"

The Department of Justice noted in court filings that Mehanna's recruitment activity was, "particularly concerning given that Mehanna apparently has been teaching his interpretation of religion and science to fifth- to eighth-graders at a local school." That school was the Al Huda Academy, run by the Islamic Society of Greater Worcester, where one of the Lashkar-e-Taiba brothers, Hafiz Hamid, was an imam.

Mehanna's access to and recruitment among Boston Muslim youths as young as ten was especially worrisome considering just how extreme his views actually were. Mehanna lionized Osama bin Laden, saying that he "look[s] to him as being my real father, in a sense." He and Abousamra talked about the 9/11 hijackers as heroes, and, according to the FBI, "studied personal details of the hijackers' lives like others their age might talk about sports or political heroes….They were particularly thrilled that 'mohammed atta was in boston' and speculated that maybe 'we saw him at the isb [Islamic Society of Boston] or something.'"

Their admiration for the 9/11 hijackers mirrored their contempt for the 9/11 victims. Mehanna visited the World Trade Center Ground Zero in New York City and took a picture standing in front of the site with a huge grin and his index finger pointing up in the style of the al-Qaeda and ISIS *tawhid* "gang sign." Mehanna flaunted his malice for those murdered there, telling one of his co-conspirators over Instant Messenger:

> "the people who say for Allah to have mercy upon the kuffar
> [infidels] who were in it"
> "so I say"
> "may Allah have mercy on just the buildings"
> "not the kuffar that were in it"

"as at least the buildings weren't kuffar"
Abousamra shared the sentiment:
"i just hate this stupid kufr land"
"i hate being surrounded by kaafirs."

For Mehanna and Abousamra, even moderate Muslims deserved the worst fates. One day, Abousamra sent Mehanna a statement by the Canadian human rights activist and moderate Muslim leader Farzana Hassan-Shahid, who was then the president of the Canadian Muslim Congress. She was commenting on the arrest of seventeen Canadian Muslim youths, who were caught with three times the amount of explosives used in the Oklahoma City bombing and with plans to blow up buildings in Ontario. Ms. Hassan-Shahid made a commonsense statement: "It's about time Muslims owned up to the fact it's a Muslim problem....We need to be more proactive, rather than issue statements of condemnation."

"She needs to be raped with a broomstick," Mehanna wrote back. "[L] ol" was Abousamra's response.

Mehanna, Abousamra, and their friends' most twisted obsession was watching jihadi murder videos: the videotaped beheadings and mutilations whose distribution online as a recruiting tool was pioneered by al-Qaeda in Iraq and perfected by its successors in the Islamic State. According to the FBI, "Mehanna and his coconspirators, who shared videos and took real pleasure in the deaths of American servicemen, seemed to delight in the most horrific atrocities." FBI intercepts of Mehanna's conversations described Mehanna sharing with his friends a video in which al-Qaeda in Iraq terrorists rip open the ribcages of U.S. soldiers, pour gasoline into their chest cavities and set them on fire. "[N]ice juicy BBQ," Mehanna gloated to his friends. "Texas BBQ is the way to go. I want more BBQ sauce videos."

Mehanna and Abousamra loved watching extreme scenes of violence and took much pleasure in human suffering. Their greatest hope in life was to murder Americans in the most gruesome ways, to see them suffer as much as possible, and then to become martyrs for Allah in the name of Islam. And while Mehanna did not get his death wish, his recruiting efforts in the Boston area apparently paid off. The Justice Department learned the hard way just how popular Mehanna and his views had become within the Boston Muslim community.

As soon as Mehanna was arrested, the Islamist network in Massachusetts erupted with rage at the FBI, the federal prosecutors who built the case against Mehanna, and the U.S. government in general. It was a repeat of the grievance theater put on after Imam Masood was arrested, with pretty much the same actors. Mehanna's supporters insisted that the twisted mind revealed in FBI-recorded conversations was actually a gentle soul who loved children and enjoyed playing with his cat. They launched a petition for him online that read, in part:

> He is a devout and tolerant Muslim who is not only respected in the local Islamic and interfaith communities, but who also gives back to his Islamic community by fulfilling the roles of brother, educator, mentor, scholar, and friend. Tarek is described by those who know him well as humble, reserved, warm, peaceful, intelligent, knowledgeable, reflective, pragmatic, dedicated, and straightforward. He is a person with strong ethical values.

Mehanna's petition gathered nearly 2,300 signatures. Led by Tarek's brother, Tamer Mehanna, the Free Tarek movement was born. Tarek's supporters claimed that Mehanna's arrest was nothing but a witch hunt by the FBI (because the FBI "hated Muslims") and incited Boston Muslims against the U.S. government by painting Mehanna as a helpless victim of religious intolerance. Over the next several years until Mehanna's sentencing in 2012 to seventeen years in federal maximum-security prison, the Free Tarek movement waged a PR and intimidation pressure campaign against the Justice Department and other law enforcement branches.

Just like Mehanna himself, the Free Tarek movement operated both online and on the ground in Massachusetts. Online, it took advantage of the social media explosion in the decade following the 9/11 attacks. The Free Tarek Facebook group had 4,283 members. There was also a MySpace page, a Twitter account, and a YouTube channel, where "friends" of the channel used slogans like "Close Guantanamo Bay, Reopen Auschwitz" as their profile pics.

Many of the individuals active online in support of Tarek Mehanna were familiar faces locally. Syed Asif Razvi, a physician who has held various positions at MAS and was at one point the president of the Islamic Council of New England, signed the Free Tarek petition, commenting:

"Tarek is INNOCENT." Dr. Razvi was also involved in Muhammad Ali Salaam's BRIDGES law enforcement outreach and dialogue program—which, again, became the vehicle for blackmail-type threats against counterterrorism efforts. As Rizvi told the *Boston Globe* after Mehanna's arrest: "We work very hard to build bridges, and it kind of wipes out all we've done for a period of time."

MAS and ISBCC Outreach Coordinator Ahmed Elewa had joined the Free Tarek Facebook group. The spring before Mehanna was arrested, Ahmed Elewa received a Community Leadership Award from the Justice Department for his role in the BRIDGES program. Assistant U.S. attorney Aloke Chakravarty—one of the lead prosecutors on the Mehanna case and a favorite target of abuse for the Free Tarek crowd—personally presented the award. Elewa didn't see any contradiction between getting an award for building bridges with law enforcement on the one hand, and belonging to the Free Tarek movement, which was actively burning those bridges, on the other. "I don't believe that sympathizing with an enemy of the United States is a crime," he told the *Washington Post*. Sympathizing is not. Material support is.

The huge number of Tarek Mehanna supporters on social media allowed me to use social network analysis to quantify the extent of support for Mehanna among the members of ISB/MAS and other Muslim Brotherhood organizations in New England. This was back when Facebook groups instead of pages were the primary activist vehicles on Facebook—and their membership was public. My hypothesis was that Mehanna and Abousamra operated within and were products of the Muslim Brotherhood network in Massachusetts. Therefore, one would see significant overlap between the Free Tarek Facebook group members and the various ISB/MAS-affiliated Facebook groups.

The results neatly matched my assumptions. The largest overlap was with the "I Grew up under Imam Masood" Facebook group. Twenty-six percent of this group's members were also members of the Free Tarek group. The second largest overlap with Mehanna supporters was among members of the "I Love the ISB" group, with 25 percent of its members also being members of the Free Tarek group. Twenty-two percent of the Facebook group for the Muslim Students Association at the University of Massachusetts Boston, where both Mehanna and Abousamra had attended before Abousamra transferred to Northeastern, were members of

Free Tarek. So was 15 percent of the Boston Council of Muslim Student Associations—an umbrella group organized directly by MAS Boston's Youth Department, and officially affiliated with the oldest Muslim Brotherhood organization in America, Muslim Students Association National. Fourteen percent of ISB Imam Basyouni Nehela's Facebook friends were members of Free Tarek. So were 12 percent of MIT Muslim Chaplain Suheil Laher's Facebook friends and 11 percent of MAS president Hossam Al Jabri's. As an experimental control, I used a Muslim student group present on several Boston university campuses that I knew was not affiliated with the Muslim Brotherhood—"Project Nur." None of the Brandeis Project Nur members were part of the Free Tarek Facebook group. Only 3 percent of the Boston University Project Nur membership was part of Free Tarek. At Northeastern University, a center of Islamic extremist student activity where Ahmad Abousamra studied before transferring to University of Massachusetts Boston, and where Tarek Mehanna frequently preached to Muslim students, only 6 percent of Project Nur members were part of the Free Tarek group on Facebook.

On the ground in Massachusetts, I could see the ISB/MAS connections with my own eyes. Before every major court hearing in the Mehanna case, the Free Tarek movement would reach out to the Boston Muslim community, urging members to pack the Moakley Federal Courthouse courtroom where the trial was taking place, and to protest outside the building in front of the media cameras set up to cover the trial. Huge numbers showed and I came, too—with a video camera for later identification.

The ISB and MAS openly supported Hafiz Masood when he was arrested. But while Masood was suspected of terrorist activity, he was only charged with an immigration violation. Tarek Mehanna, on the other hand, was charged with actual terrorist crimes, including providing material support for al-Qaeda. The ISB and MAS Boston were much more reluctant to openly support him than they were to support Masood, to the extreme anger of Tamer Mehanna, Tarek's brother. Tamer wrote on the Free Tarek Facebook wall:

> When my brother was arrested 12 months ago, he contacted MAS
> for help. He fully expected to receive their support, as he knew
> many in the organization and he thought they had a healthy
> relationship. MAS' response was to have called up Tariq's attorney

at the time, Norm Zalkind, and asked him whether he felt Tariq would be found guilty or not....Ultimately, MAS decided to keep a distance so its reputation remained "clean."

While the ISB/MAS Boston did not officially support Tarek, much of its leadership did, although quietly. I ran into MAS Boston and ISBCC president Hossam Al Jabri outside of the courtroom during Mehanna's bail hearing. (Bail was denied.) Al Jabri, remembering me from the time I called him out for his donation to Hamas, grimaced and quickly left through a back exit so that I couldn't film him later.

After the bail hearing was over, I went outside to film the protest. The Islamic Society of Greater Worcester had taken the elementary school children at its Al Huda Academy out of class, had them draw "Free Tarek" posters, and then drove them to the Moakley Federal Courthouse to chant anti-American slogans to the media cameras. Tarek's attempts to radicalize the Muslim children he taught at Al Huda seemed to have been done with the full consent of the school's leadership. Al Huda wasn't the only school like that in Massachusetts.

The Mehanna family walked out of the courthouse with Tarek's lawyer and another man as the protesters broke into chants of "Takbir!"—"Allahu Akbar." I'd seen that other man before: at the ISBCC grand opening in the summer of 2008, he had the place of honor standing directly to the right of Boston mayor Thomas Menino as the mayor gave his welcome to the mosque. The man turned out to be a Pakistani immigrant named Farooq Mirza. I saw Farooq Mirza at many Free Tarek events throughout the trial, where his sons, Ammar and Bilal, often accompanied him.

· · ·

The Mirza family had an interesting range of associations. They were apparently close to the family of Mehanna, an al-Qaeda terrorist, and also to the leadership of the ISB/MAS Boston. But they were apparently just as close to the Anti-Defamation League's New England branch. Childhood friends of Tarek Mehanna, Bilal and Ammaar Mirza had been involved with ADL's Camp Interfaith in Andover, New Hampshire since they were teenagers, first as campers and then as staffers. ADL's Camp Interfaith brings together Jewish and Muslims children for summer outdoor activities—and apparently political discussion. In a 2006 *Boston Globe* puff piece on Camp Interfaith, a teenage Jewish girl is quoted as saying: "Even if we're discussing whether Hezbollah is a terrorist group," she said, "afterward we can still be friends and go play soccer."

Only in certain circles is there any debate about "whether Hezbollah is a terrorist group": it has been so designated by the United States and many other governments for decades. With its katyusha rocket salvoes, it has tried to kill my family in Kiryat Shmona in the north of Israel on multiple occasions—and, once back in 1996, me as well. Exposing Jewish children to claims Hezbollah is anything other than a terrorist organization—and at a Jewish summer camp, no less—seems strange. But just as with its attempts at interfaith dialogue with ISB trustee Walid Fitaihi after 9/11, the ADL seemed to have gotten bamboozled again.

Bilal Mirza, in particular, seemed to be advancing at the ADL. In August 2013, he worked with the organization to expand the summer camp program into a yearlong program called "ADL Interfaith Youth Leadership Coalition." The launch was held at Babson College, where Bilal is the campus Muslim chaplain. In fact, Bilal and his father, Farooq Mirza, were prominently honored at the ADL's 2013 Nation of Immigrants Seder, commemorating the ADL's centennial anniversary. Farooq Mirza was given the honor of being a co-chair of the event together with such notables as the mayors of both Boston and Newton at the time: Tom Menino and Setti Warren.

Bilal Mirza was a member of the planning committee for the ADL Seder. ADL New England's executive director, Robert Trestan, personally introduced Bilal at the podium, and asked "those of you who came here with children, those of you who have kids at home" to consider sending them to the interfaith summer camp for some quality time with Bilal. After taking the podium, Bilal proceeded to quote a Quranic verse traditionally interpreted as rebuking Jews for deviating from divine truth. The ADL apparently did not notice.

And yet Bilal Mirza was never secretive about his support for Tarek Mehanna. After Mehanna was arrested, he told the *Boston Herald* that he had known Mehanna for years and looked up to him, saying, "He's always been a great mentor." When he signed the Free Tarek petition, Bilal left this comment about the man who said a moderate Muslim woman "needs to be raped with a broomstick" and who, according to the FBI, "seemed to delight in the most horrific atrocities":

> Tariq [sic] is a great, humble, and gentle person. His actions, mannerisms, as well as his overall demeanor exude the qualities of intrinsic humanity. He is not only a honest Muslim, but also an endearing human being....He does not deserve the things that are happening to him.

On a freezing cold and windy Saturday in January of 2012, I was filming Ammar and Bilal Mirza as they chanted "Free Tarek!" at a rally on the Boston Common. Tarek had been convicted a month earlier of providing material support for al-Qaeda in Iraq, but his supporters were unwilling to accept the verdict of an American court. Once again, I saw a familiar face: Anwar Kazmi, an ISB trustee and one of the most senior and important leaders at the ISB and MAS Boston. I was surprised to see Kazmi called to the podium as a representative of MAS, whose leaders were usually more discreet. But Kazmi let loose, attacking the American justice system as corrupt and slandering the U.S. Army with false claims of atrocities in Iraq. Kazmi told the crowd that he visited the Free Tarek website that morning and "read some of the things Tarek has written, and I was truly inspired and I'm sure that you will be inspired as well." He asked everyone to visit the website and read Tarek's writings.

A young Muslim girl read some of the poetry posted on the Free Tarek website to the audience, including this poem:

> *The reality with which we must come to grips;*
> *Is that we are hunted one after the next,*
> *PATRIOT Act foretold in the divine text*
> *They'd told us "Obama!" I said "you just wait,*
> *He is not but an employee of the state,*
> *That upon the Ummah [Muslim community] has focused its hate."*
> *And now we see that he has increased the rate;*
> *Of arrests and drone strikes and death in our land,*
> *This war on Islam, it will only expand.*

Mehanna's mother spoke at the rally and claimed that Tarek is being "persecuted for being a Muslim" and that "one day all of our kids will be in his place." It should be noted that the Tsarnayev brothers' mother has likewise proclaimed her sons' innocence and accused the United States of persecuting them for being Muslim.

A young man who claimed to represent the Occupy Boston movement told the crowd:

> I believe that Tarek is innocent of any wrong-doing....Tarek is
> an Egyptian American who empowered his community—an
> oppressed community, the Muslim community, speaking against
> U.S. wars in the Middle East. He represents in that sense a link in
> the chain of international solidarity against this global system that
> has oppressed so many of us.

He concluded by saying: "At the end of the day we are all Tarek Mehanna."

Mehanna's admirers include people who do more than cheer him on: A prayer card in support of Tarek Mehanna was found in the Boston Marathon bombers' apartment.

In inciting Massachusetts Muslims in support of Tarek Mehanna and against the United States, by far the most militant and active ISB/MAS leader was Imam Abdullah Faaruuq, the African American Muslim who was radicalized by MIT Muslim chaplain Suheil Laher and who had closely befriended Aafia "Lady al-Qaeda" Siddiqui. Faaruuq, not coincidentally, also became very close with Tarek Mehanna. As a Northeastern University Muslim chaplain, he used to invite Tarek to give sermons to Northeastern's Muslim students over dinner, at a series of events called "*Deen* [Religion] and Dine." By the time of the Mehanna trial in 2012, Faaruuq was a man on fire. Mehanna was not Faaruuq's first friend taken out of action by federal authorities over the previous few years, and he would not be the last. Faaruuq's dear friend and follower, Aafia Siddiqui—who had become the most wanted woman in the world was already in federal prison. Faaruuq had not seen her since she fled to Pakistan in 2003, where she lived for a while in her parents' home in Karachi. When 9/11 mastermind Khalid Sheik Mohammed was captured in Pakistan that same year and identified her as a top al-Qaeda operative, she disappeared into thin air.

CHAPTER 18

THE BOSTON CULT OF LADY AL-QAEDA

On July 17, 2008, local residents in Ghazni, an ancient town in Afghanistan not far from the Pakistan border, encountered a strange woman crouching on the ground outside of a mosque. She was wearing the blue burka that women in Afghanistan have been forced to wear since the Taliban took over. No one could see her face, but she was acting suspiciously and the locals were afraid she might be a suicide bomber. So they alerted the Afghan National Police, who arrested her on suspicion of attempting an attack against the governor of Ghazni Province. As she was taken to the police station, she screamed at them in Urdu: "You are infidels; don't touch me!"

The woman was Aafia Siddiqui. According to government filings in her trial, a search of her possessions revealed pre-printed documents with instructions on how to make explosives, as well as handwritten notes on making weaponized Ebola and various other chemical, biological, and radiological weapons.

An MIT-trained scientist, Siddiqui seemed to know at least something about what she was doing. Her dirty bomb recipe read:

Dirty Bomb: Need few oz. radioactive material (e.g. cobalt 60 from food irradiation facility)...wrap cobalt 60 around a [u/i] bomb, detonate it & shower a city w deadly fall out....To detect dirty bombs, gamma and other radiation sensors @ airports [or] seaports

[or] police depts (but still not all covered in America)....Practical dirty bomb would work by causing FEAR, not much deaths.

Some of Siddiqui's handwritten notes show that she was using her scientific training and her, perhaps by that point fevered, imagination to brainstorm "inventive" weaponry ideas:

Do the unthinkable: Attack enemies on gliders....Attack using laser beams.
Need booby traps "dummy" shelters (metal deposits) to fool enemys radar.
To kill or "mess up" drones. etc. How about thin pointed "charged towers" that discharge their electricity upon the drone as it approaches near or over them.

There were also handwritten notes referencing a mass casualty attack on New York City, focusing on landmarks like the Empire State Building, the Statue of Liberty, Wall Street, the Brooklyn Bridge, and the Plum Island Animal Disease Center, where biological weapons research was done during the Cold War. Siddiqui carried a thumb drive, which, according to the U.S. government, "contained correspondence that referred to specific 'cells' and 'attacks' by certain 'cells.'" Other documents referred to "enemies," including the United States, and discussed "recruitment and training" for jihad. Siddiqui was also carrying 1,800 grams of sodium cyanide and might have been planning to poison a well somewhere. A third of a gram of cyanide can kill an average person.

Siddiqui had a document that described various poisons and how to use them against civilians:

For enemy land: a) Can go into supermarkets and randomly inject fruits with poisons, as well as other items that are usually eaten raw....This may not kill as many people, but the panic, fear, and economic loss will be substantial if done properly. inshaAllah.

Siddiqui's thumb drive also contained discussions of jihadist training and recruitment, repeated references to ways to attack the United States, and materials on building chemical and biological weapons. Almost comically, in light of the other documents she was carrying, the thumb drive also contained "a biographical essay by Siddiqui titled 'I am Not a Terrorist.'"

The Afghan National Police notified the U.S. Army about Siddiqui's arrest and turned her possessions over to Army personnel at Forward Operating Base Ghazni. Phones at the FBI headquarters in Washington began ringing—the capture of one of the seven most wanted al-Qaeda terrorists, especially one who had been completely off the radar for five years, doesn't happen every day. The next morning, an interview team consisting of two FBI agents, five special operators, two interpreters, and a medic, set out from the U.S. Army's Forward Operating Base Ghazni toward the compound where Aafia Siddiqui was being held.

By the time the Interview Team had arrived at the Afghan National Police compound, Aafia had already tried twice to escape, at one point biting one of the officers and threating to blow him up. She begged the Afghans not to turn her over to American custody. When the team arrived, they were taken to a dimly lit room full of Afghan police personnel and partitioned by a yellow curtain that ran the length of the room. They had no idea that Aafia was sitting behind the curtain, unsecured and unrestrained.

A chief warrant officer with the team walked over to the curtain and checked behind it, but did not see anyone. Aafia was likely hiding in a corner and shielded from view. The Chief Warrant Officer sat down next to the curtain and put down his M4 rifle. Suddenly, two hands came out from behind the curtain, grabbed the rifle and pointed it at the Americans.

The commanding Army officer, Captain Robert Snyder remembered staring directly down the barrel of the rifle, with the look in Aafia's eyes being "a vision of hatred" as she screamed something to the effect of: "May the blood of [something] be on your either head or hands." Interpreter Ahmed Gul threw open the curtain and lunged at Aafia, who fumbled with the rifle at first, but then successfully opened fire. The team's medic, Dawn Card, "remember[ed] thinking that I needed to get out of the room because I was going to die if I didn't, but I couldn't move." Gul began to fight Aafia over the gun while she was still firing, at which point the chief drew his side arm and shot Aafia in the stomach. The interpreter got the rifle out of her hands, but Aafia wasn't done yet. According to federal prosecutors, she attacked the Americans trying to restrain her with "a look of hate in her eyes."

The prosecution's brief went on:

> Siddiqui punched them; kicked them; slapped them; tried to
> bite them; and spit at them. As Siddiqui did this, she repeatedly
> screamed anti-American statements. Witnesses recall her saying:
> "Death to America." "I am going to kill all you Americans. You are
> going to die by my blood." "I want to kill Americans. I want to kill
> Americans." "I want to kill Americans. Don't touch my blood or
> you will die." "I will kill all you mother fuckers."

After the wounded Siddiqui was finally restrained, she began asking "over and over again" for the interview team to "just kill me." The interview team's medic treated her wounds and the team carried her kicking and screaming out of the police station. Outside, 50 to 150 Afghan police confronted them with their weapons drawn. After a brief standoff with the Afghans, who wanted them to release the distraught and bleeding woman, the Americans transported Siddiqui, still kicking and screaming, back to the Ghazni FOB. The next day, Aafia was moved to Bagram Airbase for two weeks of medical treatment, and, from there, flown to the United States to stand trial.

Siddiqui was indicted and ultimately found guilty in 2010 by a New York jury on the charges of attempting to kill United States nationals, attempting to kill U.S. officers and employees, armed assault of United States officers and employees, discharging a firearm during a crime of violence, and assaulting United States officers and employees.

The Pakistani government paid for Siddiqui's defense attorneys, whom she tried to have dismissed from representing her because they were Jewish, writing to the court that Jews are "cruel, ungrateful, backstabbing" people. When it came time for jury selection, she demanded that there be no Jews on the jury, and that potential jurors be given a DNA test for Jewish ancestry to be sure that a Jew doesn't slip through.

"If they have a Zionist or Israeli background...they are all mad at me," she claimed. "They should be excluded if you want to be fair."

"I have a feeling everyone here is them—subject to genetic testing."

"This is a verdict coming from Israel, not America, and that is where this anger belongs. I can testify to this, and I have proof."

Siddiqui was sentenced to eighty-six years in prison.

• • •

Back in Boston, Imam Abdullah Faaruuq became Aafia Siddiqui's most vocal defender during her trial. She was his close friend and his partner in raising money for Care International's terrorism-fundraising efforts. Under Faaruuq's influence, the Free Tarek movement adopted her cause as well. Faaruuq gave impassioned sermons at mosques and community centers around Boston defending Aafia Siddiqui and Tarek Mehanna and attacking the U.S. government for prosecuting them. But he never did so just in the context of their individual cases—for him it was all about an infidel America that was attacking all Muslims as a group. And because Muslims were being attacked as a group, Faaruuq would preach that it was incumbent on all Muslims to strike back.

On March 6, 2010, Abdullah Faaruuq gave a sermon at the Yusuf Mosque in Boston's Brighton neighborhood that was emblematic of how he, and extremist imams in general, incite Muslims toward terrorist causes. Just as Aafia had done in the 1990s with Bosnia and Chechnya, Faaruuq started out by framing jihad as a noble defensive act mandated by Allah on behalf of the weak and oppressed. "As Allah the exalted has said in his book," Faaruuq intoned, tracing the Quranic verses with his finger. "And why should you not struggle, fight if you have to in the way of Allah when those who are weak amongst you from amongst the ill-treated and oppressed, men and women and children whose cry is 'our Lord rescue us from this town whose people are our oppressors.'"

Faaruuq then proceeded to divide the world into Muslims and non-Muslims, engaged in a struggle: "Who do you think it is? Who do you think He [Allah in the Quran] is talking to? The Christian? Is He waiting for the Jew to help us?"

The next step in taking the congregants of Yusuf Mosque toward jihad was to tell them that they could not be true Muslims unless they were brave enough to "pick up the gun and the sword." Faaruuq preached:

There is a word, *shaja'ah*. What does *shaja'ah* mean? It means bravery. You know, and if anybody in the world is to be brave it must be us. Because we are the people that Allah says: "We are the best of people taken out of humanity." If this is the case, then you—this black man and this medium brown black man, and this other black man from Pakistan and you, wherever you come from—if you are not the people that Allah is talking about when he says *shaja'ah*, then you should leave the religion. You should leave. But if you are claiming that you are these people, then you must grab onto this rope, grab on to the typewriter, grab onto the shovel, grab onto the gun and the sword. Don't be afraid to step out into this world and do your job.

The actual nature of this job that requires a gun and a sword is not revealed until toward the end of the sermon, when the worshippers have already been prepped with soaring rhetoric about how important and holy that job is. Then came the punch line. Faaruuq showed everyone a flyer with a sweet and smiling MIT student Aafia Siddiqui on it:

I brought some papers tonight that I am going ask if I can give out regarding a woman who is presently suffering—this woman, Aafia Siddiqui. Some people are afraid to get involved with politics and things that are going on, but you know, after they finish with Aafia, they're going to come to your door, if they feel like it. You know this PATRIOT Act permits them to come anywhere they want at any time. I am not inviting them, but I am not afraid to speak on her behalf and for the behalf of every man and woman who has a difficulty and there are some, many of us, who are being oppressed in this world.

Faaruuq pointed to a little child in the audience:

"I want this little boy to be saved."
He then began to pray:
    Help us who are here in America to [not] be afraid, and to speak of the case of Tarek Mehanna and Aafia Siddiqui, but help us to learn how we must do it so that we don't bring destruction on ourselves. Because we don't want the heavy hand of the oppressor to snuff out the flame of Allah near us.

He finished with the Muslim battle cry "takbir!" and chastised the men for not screaming "Allahu Akbar" back loudly enough, joking, "I thought they were afraid to say it. Maybe the FBI is around. Allahu akbar."

In 2011, at a fundraiser for Siddiqui at the Islamic Society of Greater Worcester, the Jamaican-born Faaruuq lauded Aafia's attempted murder of American soldiers and law enforcement officers:

> They say she took up a machine gun while they held her captive in the other room and was ready to attack her capt[ors]. What a brave woman she is. And if my mother was in the same place, she would have taken her West Indian machete and cut her way through those kafirs [infidels].

By this point, it should not surprise the reader to learn that, although Imam Faaruuq routinely bashed law enforcement agencies during his sermons, and one of the most unapologetic defenders of convicted terrorists in Massachusetts, he was also one of the Muslim leaders that Massachusetts law enforcement agencies and politicians most closely embraced. In March 2010, for example, Faaruuq gave the sermon in Brighton urging Boston Muslims to take up arms against American law enforcement officers in order to defend a top al-Qaeda terrorist who tried to murder law enforcement officers. Two months later, the ISB chose him to stand on stage with Massachusetts attorney general Martha Coakley at the ISBCC event with Massachusetts governor Deval Patrick and announce the $50,000 grant that Healey gave to the ISBCC's leaders for training Massachusetts cops in Muslim sensitivity. As it was his turn to speak, Governor Patrick warmly embraced Faaruuq on stage. The ISBCC leaders had a list of demands they presented to Governor Patrick, among them this one:

"Recognition of Pain: Will you Governor convene heads of law enforcement agencies (federal and state agencies) that operate in Massachusetts for a meeting with Muslim representatives to discuss the need for cultural awareness trainings?"

The ISBCC event with Healey and Patrick was co-organized by the ACLU and paid for by Islamic Relief—the Islamic charity that both Israel and the United Arab Emirates consider a terrorist organization, and which even the notoriously money-laundering HSBC bank in the United Kingdom dropped as a client due to terrorist-financing concerns.

• • •

A year later, on September 24, 2011, MAS Boston hosted at the ISBCC an event that was both very similar and very different when compared to the one with the governor. This event was also co-organized by the ACLU and featured Imam Abdullah Faaruuq. But this time, it was Free Tarek activists, rather than the Massachusetts governor and attorney general, who were center-stage. The Tarek Mehanna Support Committee also helped the ISBCC organize the event, called "Reclaiming Power and Protecting our Communities." According to an announcement on the ISBCC's website, the event promised to teach the attendees "how you can protect yourself from profiling and preemptive prosecution." The event would "shed light on the conditions of families and communities suffering under the war on terror, mobilize our communities to change the repressive injunctions and establish alliances across all communities for collective strength and positive social change."

The advertisements were otherwise cryptic: a bare poster with a picture of the ISBCC façade that made the vague announcements: "3 states, 4 families, 1 place...are you ready?" Another poster featured two silhouetted figures with question marks over them and said:

They are finally coming to Boston...are you ready?
Only @ ISBCC.

"They" turned out to be the families of four convicted terrorists; along with Imam Faaruuq, his friend Mauri Saalakhan, aradical D.C.-based activist who made Aafia Siddiqui his national cause célèbre; and several other extremists. Tarek Mehanna's brother, Tamer, spoke on behalf of his brother, apparently having forgiven MAS Boston for its earlier silence regarding his cause. Another speaker, Faisal Hashmi, was at the ISBCC on behalf of his brother, Syed Fahad Hashmi, a Pakistani immigrant from Brooklyn who pleaded guilty to conspiring to provide military gear to al-Qaeda a year earlier. Yet another terrorist family member, Sharmin Sadequee, spoke on behalf of her brother, Ehsanul "Shifa" Sadequee, a Bangladeshi-American from Roswell, Georgia, who tried to join the Taliban in December 2001 and was convicted of casing Washington, D.C., landmarks, including the U.S. Capitol, the World Bank, the D.C. Masonic Temple, and a fuel tank depot—all in the service of Lashkar-e-Taiba. Finally, Laila Yaghi spoke on behalf of her son, Ziyad Yaghi, and the Raleigh Seven Support Committee. Ziyad Yaghi was a member of the so-called Raleigh Jihad

Group, comprising seven North Carolina men led by Daniel Patrick Boyd, a white American convert to Islam who received terrorist training in Afghanistan and Pakistan. Yaghi traveled to Israel to join the Palestinian jihad against the Jews and was convicted of conspiring to provide material support to terrorists and conspiring to murder, kidnap, maim and injure persons in a foreign country. He was sentenced to thirty years in prison.

The three-hour-long event, which I found on YouTube, followed the familiar pattern at work in Faaruuq's sermons and in Muslim Brotherhood indoctrination tactics in general. The first couple of hours were filled with idealistic anti-racist speakers who spoke of the history of the American civil rights movement. Then, the families of the convicted terrorists linked their fight against the U.S. government to that legitimate movement for civil rights. Then, finally, Imam Faaruuq and Mauri Saalakhan got the mic.

Mauri Saalakhan insisted that the ISBCC should not be concerned about the scrutiny of its critics, like Americans for Peace and Tolerance, and fully embrace pro-terrorist activism, telling the gathered ISBCC members and guests:

This beautiful center, the largest center in Boston, the largest center in this area, in this metro area and a center that was born out of controversy, a center that was born out of controversy and opposition. There were people in this country, Islamophobes with a capital "I" who did their very best to prevent this center from being built.

And at the end of the day, by the grace and mercy of Allah, to Allah it was built, it was established. But now the question arises, not just for this center but many other large centers around the country, brothers and sisters, should we allow the very people who stood in the way of us establishing our institutions, should we allow them now to have veto power over our institutions? Should they be able to wield veto power from the shadows?

No, the answer to that is no. And let me say I'm speaking for myself, so if anyone gets angry with anyone, just get angry with Mauri Salaakhan, just him, nobody else. But I'm saying we should not allow the opposition to have veto power over what we do in our centers, in our *masaajid* [mosques] centers and around the country. All over the country, what I find over and over and over again is some of our largest, most well established centers are reluctant to deal with issues that need to be dealt with and, *subhanallah* [glory to Allah], just hurts us. This hurts us. It does damage to the psyche, especially of young Muslims who are tearing along the edge."

Saalakhan urged the ISBCC leadership to never cooperate with the FBI:

And this leads me to another point, we should not allow the FBI to have access to our *masaajid* centers. That's my opinion....especially given with what we know they do, . . .

And let me speak...to our "friends" in the FBI because I know they are listening, I know they are listening. *Subhanallah* and that's alright because we have nothing to hide, we're not doing anything illegal, we are within our constitutional rights, we have nothing to hide.

As an agency, I think this organization is sitting on the precipice of evil.

As with Faaruuq's sermon on behalf of Aafia Siddiqui a year earlier, Saalakhan told Boston Muslims that they would be betraying Islam if they didn't support convicted al-Qaeda terrorist Tarek Mehanna's fight against the U.S. government:

"For those of us who are not involved, we need to become involved and one of those important ways you can do this is by becoming involved in the Tarek Mehanna case," Saalakhan urged. "All over the country, I say to my brothers and sisters, there is the case and you have a responsibility to respond to it. If you don't, you are betraying what prophet Muhammad from Allah has instructed us to do."

Saalakhan urged Boston Muslims to fight the jihad, even if it comes at the expense of their lives:

"We have verses like, 'not equal are those believers who sit at home and receive no hurt, and those who strive [Ar. *jahadu*] with their property and their persons in the cause of Allah.' We have these verses...for the purpose of reminding us that just as the prophet and his companions had to struggle, just like Allah made them the best among mankind.

"[They] struggled and sacrificed and paid a price, some of them died, they were killed, they suffered all kinds of indignities, but at the end of the day because they were resolute in their faith, they ended up being victorious. Well, the same thing has to happen with us. We have to be willing to struggle and to sacrifice."

Imam Abdullah Faaruuq spoke next and told the audience about his personal relationship with Aafia Siddiqui:

"Now Aafia was a member of my masjid," he told the audience. "She had a Dawa Resource Center there and she spent a lot of time in providing and raising money to get books about Islam so the people could come and learn about what the religion of Islam means, not only from her own standpoint but from original sources.

"So I know her personally. I ate at her home. My wife and I...ate from her hand. We listened to her speech and I've watched her over a period of 10 years...as she graduated from, I believe, MIT. She had eaten at my home and I ate at her home and this is a woman they say was a threat to the United Sates government. It goes to show you how weak the United States is. If they're going to target this young woman and beat her down and do the things that they are doing to her, this shows the weakness of our nation. And I'm here to advocate on her behalf."

Faaruuq launched into a full frontal attack on America, threatening it with destruction over its sins:

[The U.S. government is] trying to send a message here to the people of the United States that for you women and men who are gathered here today that you should be weak and you should cower, you should kowtow to the authority—but never will we, not if we want to speak the truth. And so this young man Tarek Mehanna who I came to know because he attended the masjid, used to go into the meetings, the *halaqas* [study groups] over at Northeastern University, the sweetest young man you'd ever want to know....If you want to know who Tarek Mehanna is, he is a lovely young man, a PhD who had a whole future ahead of him....Of course, he was spirited. He is concerned as you are – I guess that's why you are here for the concerns that are going on to the world. Why is the world the way it is today?...The world is in the condition that we are right now presently because we refuse to obey God and we want to put the Constitution, this one nation over God, we want to put this one nation over God instead of one nation under God....We cannot let this nation just do whatever they want and expect for it

to find life and continue with existence. This nation, by God, will
be brought to its knees....And you feel that you are a great nation
America....It is called the land of the free, the home of the brave
—I call it the land of the coward, the home of the slave. This is
America. Make sure that you are not one of those slaves by [speak-
ing] up against the wrong-doing and what's going on.

Faaruuq ended his speech with a direct challenge to the U.S. government:

They're trying to prosecute [Muslims] thinking that if they do
this then they will stop it. They won't, though. Come and get me
because I'm in a jihad straight up against any wrong-doing wherever I find it. Come and get me because I will continue to speak
on behalf of those who...are being harmed and against the wrong
doing, here I am. Abdullah Taalib Faaruuq, 724 Shawmut Avenue, if
you want, come and get me. Know that my voice will continue to be
raised on behalf of those who are being oppressed.

Faaruuq continued to raise his voice, and some of his disciples would soon
take him up on his challenge.

CHAPTER 19

THE SEVENTY-FIVE RABBIS

In the spring of 2010, Charles and I tried once again to educate Rabbi Ronne Friedman of Boston's largest synagogue, Temple Israel, about the true nature of the ISBCC's owners and leaders. This was the same rabbi who was snookered by Walid Fitaihi, the wealthy and anti-Semitic ISB trustee from Saudi Arabia who had been the rabbi's dialogue partner after 9/11.

"This is alarming, but I'd need to see a smoking gun," he told us after we'd spent an hour in his office walking him through mounds of evidence that linked the leaders of the Islamic Society of Boston to terrorism and hate speech against Jews and Christians. He wouldn't, he explained, speak publicly about the doubts he now had for fear of giving offense; for fear of breaking with a certain understanding about these things. For many years, that exact sentiment has epitomized the thinking of Boston's cultural and political elite.

Nine days after we met with Rabbi Friedman, Governor Deval Patrick and future attorney general Maura Healey made their visit to the ISBCC and embraced Imam Abdullah Faaruuq, the al-Qaeda terrorist supporter. It was election season, and Republican state treasurer Tim Cahill, who was campaigning as an independent, was challenging Deval Patrick. Cahill charged Patrick with "pandering to terrorists"—and of not taking the threat of terrorism seriously. Considering the nature of the visit, that was a fair claim to make.

In response, the ISBCC gathered its interfaith allies at the mosque in a press conference and charged Cahill with bigotry. Prominently noted and photographed by the *Boston Globe* was kippah-wearing Rabbi Eric Gurvis, of the heavily Jewish Boston suburb of Newton, hugging Bilal Kaleem, the ISBCC's executive director, as Imam Abdullah Faaruuq creepily looked on in the background. I had met Rabbi Gurvis at the JCRC meeting with Kaleem and the other ISBCC leaders back in 2007. Gurvis was also one of the Jewish leaders with whom we shared our data from the ISB case file. In both situations, I remember him as being the most obstinately doctrinaire about "interfaith dialogue," no matter the consequences, when it came to his support for the ISB. He was even more headstrong in that regard than Rabbi Friedman.

Shortly after the press conference, Americans for Peace and Tolerance released a video showing Deval Patrick hugging Imam Faaruuq, Imam Faaruuq giving Attorney General Martha Coakley $50,000 for police sensitivity training, and, of course, Faaruuq advocating on behalf of al-Qaeda terrorists. Accompanying the video, which racked up more than 100,000 views on our YouTube channel, was an article by Charles Jacobs in the *Boston Jewish Advocate*. The article criticized Rabbi Gurvis for his moral narcissism and disinterest in the facts about ISB/MAS. Charles wrote:

> Why does Rabbi Gurvis refuse to acknowledge what he has
> been shown in official documents: that the MAS is a Muslim
> Brotherhood organization; that the mosque was funded by
> Wahhabi Saudis, not known to fund moderate mosques; and that
> the MAS/ISB leaders have invited defamers of Jews and Christians
> to "educate" the historically moderate Boston Muslim commu-
> nity? Rabbi Gurvis knows all this. Maybe for him it's "my Muslim
> friends, right or wrong." Or maybe the rabbi's need to demonstrate
> his moral superiority by caring for the "other"—no matter how
> radical or extreme—trumps any foreseeable consequences.

The leftist Reform rabbinate in Massachusetts was not happy. Rabbi Gurvis had just finished a stint as the President of the Massachusetts Board of Rabbis—a leftist powerhouse whose policy statements have little to do with Judaism, but everything to do with left-wing causes, such as Syrian refugee resettlement, transgender inclusion, Black Lives Matter, gun violence,

violence against African refugees in Tel Aviv, food justice, working conditions of Immokalee workers, labor, immigration, and the environment.

Seventy-five Massachusetts Reform and Reconstructionist rabbis and rabbinical students struck back at Charles and APT for questioning Gurvis's wisdom in embracing anti-Semites and terrorist supporters. In a letter to the Jewish Advocate, they wrote:

> We were shocked and appalled by the vicious, personal attack written by Mr. Charles Jacobs and printed in the Jewish Advocate. We denounce this attack, and call upon Mr. Jacobs to discontinue his destructive campaign against Boston's Muslim community, which is based on innuendo, half-truths, and unproven conspiracy theories. We call upon members of our community to reject the dangerous politics of division that Mr. Jacobs fosters....We refuse to allow Mr. Jacobs to spread his calumnies and paralyze our community in fear.

The rabbis did not provide a single fact to support their allegations. Rabbi Howard Jaffe of the Reform Temple Isaiah in Lexington orchestrated the letter. He reached out to all the other rabbis, drafted the letter, and got all the signatures. Apparently, Rabbi Jaffe was Rabbi Gurvis's best friend and he was pissed off, to put it lightly. Charles and I went to see him in Lexington after the letter came out. Also present at the meeting was Rabbi David Lerner of the Conservative Temple Emunah in Lexington.

Rabbi Jaffe is a testament to the declining quality of the Reform rabbinate in the United States. He is a thickset man, intumescent in physiognomy and character. On that hot summer day, his face was glistening with sweat and red with anger. He took offense several times during my presentation, including at me quoting a passage from the New Testament—ironic, considering he would never do the same if someone quoted the Quran to him. Off the bat, he told us that he's not interested in the facts about the ISB's anti-Semitism and extremism. We were mean to his best friend and there was no talking sense to him. He all but kicked us out of his synagogue.

In a hopeful sign, major blowback ensued from the rabbinical mass denunciation letter. It was the beginning of a major controversy within the Boston Jewish community that would play out directly over the next few months and continues to this day. The mainstream Jewish organizations sought to play the middle, but Boston's pro-Israel and Russian communities openly supported Americans for Peace and Tolerance. Eighty-four interfaith leaders from around the Boston area, including the heads of Christians and Jews United for Israel, wrote to the rabbis directly:

> Dr. Charles Jacobs helped emancipate tens of thousands of slaves in Sudan over a ten year period. The anti-slavery movement he built led to the freedom of the world's newest nation, South Sudan, which is now an ally of Israel. The redemption program depended on a close alliance with Muslims who helped the Christian Dinka tribesmen reunite with their enslaved wives and children....Yet you - as a group - for political reasons which many of you have admitted overstated your case—defamed this man, accusing him of anti-Muslim bigotry and in doing so you have placed him and his family in danger. Every day that passes that you do not publicly retract your defamation is a day that you are committing a sin against a Jew, a brave one, and against Jewish ethics and Jewish morality.

Eighty-one leaders of the Russian Jewish Community Foundation and other Russian Jewish organizations signed a letter to the Jewish Advocate rebuking the rabbis. They wrote:

> Our leaders' goodwill and credulity have no limits when it comes to Islamist radicals. Everything changes, though, when dissent comes from within the community. Just look at the vicious attack unleashed by self-selected community leadership on Charles Jacobs. While official Jewish leadership was silent, the media oblivious or intimidated, Jacobs and his group of volunteers have been providing well-documented facts about the danger of Islamist hate surrounding us. Our Jewish leaders, who were as tame as lambs in front of the Islamists, roared as lions against this brave and lonely voice of dissent. Back in the Soviet Union, authorities would put a man like Jacobs behind bars for anti-Soviet propaganda. In the United States we are dismayed by attempts to ostracize and silence him.

Soviet Jews are well aware of the type of Jew represented by these far-left rabbis. After World War II was won, Stalin needed a new enemy. He saw how well the Jews worked in the enemy role for Hitler and picked them for the same role in the Soviet Union as the "cosmopolitan" agents of Western imperialism. Leaders of the Soviet Jewish Joint Anti-Fascist Committee, which raised millions of dollars for the Soviet war effort from American Jews, were accused of working for the Americans, and thirteen of them were executed.

On January 13, 1953, the Soviet newspaper *Pravda* printed an announcement that a group of Jewish doctors had been arrested for murdering several Soviet leaders by deliberately sabotaging their medical care. According to *Pravda*, the "Doctors' Plot," as it came to be known was hatched in the service of the Joint, "an international Jewish bourgeois-nationalist organization created by American intelligence services." In reality, this was all a pretext hatched by Stalin, who was growing increasingly paranoid over Soviet Jewish ties to Israel and the United States. Stalin used the Doctors' Plot as a launching point for a mass campaign of anti-Semitism in the Soviet Union that was intended to culminate in a planned mass deportation of Soviet Jews to a tiny territory in the Siberian Far East on the border with China—had Stalin not died in 1954. Stalin already pulled off similar ethnic cleansings against the Poles, Crimean Tatars, Chechens —including the Tsarnaevs' paternal family—and other minority peoples.

At the urging of Stalin, a group of some of the most prominent Jews in the Soviet Union wrote a letter of denunciation against the Jewish "doctor-murderers." Among the fifty-seven signatories were generals, Heroes of the Soviet Union, a recipient of Stalin's Prize for Strengthening Peace among the Nations, scientists, writers, film directors, composers, conductors, ministers, and engineers. This cream of the crop of Soviet court Jewry obliged Stalin's wishes, writing:

"Together with the entire Soviet people, with all the progressive peoples of the world we brand with infamy this clique of murderers, these monsters among the human race.... Every honorable Jewish worker must actively struggle against Jewish bourgeois nationalists, these notorious enemies of the Jewish worker. One cannot be a patriot of his Soviet Motherland and a fighter for the freedom of nations without waging the most irreconcilable struggle against all forms and manifestations of Jewish nationalism."

In an earlier draft of the letter, these Soviet leftist Jewish leaders actually endorsed the mass deportations of Jews being planned by Stalin:

"[W]e completely approve the just measures of the party and of the government, taken with the aim of giving the Jews the task of developing the vast lands of Eastern Siberia, the Far East, and the Extreme North. Only with honest and selfless labor can the Jews prove their loyalty to the Motherland and to the great and beloved Comrade Stalin, thereby restoring the good name of the Jews in the eyes of the entire Soviet people."

Leftist Jewish leaders slandered the Jewish doctors as anti-Russian. Leftist Jewish leaders slandered Charles as anti-Muslim. But in both cases, the audience wasn't really the Jewish people. It was the anti-Semites among the Russians and Muslims whose purposes the leftist Jews served. In both cases, the quislings rushed to declare emphatically:

We're not Jews like Charles or the doctor-murderers. We're the good Jews. We'll gladly go even further than you in demonizing them. We'll say whatever you want us to, as long as you don't go after us. It will even make us feel morally virtuous to say it.

In both cases, the goal was to run interference for anti-Semites, whether Stalin or the ISB, for the sake of leftist ideology and solipsism. And in both cases, the letter-signers sought to make themselves seem more powerful as part of a larger collective. Instead, they just diminished themselves as individuals in comparison to Charles.

Dr. Zuhdi Jasser, the moderate Muslim leader of the American Islamic Forum for Democracy, also rebuked the rabbis—and Governor Patrick—in an article in the *Daily Caller*, writing:

Governor Deval Patrick, Rabbi Gurvis, and other leaders should not elevate Islamists like Imam Abdullah Faaruuq and his team. By doing so, they make reformists irrelevant and kill any hope for a battle of ideas....And we wonder why the reformist Muslim voices appear so silent? Political correctness has made many blind. I ask Rabbi Gurvis to wake up to the threat. I love my faith and yearn for a day that my children can realize an Islam that separates mosque and state and puts the "Islamic state" in the dustbin of history....This is not a war against a generic "violent extremism."

The Islamist problem continues to get exponentially worse because communities like Boston are not addressing the root causes. When a Governor, some rabbis, and other leaders play the religion card while ignoring the entrenched Islamist problem, they put our security in peril.

At the end of June 2010, over four hundred community members crowded into Charles's synagogue for a defiant event in support of Charles and APT. The community had never been so deeply divided. In the end, Gurvis, Jaffe, Friedman, and the rest of the letter-signing rabbis retreated into their cloisters and refused to listen. They would issue many more letters, but, like the various leftist canards against those who disagree with them, these letters had significantly devalued their own currency. Dennis Hale wrote in the Jewish Advocate about the reasons why the rabbis are unwilling to consider the evidence against the ISB:

> Rabbi Gurvis and his colleagues are so determined to be considered "tolerant" and "multicultural" that they will ignore all of the evidence about the leaders of the Roxbury mosque and the dangers that they present, not only to Jews, but to Christians and moderate Muslims as well. This is especially disturbing in the case of Rabbi Ronne Friedman of Temple Israel Boston, who has been fooled by these people once before, by mosque trustee Walid Fitahi – who was spreading poisonous anti-Semitic propaganda in the Arab press at the very moment he was engaged in "interfaith dialogue" with Rabbi Friedman's congregation.

Rabbi Friedman and his congregation would be fooled by these people many times again.

CHAPTER 20

I'M ON THE TRAIN!

Yet another Islamist Boston imam was in trouble. On February 15, 2010, ISBCC executive director Bilal Kaleem wrote to the ISB/MAS member list:

> [D]ear brothers and sisters, Insha'Allah, Shaykh Basyouny Nehela, Imam of the ISB and board member of MAS Boston, is embarking today on a trip for a number of months, going on a sabbatical to research and teach for 1 to 2 semesters at University of Qatar. He will be returning a number of times to Boston during those months to share with us some of his experiences and to deliver a couple of seminars. Shaykh Basyouny has worked with a number of dedicated members of the ISB community to delegate his responsibilities to a capable team in his absence. We will miss him during these months but we trust insha'Allah that this is an opportunity for Shaykh Basyouny to grow even more, and benefit the community greatly upon his return. May Allah accept his travels in His path, and guide him and us all.

ISB Imam Basyouni Nehela had another, non-pretextual, reason for leaving the United States. His U.S. citizenship application was stalled and the Department of Homeland Security wasn't saying why. In 2005, Nehela and his wife had their interviews with the U.S. Customs and Immigration

Service and took their citizenship exams. Imam Nehela's wife passed her interview, was given a naturalization oath ceremony notice, and went out into the waiting room while her husband wrapped up his own interview with the immigration official. Suddenly federal officers entered the room and took her oath ceremony notice out of her hands without explanation. For three years, Nehela was told that his "name check" hasn't cleared yet. In 2008, he and four other New England Muslims whose citizenship was likewise in limbo sued in federal court with a demand that they be naturalized as American citizens. The court quickly dismissed the case and remanded it back to the Customs and Immigration Service. Whatever the problem was with Nehela's "name check," he wasn't getting his citizenship. In 2010, the situation with his immigration status seemed to have come to a head and it was likely decided that it was best if he leave. He now lives in Qatar with many other Muslim Brothers in semi-exile, but still occasionally comes back to Boston.

Finding a replacement for Imam Nehela proved to be extremely difficult for the ISB. A year and a half after it opened, the ISBCC was still without an imam. WBUR, one of Boston's two National Public Radio stations, had Bilal Kaleem on a news show to talk about the imam search.

"This place has a very high profile and is always in the crosshairs," complained Bilal about APT's watchdogging. "We know whoever is the imam here is going to get the third degree. Sometimes imams don't want to go through that. So even if they like the whole vision here, they're nervous about dealing with the challenges of being an imam here."

Bilal was not wrong. Nevertheless, by the end of 2011, the ISBCC scored a rising rock star of the American Islamist community as its new imam and Imam Basyouni Nehela's replacement. Bilal Kaleem made the announcement in a video message to the ISBCC community:

> Assalamu alaikum. I am so excited and happy to share the incredible news that Imam Suhaib Webb will be starting as the Imam of the Islamic Society of Boston Cultural Center in just a little more than a month on December First, inshallah [Allah willing]. As you all know, Imam Suhaib Webb is one of the most dynamic and knowledgeable imams in America and he's going to be an asset to the New England Muslim community and all its institutions....I personally am very excited. There is such incredible potential in

the ISBCC to really make a mark not just on Boston or even New England, but for Islam in America in general. With Imam Suhaib here, we will enter a new stage of programs – programs of community development, development of youth and students, media outreach, academic outreach, even economic developments.

Hopes were up and optimism was in the air at the ISBCC in anticipation of Webb's arrival. For his part, Suhaib Webb was excited about the big raise he was getting with the ISBCC job, and bragging about it to his flock at the Muslim Community Association of the San Francisco Bay Area, where he was imam at the time:

"Now, I got a job offer in Boston. It's a $40,000 raise. You think I considered moving? Heck yeah," Webb hammed, raising his voice to a falsetto pitch. "It's not four! It's four-o! Times two, it's eighty-thousand-something ringing! Hello? I'm on the train! You know? Tshoo!"

William "Suhaib" Webb is a white convert to Islam who was born in Oklahoma in 1972, son of a female bank executive and grandson of a fundamentalist Christian preacher. Despite his privileged upbringing in the suburbs of Oklahoma City, Webb began running with the wrong crowd at fourteen, joined the Bloods gang, and was even involved in a drive-by shooting. He dabbled in both weed and hip-hop, even putting out two albums as the DJ of a rap group called "AK Assault." One night, while smoking some weed with Webb, a rapper named Chilly D told Webb some stuff about Islam. As Webb recounted to the *Washington Post* in 2017, he thought to himself:

"Wow, this is dope! I need to do this."

Webb converted to Islam in 1992, professing the Muslim testament of faith in front of an imam from the notorious Al Farooq Mosque in Brooklyn. It was the same mosque from which bin Laden's Al Kifah charity operated until 1993, when its members tried to blow up the Twin Towers and it had to move its operations to Boston. Instead of "AK Assault," his new moniker would be "Suhaib." Webb quit drinking and smoking weed, although he tells his followers that "we will get to smoke lots and lots of weed" in Muslim heaven. He studied Islam with local Islamic scholars, and he studied education at the University of Central Oklahoma, where he got a bachelor's degree. This dedication, together with his charisma, got him hired as Imam at the Islamic Society of Greater Oklahoma City—another example of the mosques named "Islamic Society of [City X]" established across the country in 1983 by the Muslim Brotherhood under the ISNA umbrella.

In 2014, a man who calls himself Noor al-Amriki spoke out publicly, but with his face disguised, on Fox News about Suhaib Webb's time at the Islamic Society of Greater OKC. The context? A worshipper at the mosque became radicalized and beheaded one of his co-workers in September 2014. According to al-Amriki, who claimed he converted at the Oklahoma mosque in 2001, while Webb was an Imam there, the mosque had long been associated with violent extremism. al-Amriki has claimed that:

> Suhaib told me bluntly that Islam teaches that when Muslims meet the kuffar (infidels or unbelievers), they are to offer them three choices. They are first to be invited to become Muslims, to embrace Islam. If they reject that, they are to be offered the choice to keep their religion but live under Islamic rule and pay the jizya [protection money]. If they reject that, the only option left is to fight them in jihad.

Two days before the September 11, 2001, attacks, Suhaib Webb appeared at a fundraiser for the Atlanta cop-killer Jamil Al-Amin, also known as H. Rap Brown. Webb raised $100,000 for the murderer that night, and he did it together with Anwar al-Awlaki, the Yemeni al-Qaeda leader assassinated by President Obama via Predator drone in 2011. Ten years before Awlaki's death, when Webb joined him at the fundraiser, Awlaki was already under surveillance by the FBI due to his relationship with the 9/11 hijackers.

Webb was at the fundraiser on behalf of the Muslim American Society. Since its early college days with the Muslim Students Association, the American Muslim Brotherhood movement has been focused intensely on recruiting the youth. The Muslim American Society maintains a very active youth section within its organizational structure; and many of its leaders, like Hossam Al Jabri, Bilal Kaleem, and even Suhaib Webb, were first brought up through the ranks from the Youth section.

As any American religion would know, attracting the youth is pretty hard. Many religious movements and denominations go to extreme lengths to appear hip to the kids. The MAS therefore likely saw the charismatic young imam who could tell Biggie apart from Tupac and said stuff like, "wow, this is dope," as a major asset for the movement. In 2004, the MAS shipped Suhaib Webb off to Egypt on a full scholarship to study at Al Azhar University with Muslim Brotherhood clerics. He would stay in the Middle East until 2004, honing his religious knowledge and forming many connections. Among these were with Yusuf Qaradawi's deputy, the Saudi-based cleric Abdullah Bin Bayyah, whom Webb considers as his "emir," or spiritual leader. Bin Bayyah has legitimized the killing of U.S. soldiers in Iraq and has called for Israel's destruction.

To stay in touch with the zeitgeist stateside, Webb would go online. He set up his own website and eagerly embraced Facebook, Twitter, and YouTube to get his message across. On his trips back to the United States, he would be a highly sought after speaker at Islamic conferences, mosques, and Muslim student groups. By the time Webb became imam at the ISBCC, he had a massive following online and among the youth membership in the constellation of American Muslim Brotherhood front groups.

I didn't quite get the hipness angle. Perhaps it was because I acted like Webb when I was seventeen but grew out of the hip-hop phase sometime during college, when I was writing ludicrous op-ed articles about the sublime meaning in (Muslim) Mos Def's lyrics. When I first saw one of Webb's sermons online, his awkward affectations brought to mind Sacha Baron Cohen's parodic character Ali G—a cringeworthy mix of cultural appropriation, poserism, and banality that would make Rachel Dolezal blush through her spray tan. Some representative wisdom that Webb has dropped on the young members of his flock included lines like these, delivered in a Chris Rock–like falsetto:

> Shaitan up in my heart telling me to ask that girl's number, go to the club.…Check yourself before you wreck yourself.
>
> Sometimes I see sisters coming to the masjid wearing very tight clothing. You are at a masjid, you ain't at the club. This is the house of Allah.…If I'm perfectly able to dress in the right way and I come to the mosque looking like Nicky Minaj with a hijab on, then I have to really ask myself, "Why am I here. Am I here to catch Allah or am I here to catch a man."

Unfortunately, Webb's influence on Boston's Muslim youth became pretty far from a joke.

CHAPTER 21

THEY PLANT A BOMB IN THE HEART

The Muslim Brotherhood–planning documents that I read from the Holy Land Foundation trial called for great efforts at indoctrinating Muslim youth and bringing in new recruits through proselytization. ISB trustee Jamal Badawi is particularly noted in the HLF trial documents for his proselytizing work. Huge emphasis is placed by the Brotherhood on specific training and teaching curricula. Suhaib Webb has long been involved in developing these curricula for the Muslim American Society on a national level. I remembered what Eric Trager, the Egyptian Muslim Brotherhood expert at the Washington Institute for Near East Policy, told me:

"The process of educating Muslim Brotherhood youths and new recruits is called *Tarbiya*, which literally means upbringing or education."

My moderate Muslim friend from the ICNE Sharon mosque had also told me how "these people have a system in which they raise the level of connected people. So, you get a young person. You groom him. He comes at a higher level. Then more indoctrination, he comes at a higher level. And, then the levels are increased."

Through some colleagues, I had obtained several *Tarbiya* curriculum documents from MAS, which describe exactly what is taught and when, with assignments detailed down to book and page number. I looked especially closely at a particular Tarbiya program called "Young Muslims" because Suhaib Webb had explicitly endorsed it in one of his YouTube videos—in his phony urban accent:

> Hey, salam alaikum, this is Imam Suhaib Webb with you, live and direct with Young Muslim TV, taking it to the streets. I just want to encourage everyone to support Young Muslims. I am Young Muslims and Young Muslims is me. You know, we're like bread and butter, we'll never be separated.

The Young Muslims *Tarbiya* curriculum lists books that all participants must read, and even includes page numbers for specific assignments. The authors of many of these books are among the "who's who" of radical Islamist ideologues. A lot of the books had been available in the ISB's library in Cambridge for decades. Seeing them alarmed Sheikh Mansour so much that he fled the Cambridge mosque, telling us later about these teachings: "They plant a bomb in the heart." Major focus in the Young Muslims curriculum is given to books by Hassan al-Banna, the founder of the Muslim Brotherhood; Sayyid Qutb, the father of modern jihadism; Maulana Maududi, the father of political Islam on the Indian subcontinent; and Yusuf Qaradawi, the spiritual leader of the Muslim Brotherhood. Some of the books on the "must-read" list have nothing to do with Islam, such as several books written by Howard Zinn, Noam Chomsky, and Michael Moore. Having young Muslims read books by far-left atheists of Jewish and Christian backgrounds shows that the goal of *Tarbiya* is not just to develop a Muslim's spirituality, but also to develop within him a deep animosity to Western democracy.

The Muslim American Society is very open about the program's existence and even has websites dedicated to it. MAS teaches *Tarbiya* at each of its dozens of chapters across the United States, including in Boston. The entire national MAS *Tarbiya* program was developed and led by Suhaib Web's precursor at the ISB, Ima Basyouni Nehela. MAS describes *Tarbiya* in these terms:

> MAS aspires to raise a generation of committed and disciplined Muslims who will spread the message of Islam and implement the Movement's vision in all fields of Islamic work. . . MAS delivers

a rigorous educational curriculum to its current and potential members.…The focus of *Tarbiya* is to groom members who…are equipped with the necessary knowledge, understanding, and skills to make a difference in the society by taking an active role, both individually and collectively, in the reform process that seeks the betterment of our community, our country, and the whole world.

Such an intense "self-development program" is usually more the province of cult-like organizations, rather than something mandatory in traditional church, synagogue, or mosque activity. Still, on the surface, the description makes it seem like yet another benign New Agey spirituality and growth system. That's because, while the program is openly advertised, the extremist and jihadist aspects of its curriculum are not—both for the sake of keeping this radical indoctrination from outside scrutiny and for the sake of keeping it, at first, from the Muslim youths who are thinking about joining it.

Indeed, a "Young Muslim" first entering the program will not be reading any extremist authors for a very long time. The first phase of the program is dedicated to completely legitimate religious learning. Participants read the Quran and other Islamic religious texts. They learn about the life of the Muslim prophet, Muhammad, and they study the importance of the Five Pillars of Islam: the declaration of faith, prayer, charity, fasting, and pilgrimage.

But soon, those participants who show a high level of dedication, zeal, and religiosity—of willingness to internalize everything that has been taught to them—are told that simply praying and giving charity are not enough. At this next stage of *Tarbiya*, they are assigned books, such as *Let Us Be Muslims* by jihadist ideologue Maulana Maududi, who provides them with the core Islamist idea: Muslims need to be more than pious; they need to rule over all mankind:

"Brothers in Islam! The Prayer, Fasting, Almsgiving, and Pilgrimage are so important that they are described as the pillars of Islam," reads the Young Muslims assignment. "They are not, however, like the worship rites in other religions.…These acts of worship have in fact been ordained to prepare us for a greater purpose and to train us for a greater duty.…What exactly is that great ultimate purpose? Stated simply: the ultimate objective of Islam is to abolish the lordship of man over man and bring him under the rule of the One God. To stake everything you have—including your lives—to achieve this purpose is called Jihad."

Having thus channeled the zealous young Muslim's sincere religious devotion into an extremist agenda, the third stage of *Tarbiya* indoctrination consists entirely of incitement to violent jihad, hatred for America, and of Western civilization in general. It is in this stage that young Muslims study in detail the Islamist corollary to Mein Kampf or the Communist Manifesto—said Qutb's *Milestones*—which outlines a road map to establishing a global Islamic State ruled by Sharia law through violent, murderous jihad.

By the time a young Muslim *Tarbiya* participant reaches this phase, he has already bought in to all the indoctrination in the previous phases that brought him there. Backing out or refusing to do what MAS tells him at this stage may well be psychologically difficult. The book chapters that he studies toward the end of his indoctrination, such as those from *To Be a Muslim* by Lebanese Muslim Brotherhood leader Fathi Yakun tell him:

> A Muslim must always worship Allah and wage jihad until death in order to reach his ultimate goal....Obedience for a Muslim means to obey every command and implement it whether in time of happiness or hardship, and whether one likes it or not....He will not act against the leader in agreed matters, and will be loyal to him in every action, regardless of his personal likes or dislikes....Dissociate yourself from every gathering or organization that opposes your ideological standpoint, especially when the Movement asks you to do so.

A key component of *Tarbiya* is not just the material taught, but the structure of the program, in which recruits are organized into intimate cells called *usras*. This structure, which was also revealed in the HLF trial documents, mirrors the organizational structure of the Egyptian Muslim Brotherhood, as Eric Trager explained to me:

"At the lowest level of the Brotherhood structure is what's called an *usra*, or 'family.' You can think of this as a cell. This is a group of five to eight Muslim Brothers. They meet weekly for about three hours. They discuss the Quran, religious texts, the Brotherhood's curriculum, politics. They share their personal lives. The members of this group become a Muslim Brother's best friends. The people that you work most closely with are in your *usra*. The *usra* is a mechanism through which the Brotherhood embeds your social relationships into the organization so that you're less likely to disobey it due to peer pressure and you're less likely to leave it because you'll be leaving your best friends."

This is exactly how MAS Boston had described its *usras* on its website:

> The *usra* is an intensive, spiritually-focused, activism-oriented program that develops the individual and invites him or her to join hands with MAS and work for the sake of Islam as a central priority in life. There are weekly assignments prior to and following each *usra* [gathering]. Each member is expected to spend approximately 3-6 hours a week on *usra* and *usra*-related activities (*usra* attendance [~ 2 hours], *usra* assignments [1-2 hrs], *dawah* work (example MSA work, MAS Youth work, or other Islamic work, etc) [3 hrs], social activities [2 hours /month].) Each *usra* generally contains around 5[–]7 members.

MAS demands that those entering its *Tarbiya* program be "willing to be committed to the *usra* and hold working for Islam as a central priority in life." Imam Suhaib Webb defines the *usra* as:

> The *usra* is you're in the ocean swimming, you're lost, your boat sunk and suddenly you see some people on the boat, you get there and they give you a blanket and a cup of soup, that's the *usra*.

All of this makes leaving the MAS/ISB program extremely difficult. It also makes it extremely likely that, if a young Muslim participant is encouraged by his *usra* leader to do something terrible for the sake of the movement, he will gladly comply, even if this means prison or death. The *usra* system of the *Tarbiya* program is less similar to a religious requirement than it is to the demands of a criminal enterprise. These methods used by MAS/ISB are much like the techniques that gangs and mafia groups use to recruit and maintain a death grip on their members. As Suhaib Webb has said about Islamists in America:

"We have a job to do here. We are not here simply to protect cultural clubs; but we have been commissioned by our Lord, unequivocally, to deliver the message of Allah to humanity – by any means necessary, as long as it's *halal* [permitted by Sharia law]."

CHAPTER 22

BOMBS WILL BE PLANTED
IN THE STREET

I have a pretty good idea of how the Tsarnaevs might have felt upon their arrival in Boston on a ninety-day tourist visa, after which they immediately sought asylum as refugees. I also came to the United States from Russia, ten years before than they did, though not as a refugee. Dzhokhar was eight when he came, just two years younger than I was when my family immigrated. I am sure that the Tsarnaev children—Tamerlan, Dzhokhar, and their two sisters—felt the same excitement as I did from the tall buildings and all the food, which had been in short supply both in the 2002 Caucasus of the Second Chechen War and in the 1992 Siberia of the immediate post–Soviet Union collapse. I can relate to the awe they must have felt at the conspicuous wealth surrounding them, and also to the disappointment at the realization of just how poor they were by comparison with their new society.

From the accounts of their life shortly after arriving in the United States, I know that they were Muslim like my family was Jewish. Whatever our "ethnicity," which all Soviet citizens had listed, as was required by law, in their passports, any sort of religion had been drained out of the ideologically remolded Soviet Man, *Homo sovieticus*, by the Communist Party. My family and I had only the vaguest ideas about Jewish beliefs and practices until Chabad came around to Siberia to start teaching them to us in 1991 or so. The same seemed to be the case with the Tsarnaevs and Islam. There is a famous picture of the Tsarnaev parents, Anzor and Zubeidat, from the

1980s, holding a baby Tamerlan. Zubeidat looks like a cross between Allison from the Breakfast Club and the 1980s goth queen Siouxsie Sioux from Siouxsie and the Banshees. She liked wearing tight jeans, short skirts and makeup, and trained to be a cosmetologist when she came to America. But while it was Chabad that came around to teach me about my religion, it was the ISB that came around to teach the Tsarnaevs about theirs.

I traced the phone number in the ISB's April 2002 online bulletin seeking housing for the Tsarnaev family to a Chechen American doctor, Khassan Baiev, who used to live in Needham. The family stayed with Baiev for a month directly after coming to America, and then moved to Cambridge, a nine-minute walk to the ISB's Cambridge mosque. The radicalization of the Tsarnaevs seems not to have happened immediately. Tamerlan partied it up in the city's nightclubs, drank, smoked, and dated non-Muslim girls. Zubeidat got a job at an upscale beauty salon in Belmont, the Cambridge suburb home to Mitt Romney. But then, in 2008, around the same time that Charles and I were going around to any New England civic leader who would listen and warning them about the ISB's extremism, Zubeidat began attending the ISB much more frequently, became extremely religious, and was fired from her salon because she refused to serve male clients and constantly took prayer breaks. As *Newsweek* columnist Michelle McPhee wrote in an article on the women in Dzhokhar Tsarnaev's life:

> Tamerlan too was going through some dramatic changes....
> [H]e had been arrested for slapping his live-in girlfriend, Nadine
> Ascencao, across the face. She would later recall that when she
> met Tamerlan he was a handsome playboy, "Euro-trash," she said,
> partying in Boston's hot spots. In the summer of 2009, his mother
> insisted he change his ways, and Tamerlan began to attend prayers
> at the Islamic Society of Boston's Cambridge mosque. "One minute
> he was a normal guy, the next minute he is watching these crazy
> Muslim videos," Ascencao said.

By 2011, the KGB's successor spy agency in Russia was warning the FBI that Tamerlan and Zubeidat Tsarnaev made contacts with Chechen militants and were "adherents of radical Islam." Tamerlan was put onto the federal Terrorist Screening Database, but was then, flatfootedly, removed.

That was the year that Tamerlan quite likely took his first human lives. Tamerlan was a competitive boxer who won the New England Golden Gloves championship in 2010. His best friend from Cambridge Rindge and Latin High School, and from the training gym, was a mixed martial arts fighter and midsize weed dealer named Brendan Mess. But when Tamerlan became more religious, they had a falling out over lifestyle. Apparently, when Mess, who was Jewish, began dating a secular Muslim girl, Tamerlan was enraged.

Whatever happened, all the people who were involved, according to the FBI, are now dead. The official FBI story is that on September 11, 2011, Tamerlan Tsarnaev and a fellow Chechen worshipper at the ISB's Cambridge mosque, Ibragim Todashev, who also happened to be a mixed martial arts fighter, went to Mess's house. Mess was going through a nasty breakup with his Muslim girlfriend, who had been living with him but had gone to Florida. However, there were two other guys at Mess's apartment, both Jewish: Erik Weissman and Rafi Teken. Weissman was a bodybuilder and Teken was a personal trainer. The assailants might have struck by surprise, because the three Jews were murdered in separate rooms, but Mess had put up a violent struggle and was covered in defensive wounds. It was no use. All three Jewish men had their throats slit ear to ear, with almost total decapitation. They were sprinkled with weed and $5,000 in cash.

After the murder, Tamerlan Tsarnaev went on the lam back to the Caucasus and stayed there for six months visiting family. His ostensible purpose was to get a Russian passport, but, although he applied for one while in Russia, he never picked it up. The Russian security forces had him under surveillance, as well as his mother, who joined him later in his trip. Apparently, the two made contact with Chechen extremists while there. Most likely, Tamerlan was just laying low and seeing if the cops would catch his trail. They never did. Tamerlan returned in 2012, more radicalized than ever, and with a plan in mind. The Russian security agencies once again warned their American counterparts about Tamerlan's ties to Chechen terrorists, and were once again ignored.

Susan Zalkind was a friend of Erik Weissman's. She also happens to be a reporter for *Boston* magazine and the daughter of Tarek Mehanna's defense attorney. Boston is a small town. She wrote a definitive account of what is publicly known about the murder investigation, as did Masha Gessen, a Russian immigrant with Boston ties, who traced the story into

Russia. Zalkind reported that the Massachusetts State Police did not actively investigate the murders, instead taking the wait-and-see approach and hoping for "a suspect to shake loose." Tamerlan shook loose, all right, and within hours of him being identified as the Boston Marathon bombing suspect, the Massachusetts State Police had both him and Todashev as the suspects in the almost-two-years-old case. On May 21, after a month of intense surveillance, questioning, and pressure, first about the marathon bombings and then about the Waltham triple murder, an FBI agent fatally shot Ibragim Todashev at his apartment in Florida. According to the FBI, Todashev was writing out his confession to the murder as an accomplice of Tamerlan Tsarnaev, when he suddenly lunged at the federal and state cops questioning him with a metal pole. Both Zalkind and Gessen, as well as many others, are skeptical of that official story. I am agnostic.

What I do think is that various law enforcement agencies missed a number of red flags that were being thrown up by the Tsarnaev brothers on their way to Boylston Street on Patriots' Day 2013. These flags might not have been missed but for the Massachusetts Attorney General's Office and the Obama Justice Department's refusal to honestly deal with the threat American Islamist mosques like the ISB pose to the U.S. homeland. The Keystone Kops at the Department of Justice were handing out community leadership awards to open supporters of failed Boston terrorist Tarek Mehanna. The Massachusetts Attorney General's Office was working with alleged money-laundering terrorist financiers to train state police in diversity and Muslim sensitivity. The FBI was doing outreach with close friends of Aafia Siddiqui, whose most wanted status as "an al-Qaeda operative and facilitator" had been announced by FBI director Robert Mueller nine years before the marathon bombing.

On June 13, 2013, Representative Louis Gohmert was on the House Judiciary Committee grilling Mueller about what he characterized as the FBI's thorough job on the Boston Marathon–bombing investigation. Gohmert asked Mueller about the ISB:

"The FBI never canvassed Boston mosques until four days after the April 15th attacks. If the Russians tell you that someone has been radicalized and you go check and see the mosque that they went to; then you get the articles of incorporation as I have for the group that created the Boston mosque where these Tsarnaevs attended. You find out the name Alamoudi, which you'll remember because while you were FBI director this man, who was so helpful to the Clinton administration with so many big things, he gets arrested at Dulles Airport by the FBI, and he's doing over twenty years for supporting terrorism. This is the guy that started the mosque where your Tsarnaevs were attending and you didn't even bother to check about the mosque? And then, when you have the pictures, why did not one go to the mosque and say: 'Who are these guys? They may attend here.' Why was that not done if such a thorough job was done?"

"We went to the mosque," Mueller replied. "Prior to Boston happening, we were in that mosque talking to imams several months before as part of our outreach efforts."

Gohmert pressed on: "Were you aware that those mosques were started by Alamoudi?"

"No," was Mueller's reply.

He should have been aware. On May 1, 2009, Charles and I briefed representatives of the Boston FBI office on the Islamic extremist affiliations of the ISB mosques. I have looked over the PowerPoint slides I used during that meeting. Sure enough, FBI Boston should have known all about Alamoudi and much, much more.

Unfortunately, the Obama administration scrupulously avoided scrutinizing Islamic religious convictions as motives for terrorist acts. The Russians may have told the FBI that Tamerlan and his mother were "adherents of radical Islam." That likely meant nothing to the Obama FBI because its officials refused to believe that radical Islam results in radical violence. In 2010, then-U.S. attorney general Eric Holder was on Capitol Hill after a massive propane bomb placed by Islamist extremist Faisal Shahzad failed to explode in Times Square. Senator Lamar Smith asked him:

"Do you feel that [Islamic terrorists] might have been incited to take the actions that they did because of radical Islam?"

"There are a variety of reasons why I think people have taken these actions," was Holder's answer.

"But radical Islam could have been one of the reasons?"

"There are a variety of reasons," Holder continued insisting.

Senator Smith got to the point:

"Are you uncomfortable attributing any of their actions to radical Islam? It sounds like it."

"I don't want to say anything negative about a religion," Holder admitted. Even when suspects were explicit that they murdered Americans "for

Allah," like the Ford Hood jihadist Nidal Hasan, the Obama administration refused to impute a religious motive to their actions, labeling the Ford Hood Massacre as an act of workplace violence. During the Cold War, America's intelligence agencies had aggressively pursued intelligence research in the so-called Kremlinology, or Sovietology, fields. American intelligence agencies and academics alike sought to understand in honest terms what made the Russians tick, what their culture was like, what their motivations are, and what ideology they believed in. There was nothing racist about that. Know your enemy, know yourself. One thousand battles, one thousand victories, as Sun Tsu said. Unfortunately, when it came to learning about what makes the Islamists tick, the Obama administration's Justice Department preferred to avoid victories.

So, we got defeats, including a potentially lost opportunity to apprehend Tamerlan Tsarnaev after the Waltham murders and before he began plotting the marathon attacks. An intelligence and law enforcement approach that included an understanding of the Islamist movement as a thing in itself, as a cult which causes people to act violently, might have made the following investigative inference: A triple beheading, which occurred without a robbery, is not a drug deal gone wrong, as the Waltham police first assumed. Not only were eight and a half pounds of marijuana left untouched in the apartment, but some of that weed, together with $5,000 in cash, was sprinkled all over the bodies. This was ritualistic. What kind of a violent cult had been all over the news during the previous decade for carrying out ritualistic beheadings of its enemies; a cult that happens to have a problem with intoxicating substances? Tamerlan was in the FBI's Terrorist Screening Database, which is shared with state and local law enforcement; and intelligence from state and local cops flows back up to the Terrorist Screening Center within the FBI. This intelligence flow happens through regional intelligence centers throughout the United States. Through the years, I've met several times with FBI and local investigators at the Boston Regional Intelligence Center, run out of the Boston Police headquarters near the Roxbury ISBCC mosque. These local-federal collaboration efforts are thorough and professional. Unfortunately, actual derogatory information is stripped from intelligence reports like the one the FBI received from the Russians about Tamerlan's Islamist ties before they are entered into the Terrorist Screening Database for sharing with other law enforcement agencies.

I am fairly confident that Tamerlan would have been caught if 1) the FBI was allowed to use indicators of Islamist extremism in the intelligence that is reported and considered during investigations; and 2) federal, state, and local police were trained in the history and ideology of the Islamist movement instead of in Muslim sensitivity by the Islamists themselves. Tamerlan's phone number was in Brendan Mess's recent call records prior to the murder, and his phone was identified as being in the vicinity of the murders on the night that they happened. Knowing that Tamerlan was an Islamist radical from FBI intelligence shared via the Boston Regional Intelligence Center and being aware of Islamist murder rituals through training in the movement's ideology would have likely caused investigators to at least take a look at Tamerlan as a suspect. If that happened, he and Todashev would have been in jail and the victims of the Boston Marathon bombing might have still been alive.

It wasn't just the Russians who were aware of Tamerlan's increasing extremism. After Tamerlan returned to Boston from the Caucasus, he twice had outbursts during the Friday sermons at the ISB. It would seem that, by 2012, the student had surpassed his teachers in extremism. Tamerlan took issue with the imam saying that Muslims could celebrate secular American holidays and that Martin Luther King was a good man, even though he wasn't Muslim.

The Obama administration forbade the FBI from surveilling mosques or cultivating informants who would report fundamentalists inside mosques. So, another opportunity to identify Tamerlan as an Islamist radical and to surveil him further was lost. But how was it that in a crowd of several hundred worshippers there was no one who was willing to say something to the authorities about Tamerlan's two outbursts? Could the climate set by Islamist leaders like Nabeel Khudairi, who expelled worshippers from the Sharon mosque because they went "on the record about there being fundamentalists in the masjid," have something to do with it? And what about those Islamist leaders at the ISB in Cambridge? After his outbursts, Tamerlan was told to quiet down, but he was neither expelled from the mosque nor reported to authorities.

After the Boston Marathon bombing, ISBCC Imam Suhaib Webb and the ISBCC's new executive director, Yusufi Vali, were on WBUR, the Boston NPR station. The radio host asked Webb: "Imam Webb, what is your relationship with law enforcement?"

"We have a monthly meeting through BRIDGES," the imam assured the host. "We've met with the Attorney General of Massachusetts and talked about youth radicalization. I've been invited to attend a DHS meeting in two weeks. So I think that we know who to contact if we see something that might violate the law or threaten people."

Yusufi Vali claimed that the ISB's leaders, in Cambridge and Roxbury, "encouraged any community members who had potentially interacted with them to go to the FBI."

I knew better. On April 22, seven days after the bombing, MAS Boston sent an email to both the ISB and the ISBCC membership, telling them that "the FBI may be starting to question some of the community members about the suspects," and then asking that members not talk to the FBI before getting in touch with the mosque first because "we want to help as much as we can, but of course not put ourselves at risk either." Of course, it is extremely unlikely that any ISB leader told Tamerlan to bomb the Boston Marathon. The slow and steady work of the Muslim Brotherhood in America proceeds under the belief, realistic or not, that it can gradually move Western Muslim youths into its camp, engaging in violent jihad only after the movement is strong enough. The ISB and ISBCC have experienced tremendous success, probably beyond their expectations, in posing as moderates and becoming accepted into Boston civic society. This success includes positive coverage in the mainstream press, support from mainstream politicians, and access to new unsuspecting recruits within Boston's traditionally moderate Muslim community. Why risk all of that with a bomb that only can set the effort back? The Young Muslims *Tarbiya* curriculum repeatedly states that the time for violent jihad has not yet come—much preparation work still needs to be done.

But, the Muslim Brotherhood's indoctrination programs will always have this fundamental problem: When you tell young or dumb people that something can be a good thing to do, but "not yet," whether it be sex or alcohol—or violent jihad—you will surely find that some will jump the gun. That's what happened with Abdullah Azzam and Osama bin Laden—who had their roots in the Muslim Brotherhood and who became impatient with its slow-walking of violent jihad. That's probably what happened with Tamerlan and Dzhokhar.

Then again... As he lay wounded and hiding inside a boat stored for the winter in a suburban Boston-area backyard on April 19, 2013, Dzhokhar Tsarnaev penciled a mini-manifesto on the twenty-two-foot cruiser's walls, taking the time to list his grievances in detail.

This is what Dzhokhar wrote:

> Know you are fighting men who look into the barrel of your gun and see heaven, now how can you compete with that.

This is what kids in Imam Suhaib Webb's Young Muslims program are assigned to read:

> Regularly make the intention to go on jihad with the ambition to die as a martyr. You should be ready for this right now.

This is what Dzhokhar wrote:

> Our actions came with a message and that is la ilaha illalah [there is no god but Allah]. We are promised victory and we will surely get it.

This is what kids in Imam Suhaib Webb's Young Muslims program are assigned to read:

> We will pursue this evil force to its own lands, invade its Western heartland, and struggle to overcome it until all the world shouts by the name of the Prophet and the teachings of Islam spread throughout the world.

This is what Dzhokhar wrote:

> We Muslims are one body, you hurt one you hurt us all.

This is what kids in Imam Suhaib Webb's Young Muslims program are assigned to read:

> A Muslim has no relatives except those who share the belief in Allah.

This is what Dzhokhar wrote:

> The ummah is beginning to rise/awaken [bullet hole] has awoken the Mujahideen.

This is what kids in Imam Suhaib Webb's Young Muslims program are assigned to read:

> To be true Muslims, we must be Mujahideen. We can no more sit back passively; we must try, actively, to change history, that is, wage Jihad.

CHAPTER 23

FOOL ME TWICE AND THREE TIMES

The Tsarnaevs might have been acting according to ideology that has been taught at the ISB, but they ended up bringing tremendous harm to the organization and the entire Islamist movement in Boston. After the bombs went off at the Boston Marathon, both of the ISB's mosques were in full damage control mode. With the ISB back in the media spotlight, APT's data on the ISB was in high demand. Various media outlets began exploring our research and putting out damaging reports on the ISB. *USA Today* had a front-page story, "Mosque that Boston suspects attended has radical ties," citing a broad array of APT's findings. Everyone from UPI to CNN to Fox News was getting in touch with me or Charles and looking for information, after which they would put out honest articles on the ISB's radical ties. But, honest portrayal of the information on the ISB and the Tsarnaev brothers was only limited to honest journalists, which were, even back then, in extremely short supply in the leftist media. Honest approaches to dealing with the ISB would have also depended on honest politicians, of which there were none in the Obama administration or in Massachusetts when it came to the issue of Islamist extremism.

In 2017, a think tank affiliated with the American Muslims Brotherhood, called the Institute for Social Policy and Understanding (ISPU) put out a postmortem report called "How a Mosque Managed a Crisis: The ISBCC Response to the Boston Marathon Bombing." By the time of the Marathon bombing, Bilal Kaleem was gone as the executive director of the ISBCC. He had gotten a job as a vice president at J.P. Morgan—ironic, considering that he had previously pressured Bank of America to reinstate accounts connected to money laundering and terrorist financing. In his place, the ISB Trust installed Yusufi Vali, the Obama campaign worker and Greater Boston Interfaith Organization community organizer. Vali was clever in the way he handled the Boston Marathon bombing, but the report on the ISBCC's response to the bombing is less a testament to his public relations skills, or those of Imam Suhaib Webb, than it is to how willing Boston's media, law enforcement, and Jewish leaders were to believe their stories. All of the infiltration and subversion of Boston's institutions—the Justice Department office for the District of Massachusetts, the local law enforcement agencies, the governor, the Boston and Cambridge mayors, the Jewish rabbis, the *Boston Globe*—had paid off in spades.

The *Globe*'s religion reporter, Lisa Wangsness, seemed to have had somewhat of a crush on Suhaib Webb. When he arrived in Boston, she had written a fawning profile about him, even going so far as to gush about his blue eyes and blond hair. The profile was an embarrassment to journalism, and should have been an embarrassment to anyone but a teenage girl in love. Charles and I had met with Wangsness at the *Globe* on November 10, 2010, and briefed her on the ISBCC's deep connections to terrorism. It was no use. She looked at all our evidence, thanked us politely, and reported nothing. After the marathon bombing, Webb put Wangsness to work. According to the ISPU report:

> Ms. Wangsness spent weeks shadowing Imam Webb and visiting ISBCC while writing a profile piece on him. This experience allowed ISBCC to trust Ms. Wangsness and to open the doors of ISBCC to her, which in turn, allowed her to be receptive to working with ISBCC again. This relationship proved to be vital in ensuring that ISBCC received generous and positive coverage both during and after the bombings.

Wangsness's treatment of APT was much less generous and positive, which was to be expected from a "journalist" who had unabashedly become Webb's PR representative. In another glowing profile of Webb, tilted "In life and words, Muslim leader bridges cultures,"written less than a month after the bombings, Wangsness wrote: "The heightened focus on Boston's Muslim community offered an opportunity for Charles Jacobs, a longtime critic of the cultural center and its sister mosque in Cambridge (they are both owned by the Islamic Society of Boston but run separately), to revive his allegations — picked up by USA Today — that the mosques are breeding grounds for hatred and extremism." She went on to cite several leftists who dismissed our allegations without addressing them.

Law enforcement agencies also went to bat for Webb. According to the ISPU report:

"Because of the Islamophobia ISBCC faced during its inception, from early on ISBCC learned the importance of establishing strong bonds with local government and law enforcement agencies....In the immediate aftermath of the Boston Marathon bombing, ISBCC witnessed the dividends from the investment in these bonds. Even as there were voices from the political right accusing local mosques of playing a role in the Tsarnaevs' radicalization, local government and law enforcement agencies displayed unflinching public support for Boston's Muslims."

Even more unflinching public support came from a frequent target of ISBCC-instigated abuse, the Justice Department. True, the ISBCC and its leaders, on multiple occasions, had incited the Boston Muslim community against the Justice Department over the prosecutions of Tarek Mehanna, Aafia Sidiqui, and Hafiz Masood. But the U.S. attorney for the District of Massachusetts was a doctrinaire leftist named Carmen Ortiz. She probably secretly thought that the ISBCC was right to be upset. As the ISPU report recounted:

The ongoing relationship ISBCC had with Ms. Ortiz's office proved to be immensely helpful. After the attack but before the identity of the bombers had been established, Ms. Ortiz preemptively extended her support to the Muslim community and asked them to reach out to her if indeed it did turn out that the attackers were Muslims, which is exactly what ISBCC did. When ISBCC leaders shared their concern that ISB and ISBCC could be held responsible, the U.S. Attorney's office connected ISBCC with the Public Information Officer and tasked that office with finding professional help and guidance for ISBCC to manage media.

As with the *Globe*, Ortiz was glad to serve as the ISBCC's attack dog against APT, telling the *New York Times* that our allegations against the ISBCC were "incredibly racist and unfair." Ortiz, it turned out, however, was not a credible source on matters of character, and that was not the first time she has slandered people. She resigned in after a term filled with bipartisan outrage over her penchant for making baseless claims and "indicting the good guys." Reddit co-founder Aaron Swartz was driven to suicide after Ortiz indicted him on trumped-up charges.

Cambridge mayor Henrietta Davis came out to the ISB's Cambridge mosque for a solidarity event with ISB Trustee Anwar Kazmi. There, Kazmi said of the Tsarnaevs: "What they have done is a grotesque perversion of the teachings of our faith....The Quran teaches us that whosoever kills an innocent person, it is as if he killed all of mankind." Yet not long before he disavowed the Tsarnaevs' terrorist act, I was filming him at that cold and windy rally held at the Boston Common gazebo when he was urging the crowd to support the convicted al-Qaeda terrorist Tarek Mehanna. At the rally, Kazmi dropped the pretense that thrilled the Cambridge mayor and let loose, slandering the U.S. army with false claims of atrocities in Iraq. Tarek Mehanna, it must be repeated, was in jail specifically for the things he's written on behalf of al-Qaeda in Iraq, including various violent jihadist fantasies like his martyrdom porn poem about the seventy-two heavenly virgins.

But no one else was as useful and as idiotic in his support for the ISBCC and Suhaib Webb as were Boston's Jewish leaders. As Webb said: "It was really the Jewish community that supported me more than the Muslim community." The umbrella Jewish group in Massachusetts, the Jewish Community Relations Council (JCRC), had a new leader to replace Nancy Kaufman, who had cut off dialogue with the ISBCC. Jeremy Burton checked all the right boxes to be hired as head of Boston's left-wing Jewish community. He was a homosexual, Latin American J Street supporter. He was also willing to change the JCRC's policy toward the ISBCC. As he told the *Boston Globe*, "his group still has significant questions about the organization that manages the Roxbury mosque, the Muslim American Society." Despite these questions, however, "Burton said he has engaged with Webb in interfaith conversations and has seen him talking 'about the kind of mainstream Islamic American rooted community he is trying to build here.'"

With the umbrella Boston Jewish group getting ready to jump off the fence into Imam Suhaib Webb's arms, leading the effort to sanitize the ISB's connection to the Tsarnaevs and to various al-Qaeda terrorists was none other than Rabbi Ronne Friedman of Temple Israel in Boston. This was the same rabbi who was already once snookered by ISB Trustee Walid Fitaihi into embracing the ISB while Fitaihi was writing nasty anti-Semitic articles about him and all Jews in Arabic newspapers. When Imam Webb came to Boston, he reached out to Rabbi Friedman and convinced him that he wasn't like all the other guys who came before. Imam Webb would be different. The Friday after the Boston Marathon bombings, both Rabbi Friedman and the JCRC's executive director, Jeremy Burton, showed up at the ISBCC's evening prayers in a show of support. According to the rabbi, this show of support "was predicated very much on the relationship that had been established and the enormous trust that we felt for Yusufi and the appreciation, the affection we felt for Suhaib Webb."

That affection took on a bit of a tarnish, however, within days of the bombings. In response to the universal love affair with Suhaib Webb and the ISBCC among leftists in Boston and elsewhere, I released a couple of secret weapons. After Webb came to Boston, I had taken to listening to his online sermons while working out at the gym, just so I could get a feel for the guy. Plus, like Sacha Baron Cohen's Ali G, he was pretty entertaining in his own poserish way:

"Maryam in Palestine, she was rocking mangoes, yo," Imam Webb would tell his flock And, like, watermelons. This is dope."

"Ay yo, whaddup man, get off that camel!"

Among the pretend Eminem jive, however, I soon heard some very worrying things that Suhaib Webb was teaching to Muslim young people all over the country and, now, at the ISBCC. For example, in 2009, Webb was preaching at the Muslim Community Association in San Francisco while that year's Israel-Hamas war was in full swing—and it was Jews who were on the imam's mind.

He asked the congregation, rhetorically:

Who were the people that tried to kill Issa [Jesus] and Zachariya [father of John the Baptist]? The Jews! The followers of Musa [Moses]. When the Prophet [Muhammad] goes to Medina, who are going to be his greatest antagonizers? Think about it!

But, Webb counseled his flock, they should never let their hatred for the Jews show publicly, again taking examples from Islamic religious texts:

> Abdullah bin Mubarak is one of the greatest mujahedeen [jihad-ists]. He died on the battlefield, and he was a great scholar of had-ith [sayings of the prophet]. His neighbor in Iraq was a Jew. Can you imagine? The neighbor of Abdullah bin Mubarak is a Jewish person. Ya, salaam! If we had a Jewish neighbor now, oh man"— here, Webb's smile turns into a scowl. "Yeah, I can understand that you might have some animosity to them, but try to make some *dawa* [proselytizing], you never know what might happen."

Catching Imam Webb at anti-Semitism was one thing. Rabbi Friedman had been there and done that before. Mere Jew hatred wouldn't cause him to lose faith in his new interfaith friend. But, I had a pocket ace. In his sermons, including in sermons he gave at the ISBCC just months prior, Imam Webb touched a third rail of leftist politics—indeed, one of the forbidden holiest of holies of the left-wing religion. Imam Webb, it turned out, was quite a raging homophobe. During the summer of 2012, Webb held a series of lectures at the ISBCC centered on warning the ISBCC's young congregants against going to the beach and dressing in light summer clothing. But, he also made a jab at the LGBT community:

> I hear a lot of people get mad at the sisters for how they dress but I never hear anybody scolding brothers for their skinny jeans or their effeminate clothing. Very effeminate clothing now. And the Prophet [Muhammad] said that he cursed the man who imitates a woman and the woman who imitates the men in their dress.

At a 2012 Muslim youth conference in Washington, D.C., Webb told the kids that Muslims must speak out against gay marriage, which was then winding its way to Supreme Court affirmation through the lower courts:

"What is our position on gay marriage?" he asked the audience mem-bers. "We already know what our positions are on homosexuality. But why are we so quiet? Why? We have something to offer society, and we should ask America nicely—what on Earth has happened to your values in forty years? And not be shy!"

I released this video of Suhaib Webb on April 25, 2013, ten days after the marathon bombing. It did not go over well with Webb's new interfaith buddies. Indeed, Rabbi Ronne Friedman was part of what had happened to American values over the past forty years, having in 1992 performed the first Jewish gay marriage ceremony in the religion's 3,500-or-so-year history. The head of Boston's JCRC, Jeremy Burton, who was one step away from being convinced to change JCRC policy and embrace the ISBCC as an interfaith partner, was himself gay. One of Webb's other biggest boosters among the interfaith rabbis was Toba Spitzer, the first ever lesbian rabbi of a Jewish congregation. Massachusetts was the first state in the Union to allow gay marriage back in 2003. Many of Webb's new friends had a lot to do with that. Now, they were pissed off at Webb, and Rabbi Friedman, as Webb's biggest fan, looked like a chump for the second time in his dealings with the ISB. It wouldn't be his last.

But Webb threw a "Hail Mary" excuse. As I expected, the anti-Semitism wasn't even an issue. However, Webb wrote to Rabbi Friedman and included Jeremy Burton:

"Dear Rabbi,

My theology has evolved over the years. I was wrong with those clips. My stance on this issue changed after meeting with gay congregants and humanizing their struggles some months ago....I ask that you give me a little room to try and build this understanding in my own community."

In other words, Webb was asking Friedman to please not to force him into to be honest with his community—or with Friedman, it cannot be both—about this issue. The email was an obvious falsehood, especially considering that what Webb termed "over the years" was actually less than one—he was yelling about gays marrying and brothers dressing like sisters just the previous summer. And yet, the Hail Mary worked on the good rabbi and Jeremy Burton.

Webb was back in their good graces. Jeremy and Webb started tweeting at each other again, and in January 2014, Imam Webb returned the favor of Rabbi Friedman's visit to the ISBCC by speaking from the pulpit at Temple Israel, just like Fitaihi did exactly a decade prior. Rabbi Friedman introduced the imam, telling the assembled Jews that "we have a great opportunity for true progress in this city because of the current leadership of Imam Webb...[and] his openness to the Jewish community."

Webb called Rabbi Friedman "a mentor and...a friend and a brave person." Webb told the assembled Jews that "we have to begin to take each other as brothers and sisters...to learn not to believe the things that we are told about each other...to hug each other and love each other."

It was "Kumbaya" at its best. But, as always, Rabbi Friedman got punked for the third time. Later in 2014, Hamas decided to kidnap and murder three Israeli teens and start another war with Israel. Webb's mask slipped. In a series of increasingly hostile social media posts to his tens of thousands of followers, Webb became less than brotherly to Jews and Israel. Some examples:

"2 children massacred by the Israeli army as it 'defended itself' 2day."
"Modern Israel: Pioneers of Terror in the Holy Land."
"Israel: America's Frankenstein monster."

Webb posted a cartoon of Netanyahu sitting in a Gaza-shaped tub of blood, waving a butcher's cleaver at screaming children. "Tells the story" was Webb's comment on the blood libel.

Webb dishonestly defended Hamas, tweeting out an article titled "It Turns Out Hamas May Not Have Kidnapped and Killed the 3 Israeli Teens After All." He attacked law enforcement: "US Terrorism Prosecutions Often An Illusion." He shared an article advising Islamic radicals on how to shield themselves from the authorities, tweeting "Wondering If Your 'Jihadist' Friend Is With the FBI?" He criticized U.S. air strikes against the ISIS barbarians responsible for crucifixions and beheadings in Iraq, claiming that the reason for the strikes is that America simply wants Iraq's oil. Throughout the war, he raised money for "Gaza" through Islamic Relief, the suspected Hamas charity that's banned as a terrorist entity in Israel, West Bank, and the United Arab Emirates. According to one tweet, he raised over $200,000 for the group.

Indeed, Webb promoted the Twitter hashtag campaign #JSIL (Jewish State in the Levant), which slanders Israel by comparing it to ISIS. He compared the ISIS genocide of the Yazidis to Israel's treatment of the Palestinians. Webb also attacked President Obama for saying that "no country can accept rockets fired indiscriminately at its civilians," and that "Israel has a right to defend itself." Webb wrote that these comments said by the president "were a shame and disrespectful," and that "[t]ime and time again, Obama shows that he lacks the backbone to make ethical decisions." In one 2014 sermon, Webb really went after Obama telling Boston Muslims:

> In America, no religious community has been beaten up or slapped around in the last thirteen years like us....But if we look at the children killed in Gaza on the watch of President Obama, President Obama has been the greatest perhaps, saddest president I ever witnessed in my lifetime. I feel duped. I feel like I got played. I feel like I was tricked.

Even Rabbi Friedman had to acknowledge he was bamboozled again, writing to his congregation: "Suhaib Webb posted or 're-tweeted' certain articles or cartoons that gave rise to Jewish concern." Nevertheless, he still stood by Webb. True believers in the cult of "dialogue" will not suffer their beliefs being questioned. After the Marathon bombings, APT released videos exposing anti-Semitic and homophobic statements by Webb. We wrote about Webb's support for a cop killer, his association with Anwar al-Awlaki, and the radical indoctrination curriculum that Webb has endorsed for training Muslim youth.

In response, in a letter to his entire congregation, Friedman complained about a conspiracy "by Charles Jacobs and his minions" to subject "the Imam and the ISBCC...to a withering, pernicious and persistent attack." Defending Webb, Friedman wrote: "He is clearly seeking relationship with the Jewish community." Indeed he is; a relationship where naïve Jewish "leaders" signal to the Boston community that Webb is a man to be trusted. That's what Webb and Yusufi Vali really wanted.

The rabbi was right, however. We did subject Webb and the ISBCC to a withering, pernicious, and persistent attack. It should, by right, have been the rabbi's job and the job of ADL, but we were the ones who had to do it. We scored an immediate success right after the Boston Marathon bombings when Suhaib Webb was disinvited from a memorial ceremony with Governor Deval Patrick and President Obama, most likely due to the revelation of his ties with Awlaki. Although the leftist media tried to tamp down on our exposure of Webb's background while attacking APT as bigots, conservative and new media outlets ran our articles on Webb and we were published in *Frontpage Magazine,* the *Daily Caller,* the *Federalist,* the *Washington Times, Breitbart,* and *American Thinker,* not to mention a variety of blogs and significant word of mouth through Facebook. Fox News picked up most of these new media exposés on Suhaib Webb, and Webb was beginning to squirm.

One of the last straws was my exposé of Webb's speech at a 2013 conference of the Hamas front group CAIR. "May Allah help CAIR," Webb began his speech. "This is an incredible institution. You know, I love CAIR man. It's one of the few invites I get where I'm like "Yeah!" Right?...I mean, imagine that the FBI told us, "We don't work with CAIR....So what? We do. And if you want to work with us, you work with them."

Webb then complained about secularism being "a radical, lunatic ideology" and attacked the brave Somali American activist against radical Islam, Ayaan Hirsi Ali. "Aayan Hirsi Ali is teaching a class in Harvard on Islamic political thought?" whined Webb. "This woman is an idiot! I say that sincerely! How could she teach at the University of Phoenix, let alone Harvard? And I say that with all respect to graduates of University of Phoenix." This got the attention of Megyn Kelly and Webb was in the crosshairs fulltime. The ISPU report on the ISBCC's reaction to the marathon bombing describes what happened to Webb:

> For Imam Webb, the very visible and prominent representative of ISBCC, the attacks and the fallout were particularly ruthless....Fox News, for example, targeted Imam Webb, running a three-part special on him. The coverage included allegations that Imam Webb had met with the Tsarnaev brothers [we never made these allegations], that he knew al-Qaeda leader Anwar al-Awlaki, that he was a member of the Muslim Brotherhood and a jihadist, and that ISBCC was "a terrorist factory," an accusation that stings to this day....Imam Webb also had many invitations to speak at events that were revoked. The most obvious one was when President Obama came to Boston for an interfaith service at a local church two days after the attack. Imam Webb was scheduled to speak at the major event as a representative of the Muslim community. However, the night before, he was informed by the governor's office that he would not be speaking; despite being the imam of the largest mosque in New England and having represented the Boston Muslim community on national media, Imam Webb was replaced

by another, much lesser-known Muslim leader. To this day, no clear explanation has been provided for the change....In the entire difficult experience, what stuck out most for Imam Webb was how little support he received from his fellow Muslims. In many instances, leaders of the Jewish community spoke up to defend Imam Webb, while Muslims, nationally and locally, remained silent.

According to Webb himself, tangling with APT, "basically, it felt like you're a fighter and you're getting hit and beat, and you turn around and your manager's gone. And then someone from the crowd throws a chair and hits the guy on the head. And that was somewhat shocking because I thought that Boston would have been a little bit more used to the potential of Islamophobes after what happened with the [ISBCC] mosque....It was a very lonely place to be."

· · ·

On Friday, October 24, 2014, just under three years after Bilal Kaleem made his excited announcement about the rock star Imam Suhaib Webb coming to work to Boston, it was time for the weekly sermon at the ISBCC and Imam Webb was nowhere around. Instead, Hossam Al Jabri, the alleged money-launderer and president of the ISBCC, gave the sermon. Before he did so, he had an announcement to make:

> Many of you have seen Imam Suhaib's email that went out to the community this morning regarding him leaving Boston and having another opportunity in Washington [D.C.] that he will be pursuing, inshallah....We are proud of what Imam Suhaib has done, we are proud of what he has given us in Boston, and proud of what he will do, inshallah, in order to contribute to Islam in America. Of course, all of you know that he had a difficult time in Boston with all the attacks that were against him, and we are accustomed, unfortunately, with the attacks by Islamophobes on our institution. In fact, any individual or any institution in America today that tries to do good things and great things in America is attacked by a very small but well-funded group of Islamophobes. And these attacks are hard on the individual. They're not easy because when you see your reputation smeared, when you see your picture in the

newspaper in front of terrorists or with terrorists, these are not easy things to withstand. We are grateful for Imam Suhaib that on our behalf he withstood many of these attacks, and we pray that Allah subhanahu wa taallah will give us all the courage to support our scholars and our leaders and our institutions and be with them in these times of difficulties.

On the same day that Webb's resignation was announced, a member of Suhaib Webb's old mosque in Oklahoma beheaded his coworker on October 24, 2014, telling detectives shortly thereafter: "You know all I was doing was...what I was supposed to do as a Muslim." As with the Fort Hood Massacre, the Obama administration would again label this act of jihad as workplace violence. But, another member of Suhaib Webb's mosque, Nur Al Amriki, was now on Fox News telling the world that Suhaib Webb had been preaching jihad in Oklahoma. The ISBCC couldn't have jettisoned Webb any quicker.

On May 23, 2015, Rabbi Ronne Friedman devoted the Friday night sermon before the Jewish holiday of Shavuot to me and Charles. We had made the previous year extremely unpleasant for him and his ISBCC allies, so the rabbi seemed especially angry as he intoned:

Many of you are aware that Temple Israel and, at times, that I as your rabbi have been attacked by Charles Jacobs and Ilya Feokstitov [sic] of the so-called Americans for Peace and Tolerance. We've been depicted variously as innocent dupes, as anti-Israel, as friends of those who promote terrorism, and more. These two bad actors have recently been joined by two New York provocateurs, Pamela Geller and Ronn Torrosian.

Pamela, the courageous counter-jihadist Jewish heroine, and Ronn, a brilliant PR professional, had joined us in condemning Rabbi Friedman for inviting the left wing anti-Israel group J Street to his synagogue. The rabbi went on:

Charles Jacobs and his sidekick, Ilya Feoktistov [sic] must imagine themselves as Jewish crusaders, as defenders of the faith. But I've come to the conclusion that they are, quite frankly, Judeophobes

and misanthropes. They've amplified their animosity toward
Muslims and added to that a hatred of Jews – that is, those Jews
who disagree with them—and a cultivated animosity toward others,
political liberals in particular, who would dare argue against their
politics of fear. Those of us who choose to stand against them will
continue to be pilloried in print by them, but we have one consola-
tion: Blustering ideological bullies may achieve publicity and noto-
riety for a brief moment in time, but ultimately, they will always
be exposed for what they are. As our community continues on our
path to fulfill our promise, they will be consigned to the wilderness,
where, frankly, is where they belong. We continue on page 282...

Charles and I have, so far, avoided expulsion to the wilderness. On the
other hand, the *Washington Post* would later report that Webb moved to
D.C. "to escape the political limelight." Webb went from running the largest mosque in New England to running a small D.C.-area Muslim youth
group without its own physical plant. I want Suhaib Webb's experience in
Boston to be a clear object lesson to any Muslim Brotherhood or other
Islamist imam who is contemplating a move to Boston; although moderate
imams are always welcome. As Bilal Kaleem said before Webb took the
imam job at the ISBCC: "We know whoever is the imam here is going to
get the third degree. Sometimes imams don't want to go through that. So
even if they like the whole vision here, they're nervous about dealing with
the challenges of being an imam here."
Stay out of Malibu, Lebowski.

CHAPTER 24

DREAM COME TRUE

The last half of 2014 through 2016 was indeed a time of great difficulty for the ISB and the Islamist movement in America generally. In June 2014, ISIS declared itself a caliphate and rebranded as the Islamic State. In October 2014, the territory in which it exercised sovereignty would reach its historic maximum. ISIS was showing the world, in highly produced videos, what Islamist extremists are capable of for the sake of their ideology, and Boston would, again, play a significant role in this story.

In the fall of 2012, the FBI put out a $50,000 bounty on Ahmad Abousamra, the son of former ISBCC vice president Abdulbadi Abousamra and Tarek Mehanna's co-conspirator. Ahmad fled to Syria in 2006, and in 2012 the Syrian Civil War was really heating up. ISIS was just starting to make its presence known. I had thought to myself back then, *I bet Ahmad went and joined ISIS*. Sure enough, in September 2014, ABC reported that Ahmad Abousamra might be playing a key role in the ISIS media blitz. It turned out that Ahmad joined the al-Qaeda in Iraq affiliate in Syria, Jabhat-al-Nusra, and, when that split into the rival al-Qaeda and ISIS factions, Ahmad stuck with ISIS, claiming that al-Qaeda were the "Jews of Jihad." He took part in armed combat and was wounded fighting Bashar Assad's forces in the Halab neighborhood of Aleppo.

I had to give this to the guy: he followed his dream and made it, joining the terror group originally started by his idol, Abu Musab al Zarqawi. Back in 2004, no one wanted to take young Ahmad into his terrorist group. He

struck out with Lashkar-e-Taiba in Pakistan, as well as with al-Qaeda in
Yemen and Fallujah, Iraq. But now, unlike his friend Tarek, who was rot-
ting away in solitary at the ADX Florence supermax prison in Colorado,
Abousamra had made it big. He and Tarek used to joke about being "the
media wing of al-Qaeda in Iraq." Now, Abousamra was the media wing of
its direct and more extreme descendant, ISIS. He became the chief editor
of the dark-web ISIS propaganda magazine, *Dabiq*, when the magazine
launched in June 2014 and soon branched out to other countries, publishing
the ISIS magazines *Istok* in Russian, *Konstantiniyye* in Turkish, and *Dar
al-Islam* in French.

Abousamra was killed by a U.S. airstrike near Raqqa in January 2017.
ISIS issued a long eulogy for him, ending with:

> He departed, having known that media is for calling people to
> Allah, guiding them to His cause, and inciting them to kill His
> enemies, and having worked according to that knowledge and
> proven himself well.

Incited by Abousamra's ISIS propaganda, violent jihadists were popping
off across the United States and Europe in quick succession, starting with
the decapitation jihad by a member of Suhaib Webb's Oklahoma mosque
and a hatchet melee attack by an ISIS supporter against police officers
in Queens. Then came the Charlie Hebdo massacres in France and the
attempted massacre at a Draw Muhammad cartoon contest, organized by
Pamela Geller in Texas on May 3, 2015.

Indeed, the two ISIS acolytes from Arizona who were hoping to kill
her were not the only ones who wanted Pamela Geller dead that May.
Neither was Rabbi Ronne Friedman the only person in Boston who was
expressing his hatred for the brave woman. The FBI was monitoring one of
Imam Abdullah Faaruuq's disciples, a young man named Usaama Rahim,
who grew up attending Imam Faaruuq's mosque for most of his life and
was personally close with Imam Faaruuq. Ussama Rahim also worked as
a private security guard at the ISBCC mosque nearby and often prayed
there. His brother, Ibrahim Rahim, was a local imam who preached often
at the ISBCC and was close with the ISCC's former imam, Suhaib Webb.

Usaama, together with his nephew, David Wright, and a third man,
Nicholas Rovinsky, aka Nuh Amriki, had decided to get in on the Pamela

Geller–killing action. They were plotting a decapitation attack. Usaama bought three bowie knives on Amazon. The three men were getting their directions from ISIS operatives in Syria. They had already proved their worth by raising funds to send another American ISIS supporter, Zulfi Hoxha, to Syria, where he became a senior ISIS commander.

But, getting to Pamela proved to be too difficult and Usaama Rahim proved to be too impatient. On June 2, at 5 a.m., he called his nephew and, with the FBI listening, told him he's changing the plan:

"I can't wait that long, I can't wait that long man....I'm just going to ah go after them, those boys in blue. Cause, ah, it's the easiest target and, ah, the most common is the easiest for me." He told his nephew that he would attack randomly, somewhere in Boston, sometime within the next few days, put his knives in his backpack and left his apartment. Two hours later, Boston Police officers and FBI agents confronted Usaama Rahim outside of a CVS in the Boston neighborhood of Roslindale, where Usaama worked. In response, Usaama pulled one of his bowie knives out of his pocket and brandished it at the officers. They drew their guns and told him to drop the knife.

"You drop yours," Usaama responded and started moving toward the cops with his knife. He was shot dead. Immediately after the shooting, Usaama's brother, Ibrahim Rahim, the imam who frequently preached at the ISBCC, began claiming on social media that Usaama was shot in the back as he was waiting for a bus and talking to his father on the cellphone. According to Ibrahim, Usaama's last words to his father were, "I can't breathe." This was a cynical and fraudulent attempt to exploit the then-current story of Eric Garner—a black man who died while resisting arrest in Staten Island—and the anti-police Black Lives Matter riots then gripping major U.S. cities. Eric Garner's last words were "I can't breathe."

And yet, the Boston Islamist community ran with it; no one more so—as was now to be expected—than Imam Abdullah Faaruuq. Boston's News Channel 5 caught up with Imam Faaruuq outside of his Mosque for the Praising of Allah, where Usaama prayed. Asked to comment on the man's death, Faaruuq seemed to blame Pamela Geller for a member of his mosque trying to chop her head off:

"Another American boy – he was born here. He was like a nephew to he and I," said Faaruuq, pointing at a fewllow mosque leader. "Just another American boy caught up in the sickening malaise of Islamophobia."

Later, at a press conference with Usaama Rahim's family and its attorney, Faaruuq showed up and got his hands on the mic. "I'm going to ask for a few things here for myself, as a man who believes in God that God has mercy on the young man," said Faaruuq as the family looked on and the cameras rolled. "I don't know what his faults were, but I don't think that whatever had transpired warranted him being killed. I also want to pray for the officers that were involved, that God would guide them because they have families and I don't know how strongly they take it that they murdered a young man that they could have captured....I ask God that people overlook the shortcomings of the people – who continue to exist – that murdered the young man. I know they probably didn't want it or that's not what they intended in their hearts. But this is what they're trained—to shoot at the critical mass in an open space with cars going by and a school bus."

There was poor Yusufi Vali at the ISBCC, who had just spent the two years since the Boston Marathon bombings working his butt off on messaging the media that Boston Islamic leaders were against terrorists and condemn terrorism in the strongest terms. And here was Imam Faaruuq, in front of the cameras, on all the local news shows, and in all the newspapers, insisting that he's standing behind this ISIS supporter while faulting the police for preventing another Islamist terrorist tragedy in Boston from happening.

The incident in Roslindale intensified a mounting concern surrounding the burgeoning roster of Boston-based Islamic extremists. People around the country were asking: what's going on in Boston? And Yusufi's job got even harder. After Abousamra turned up as an ISIS leader in Syria, even CNN put out an article asking: "Why does Cambridge mosque draw extremists?" After Imam Faaruuq's attacks on the Boston Police and the FBI for killing his disciple, even the *Boston Globe* started noticing that something was not right. The *Globe* wrote a profile on Faaruuq called "An imam of fiery words and a fatherly presence." The article was co-written by Shelley Murphy, a hard-nosed, no-nonsense, deeply honest liberal reporter of a dwindling old breed, and Lisa Wangsness, the ISBCC groupie. There was palpable tension between honest reporting on Imam Faaruuq's alarming rhetoric and close ties to convicted al-Qaeda terrorists, likely done by Shelley Murphy, and dishonest attempts to rehabilitate the man, almost certainly done by Lisa Wangsness.

When Usaama Rahim was shot in that CVS parking lot, he became the thirteenth individual connected to Islamic Society in Boston (ISB) mosques and involved in terrorism. All of the thirteen are either killed, or in jail, or are fugitives from the law. Some have already been mentioned; some have not. Abdulrahman Alamoudi is the founder and first president of the Islamic Society of Boston. In 2003, he was arrested for trafficking funds from Libya's Muammar Qaddafi to a U.K. al-Qaeda cell for the purposes of carrying out the assassination of Saudi King Abdullah. He is serving an eighteen-year federal prison sentence for his crimes.

Yusuf Qaradawi is one of the founding trustees of the Islamic Society of Boston. Qaradawi served on the board of trustees from 1993 until 2000. In 1999, Qaradawi was banned from entering the United States by the Clinton administration due to his terrorist connections. Called the "Theologian of Terror" by the Anti-Defamation League, Qaradawi is the spiritual leader of the Muslim Brotherhood and has called for the murder of all Jews, the execution of homosexuals and suicide attacks against Israel and U.S. forces in Iraq. There is a "high alert" Interpol warrant out for his arrest on Egyptian charges of incitement to murder.

Aafia Siddiqui had been a leading member of the ISB in the 1990s during her studies at MIT and Brandeis. Siddiqui gave impassioned speeches at al-Qaeda–fundraising events held at the ISB and other area mosques. In 2003, Siddiqui fled Boston. She turned up in 2009 in Afghanistan, where she was arrested carrying plans for a mass casualty attack on New York City and a large quantity of cyanide. She opened fire on the FBI agents holding her prisoner and was eventually sentenced to eighty-six years in prison for attempted murder of U.S. government officials. After her arrest, various ISB leaders have portrayed her as a victim of a supposed American war on Muslims.

Tarek Mehanna had attended the ISB mosque in Cambridge and was a highly regarded Islamic teacher within the Massachusetts Muslim community. In 2009, Mehanna was arrested on charges of providing material support to al-Qaeda in Iraq and lying to the FBI. After his arrest, the ISB and various ISB leaders have portrayed him as a victim of a supposed American war on Muslims. In 2012, Mehanna was sentenced to seventeen years in federal prison after being proven guilty of the charges against him.

Ahmad Abousamra was the son of the former vice president of the ISBCC, Abdulbadi Abousamra. Ahmad was indicted along with Tarek

Mehanna in 2009 on charges of providing material support to al-Qaeda in Iraq (which gave birth to ISIS) and lying to the FBI. However, Abousamra fled the United States to Syria in 2006, shortly after the FBI first interviewed him. He surfaced in Syria in 2014, when officials reported that he had become a key leader in the ISIS propaganda effort. He died in January 2017 in a U.S. airstrike near Raqqa.

Rezwan Ferdaus began attending the ISB's Roxbury mosque while a student at Northeastern University, located nearby, where Imam Faaruuq was the Muslim chaplain. According to media reports, Ferdaus was a secular Muslim youth before college, but became increasingly fundamentalist during his college years. Ferdaus was arrested in 2011 and charged with plans to attack the Pentagon and the U.S. Capitol with remote controlled airplanes packed with C-4 explosives, and with support for al-Qaeda. He was sentenced to seventeen years in federal prison in 2012 after pleading guilty to the charges.

Oussama Ziade was a large donor to the ISB, and was indicted in 2009 for dealing in the assets of specially designated global terrorist Yassin Qadi. Ziade was the CEO of PTech, which had been raided in 2002 as part of Operation Green Quest—the Muslim Brotherhood money-laundering investigation. Ziade is currently a fugitive living in Lebanon.

Hafiz Masood was one of the religious leaders of the ISB's political arm, the Muslim American Society of Boston. In 2006, Masood was arrested on immigration charges and eventually deported. After the 2008 Mumbai Massacre, the *Times of India* reported that Masood was the brother of the massacre's ringleader, Hafiz Saeed, and that he had raised money and recruited for his brother's terrorist group while in Boston. After his arrest, ISB leaders publicly supported Masood and accused the U.S. government of a "witch hunt against Muslim leaders." After moving back to Pakistan, Masood became the director of communications for his brother's terrorist group.

Dzhokhar Tsarnayev had occasionally attended the ISB with his brother Tamerlan, who was a frequent worshipper at the ISB. On April 15, 2013, Dzhokhar and his brother Tamerlan allegedly placed two pressure cooker bombs near the finish line of the Boston Marathon and remotely detonated them, causing four deaths and 264 injuries. Three days, he and his brother allegedly executed MIT policeman Sean Collier in an opening move in a final confrontation with law enforcement authorities. Dzhokhar escaped from the ensuing shootout after running over his brother in a hijacked car and set off a manhunt that resulted in an unprecedented request for all residents of Greater Boston to stay indoors. Dzhokhar is on death row for his murder convictions.

Tamerlan Tsarnayev began attending the ISB in 2009. Despite initial ISB denials, media reports have since indicated that Tamerlan was a frequent worshipper at the ISB. According to his ex-girlfriend, Tamerlan began to change after joining the ISB: "One minute he was a normal guy, the next minute he is watching these crazy Muslim videos." The alleged mastermind of the Boston Marathon bombings of 2013, Tamerlan was caught on surveillance video placing one of the two bombs that killed four and wounded 264 spectators and participants at the marathon's finish line.

Khairullozhon Matanov met Boston Marathon bomber Tamerlan Tsarnayev while attending events together at the ISB. Hours after the Boston Marathon bombing, Matanov allegedly met with Tamerlan and Dzhokhar Tsarnayev and bought them dinner. Matanov is accused of destroying evidence and lying to federal authorities that questioned him on his relationship with the Boston Marathon bombers.

Ibragim Todashev met Boston Marathon bomber Tamerlan Tsarnaev while attending events together at the ISB. FBI agents subsequently met with him to question him about his role in a ritualistic murder of an associate of Tamerlan and two others, who were found semi-beheaded, with marijuana and cash spread over their bodies. Tamerlan is a suspect in that murder. While being questioned, Todashev allegedly grabbed a metal pole and lunged at FBI agents interviewing him. He was shot and killed as a result.

And the Islamist terrorist attacks on U.S. soil just kept on coming. On July 16, 2015, an Islamist extremist murdered four U.S. Marines and a U.S. Navy sailor at two military centers in Chattanooga. On December 2, 2015, a husband and wife jihadist team murdered fourteen of the husband's co-workers at a Christmas party in San Bernadino, California. In response to the San Bernadino shootings, Boston Police Commissioner William Evans showed up at the ISBCC and told the mosque's leaders:

"There's been some tragedy in this country, yesterday in California, in Paris, and other places. We're very much aware of the possible backlash against the Islamic community. I just want to let you know that we won't tolerate that." Instead of letting Boston's residents know that he won't tolerate Islamist extremism in the Hub, Evans was keen to let Islamists know that he's with them against a nonexistent backlash, telling the mosque:

"We're all Muslims deep down. We all yearn for peace."

After Usaama Rahim was shot, Commissioner Evans stabbed his police force in the back when he appeared at a press conference with Imam Abdullah Faaruuq and thereby legitimized Faaruuq's slanders against Boston cops. Yusufi Vali, meanwhile, shot himself in the foot.

CHAPTER 25

VIOLENT AND NON-VIOLENT EXTREMISTS

In 2015, the Obama White House decided to showcase what it considered its counterterrorism successes at the so-called Countering Violent Extremism Summit—studiously avoiding any mention of Islamist extremism. The *New York Times*'s Thomas Friedman, who loyally supported Obama in both elections, asked for the summit to be canceled: "When you don't call things by their real name," he wrote, "you always get in trouble....But it is no good for us or the Muslim world to pretend that this spreading Jihadist violence is not coming out of this faith community." Even Obama's own supporters understood that the main threat to America and the world at large comes not from just any kind of violent extremism, but from "Islamic extremism," a term that Obama was always unwilling or even unable to utter.

In the run-up to the summit, the Obama White House cited Boston as one of three pilot cities that have lead the way in "countering violent extremism." Amazingly, the White House invited Nabeel Khudairi as a representative of the joint effort to counter violent extremism in Boston. This was ludicrous. Nabeel Khudairi was a vocal supporter of Lashkar-e-Taiba terrorist Hafiz Masood, while Masood preached at Khudairi's mosque in Sharon. He engineered the lawsuit against the Boston media that were exposing the violent extremism at the ISB. And he bullied moderate Muslims in his mosque, punishing them with expulsion for telling the police about fundamentalists at the Sharon mosque. In Boston, the Obama administration picked the absolute worst partners in its stated mission to "counter violent extremism."

But in a jolt to the Countering Violent Extremism Summit—unreported by many of the journalists who covered the event, the ISBCC's executive director, Yusufi Vali, pulled his mosque out of the summit. Just days before three and a half years of relationship building between Boston's Muslim leaders and federal law enforcement were to result in a jointly agreed-upon framework to be announced at the White House CVE Summit, Yusufi Vali made a surprise announcement. He told U.S. attorney Carmen Ortiz that the ISBCC will be boycotting the summit, denounced President Obama's Countering Violent Extremism program as an Islamophobic attempt by President Obama to unfairly target all Muslims, and, in effect, largely scuttled the Boston part of President Obama's CVE initiative. This was reported by only one *Boston Globe* reporter, whose report was predictably slanted toward Vali's position, and the story never gained traction. Most of America does not know that the Islamic partner in one of the three cities touted as models of cooperation rejected the president's path, writing that, "It clearly appears that the CVE initiative is exclusively targeting the American-Muslim community."

Even President Obama was an Islamophobe to Vali. The American Muslim Brotherhood's fortunes in Boston must have looked extremely terrible to its national leaders because they sent in the big guns to the rescue. In 2015, America's most belligerent Islamist group, the Council on American-Islamic Relations (CAIR), the Hamas front, opened up an office in Boston, adding to the city's ongoing struggles with Islamist terrorism. Its mission: to counter APT's public awareness campaign targeting the embattled Muslim Brotherhood institutions in Boston. The first thing it did was to incite against President Obama's countering-violent-extremism program. The second thing it did was to write a slanderous dossier on Americans for Peace and Tolerance, attacking our moderate Muslim director, Sheikh Ahmed Mansour, personally, for his criticism of Islamic extremism.

In a mudslinging report on APT, written shortly after it incorporated in Massachusetts, CAIR helpfully detailed our work:

> They [APT] have taken out extensive advertising in local and
> national newspapers asserting ties between these organizations

and designated terrorist groups, penned op-eds in numerous news outlets presenting Boston as a "hub" of extremism, and accused local mosques of serving as fronts for the Muslim Brotherhood and promoting "violent Jihad, hatred for America, and of Western civilization in general."

CAIR would seem to be an unusual choice of damage control leader. The judge in the Holy Land Foundation trial said that the government had established "at least a prima facie case as to CAIR's involvement in a conspiracy to support Hamas." The following year, the Obama Justice Department cut its ties with CAIR.

Even the United Arab Emirates has designated CAIR as a terrorist organization. Yet CAIR has successfully fooled many leftist media out-lets, such as the *Boston Globe*, that its goals are to protect the civil rights of American Muslims. It is alarmed that APT has consistently exposed its real mission here in New England: to support and defend the radical Islamist leadership of Boston's largest Islamic institutions, such as the Islamic Society of Boston (ISB), in order to help the continue radicalizing the historically moderate Muslim community here.

CAIR's attack on APT comprised an assortment of false accusations and wild claims. Without any real substance to include, CAIR instead turned its fury onto APT's Muslim allies. It named Islamic leader Ahmed Subhy Mansour and groups such as the Center for Islamic Pluralism as "native informants" participating in some grand "Islamophobic" conspir-acy—a pretty racist statement considering who was in charge at CAIR Massachusetts.

The Massachusetts branch of CAIR would be headed by John Robbins, a convert to Islam and a PhD who was squeaky clean. CAIR must have been carefully grooming him for years. But, I noticed another name among CAIR MA's three founding directors. It was the name of Cambridge city councilor Nadeem Mazen. Mazen was a graduate of MIT and another student of MIT Muslim chaplain Suheil Laher, who had radicalized Aafia Siddiqui, raised money for al-Qaeda, and exhorted Boston Muslims to jihad in the 1990s. Mazen worked closely with Laher and was elected president of the MIT Muslim Students Association. After graduating, Mazen seems to have kept his Islamist sympathies out of the public eye. In 2013, courting the hipster and student vote, the "man bun"–sporting Mazen was elected on a progressive platform to Cambridge City Council.

I actually met Nadeem at the ISBCC's grand opening in 2009 and talked to him at length. He seemed like an intelligent, moderate Muslim, and I was extremely disappointed to see him involved with CAIR. But, as I dug deeper, I had realized that he had totally bought in to the Islamist cause. I checked his campaign donations and saw that he was elected to Cambridge City Council with a slew of donations from local and national Muslim Brotherhood figures like ISB Trustee and Muslim Brotherhood leader Osama Kandil, as well as ISB Trustee and al-Qaeda terrorist supporter Anwar Kazmi,

After his election, Mazen increasingly began associating with other Islamist groups and preachers. He founded a group named MassMuslims, which has promoted events with radical Islamist preachers who describe homosexuality as a "disease" and a "repugnant shameless sin." Moreover, Mazen's willingness to speak out publicly against Israel while in office during the 2014 Hamas-Israel war made him a perfect recruitment prospect for the Council on American Islamic Relations (CAIR).

Mazen has also spoken out publicly against moderate Muslim groups that "foist secular attitudes on Muslims," telling the proudly secular Jewish Workmen's Circle that:

> "There's actually like a Boston-based and now nationally-based program of: "Muslims should have a secular alternative."...So, you know, that project exists, and to the extent that that and projects like it are being projected, imperialist style on to our population, I think people are going to be very hesitant to follow anything like that.

That was an interesting comment to make because, throughout 2016, Mazen was not at all hesitant to be blowing up Tinder, the promiscuous sex app, allowing it to project, imperialist-style, some fine examples of the Boston and Cambridge female population for Mazen to hook up with. This is a bit incongruous, considering that nonsecular "non-imperialist" Islam at the very least seriously frowns at sex outside of marriage, and sometimes even calls for adulterers to be stoned to death. This punishment for adultery is still on the books in many countries, including Iran and Saudi Arabia;

and Mazen could theoretically put himself in legal jeopardy by going on pilgrimage to Mecca. But, Muslims have their own hypocritical Puritans, too, and Mazen seemed to be one of them.

It was fairly easy to find Mazen on Tinder through the Swedish website Swipebuster.se. For a small fee, Swipebuster will crawl the public part of the Tinder user database, the stuff users like Mazen put out there for the world to see—profile pictures, brief bio, age, occupation or school, and the last time the app was used. Mazen appeared to have two Tinder profiles, one with his real age and one that claims to be ten years younger. He's covering all the bases, I guess. I monitored Mazen's use of the app for a couple of months in 2016 and he was definitely a frequent flyer, sometimes signing in more than once a day.

Mazen e seems to have gotten over Tinder in 2017. His ISB handlers certainly would have approved. Suhaib Webb, for example, has given sermons calling American girls "bad people" because they "don't wear any clothes," and told young Muslim men that their faith will go "right out the door," even if they see a girl one the subway and give her: "One wink, one blink, one number, one digit, one note."

In November 2015, flush with ISB and Muslim Brotherhood campaign cash, Nadeem Mazen was reelected as Cambridge city councilor, getting the highest number of votes among all his colleagues. After his reelection, APT wrote an exposé on Mazen in Breitbart—leaving out the Tinder bits, but questioning why a leader of the Hamas front group CAIR is serving as an elected official in America. In response, the entire Cambridge City Council passed a unanimous resolution "denouncing the anti-Muslim libel spread by Breitbart and similar organizations." It was chilling to read the wise leaders of the People's Republic of Cambridge, as it is derisively known, claim that Breitbart and other right wing media are "illegitimate."

There was a lot of that delegitimizing going around back then, and even more would come. The U.S. presidential election was heating up and the left wing was in attack mode. We all know how that turned out.

CHAPTER 26

TRUMP DERANGEMENT IN BOSTON

Ever since President Trump's election, repeating a pattern happening across the country, Boston leftists let their emotions overwhelm their common sense. For the Jewish community, in Boston and elsewhere, a deeply unfortunate consequence of that fact has been the subversion of Jewish communal institutions into the spiritual arms of the Democratic Party. This was true for ADL, for the Reform movement, and for Boston's JCRC. After President Donald Trump's election, the JCRC, and especially its executive director, Jeremy Burton, refused to accept the legitimacy of the election results, and adopted an aggressively hostile posture toward all branches of the federal government.

On November 11, 2016, JCRC executive director Jeremy Burton responded to the presidential election results on the organization's website by pointing out that the majority of American Jews did not vote for Donald Trump. A week later, sounding like a Georgia plantation owner after Abraham Lincoln took the White House, Burton strongly suggested that the Jewish community must be prepared to take an adversarial stance vis-à-vis the president-elect, tweeting: "It is important to not normalize the coming Trump presidency." By November 22, long before Trump was even sworn in, he was dreaming of impeachment, hallucinating an impeachable offense in Trump taking a call from the Argentinian president. On December 6, Burton decided to join the #resistance: "[W]e need to break out of normal operating modalities & have new/exceptional rules for working in context of Trump admin," he bravely tweeted. By late December, he was saddling up for battle:

"We are entering an era where our duly elected President lacks a popular mandate (or even a plurality of the vote), yet is promising radical and disruptive change. Normally, we would find ways to embrace working with any administration—even when nearly 80% of our own community voted for different candidates—whereas today, we are entering an era of unusual and significant challenges to the norms of our constitutional democracy."

These are confusing and contradictory times for leftist partisans. On December 23, 2016, Burton wrote that: "[W]hile the majority of our community did not support the President-elect, JCRC stands firm in our belief that we should not demonize those who voted for this direction." He then proceeded to demonize those who voted for this direction, quoting Trump opponent Evan McMullin: "We can no longer assume that all Americans understand the origins of their rights and the importance of liberal democracy." Indeed, Burton at first seemed to claim that Trump's election gave the leftists at the JCRC license to dispense with civility altogether, writing: "In cases where JCRC is opposing a position or appointment by the new administration, we will sometimes be asserting our institutional voice beyond the norms of traditional Jewish communal politeness." And in the very next sentence, he contradicted himself: "JCRC will strive to set an example of civil discourse, even whilst the President-elect sets a new bar for intemperate discourse." Some examples of Burton's civil discourse on Twitter include small penis jokes about Trump's "mandate," accusing Trump of a dastardly "cold + calculated plan to discount certain American lives," and pretending to hear an "antisemitic dog whistle at the heart of President Trump's inaugural speech."

But, there was no topic on which the JCRC and Burton engaged in more politically opportunistic moralizing, chest beating, and virtue signaling than in their embrace of the ISB. There is one issue that unites far-left Jews and far-right Muslims: hatred of America's current government and of Jews who dare to criticize Islamic extremists. On March 24, 2017, the *Boston Globe* reported on the JCRC's embrace of the ISBCC since Trump was elected: "In Boston and across the country, a winter of persecution [!] has brought a new warmth and vitality to Muslim-Jewish relationships." The *Globe* quoted Jeremy Burton declaring that: "In this moment of crisis for both communities...there's been a clear sense that we need to be able to stand together where we can..."

Trump's election did not create a moment of crisis for the Jewish community; it created a moment of crisis for far left Democratic activists posing as Jewish community leaders. American Jews have the first Jewish First Daughter and one of the most pro-Israel presidents in history now in the White House, whose fierce battles on behalf of Israel at the United Nations stand in stark contrast to the Obama administration's last-minute betrayal of Israel in the Security Council.

American Jews also have an administration with unparalleled commitment to fight Islamic terrorists, some of whose most frequent targets have been Jews. In that sense, this is a moment of crisis for the ISB. Since 9/11, its mosques in Cambridge and Roxbury have been home to thirteen mosque leaders, donors, and worshippers who have been either imprisoned, killed by law enforcement, or are fugitives from the law due to their involvement in Islamist terrorism. ISBCC speakers have called for jihad against America and demanded that Muslims fight to bring this nation "to its knees." The ISBCC event at which Imam Faaruuq made those comments was held in support of no fewer than twenty-two U.S.-based individuals convicted of material support for al-Qaeda, the Taliban, Hamas, Palestinian Islamic Jihad, and several other designated terrorist groups.

The JCRC has been naïve to think that the ISB's problem with America's counterterrorism efforts began only with the Trump administration and that the ISB's leaders will just go back to being patriotic Americans once a Democrat is again in the White House. That pro-terrorist event at the ISBCC was held in 2011, in the middle of the Obama administration, and ISBCC speakers accused President Obama of masterminding a broad conspiracy to falsely convict and imprison American Muslims as part of a general war against Islam. In 2014, the ISBCC's imam condemned President Obama personally for saying Israel has the right to defend itself from Hamas violence. In 2015, its executive director, Yusufi Vali, condemned and boycotted President Obama's Countering Violent Extremism program. Even if Bernie Sanders was in the White House, ISBCC leaders would still be singing the same jihadist song.

Nevertheless, doing its part for the Democrat Party, on December 11, 2016, the JCRC co-sponsored an anti-Trump political rally at the ISBCC, called "Out of Many, One," and paid for buses to take suburban

Jewish community members out to the anti-Semitic mosque. Attending the event were Senator Elizabeth Warren, Boston mayor Martin Walsh, and one of our activists—who snapped Mayor Walsh shaking hands with the al-Qaeda terrorist supporter, Imam Abdullah Faaruuq on stage at the ISBCC. According to the *Boston Globe*, the idea was to "stand together against a wave of incivility, hate speech, and violence that has followed the presidential election." JCRC's associate director, Nahma Nadich, took personal part in the slander, telling the *Globe* that "in my lifetime, I haven't seen the expression of anti-Semitism in America like this, ever." On February 9, 2017, Nadich tweeted out a call for Jews to form a human "Chain of peace" around the ISBCC on February 10, 2017. Rabbi Sue Fendrick, Editor at the Center for Global Judaism at Hebrew College and one of the main organizers of the Chain of Peace event, repeatedly compared Trump's election to Hitler's and predicted another Holocaust as its result.

There are a variety of reasons for why the JCRC and its leaders would go out of their way to support anti-Semitic terrorism-connected Islamic extremists. An uncharitable hypothesis is that personal desire for access coupled with foolish ideological inflexibility means more to them than the interests of the Jewish community. The ISB has major clout among Boston's leftist circles in government and civic life, especially within the politically powerful Greater Boston Interfaith Organization. As the only faith community holdouts in embracing the ISB as late as 2009, the JCRC, representing the organized Jewish community, faced enormous pressure to abandon Jewish interests in order to "fit in" with the rest of the leftist crowd. The social pressure might have turned out to be just too much.

A more charitable explanation is that Jeremy Burton and his fellow JCRC leaders believe that they are in a sort of quid pro quo bargain with the ISBCC. The JCRC will protect the ISB from scrutiny and criticism in the Jewish community by marginalizing and demonizing its critics. In return, the ISBCC will keep a lid on anti-Semitism in the Muslim community, or at the very least refrain from officially promoting anti-Semitism through its own activities. But the ISB has never kept up its side of the bargain. It didn't after Boston Jewish leaders first reached out to the ISB after 9/11. It didn't after the JCRC resumed its official support for the ISB after the Boston Marathon bombings. And so, Jeremy Burton will continue to trudge over to the ISBCC for "honest conversations," and the ISBCC will continue making him look like an idiot by inviting notorious anti-Semites to speak at the ISBCC just a week later.

Indeed, Jeremy Burton and other leftist Jewish Boston leaders no longer even pretend to get upset when the ISBCC is caught hiring another anti-Semitic imam. The ISBCC hired two imams to replace Imam Suhaib Webb. In 2015, Imam Yasir Fahmy was hired as the head imam. Fahmy hailed from the New Jersey mosque, the Islamic Society of Passaic County, where he was assistant imam to a former Hamas member, Muhammad Qatanani, who had done time in Israeli jails. Jeremy Burton continues to partner with Imam Yasir Fahmy in interfaith dialogue.

In 2016, Imam Abdul-Malik Merchant was hired as an assistant imam and as an interfaith coordinator. Merchant has a habit of publishing things on Facebook like the February 5, 2013, post claiming that: "The Jews wanted to kill Jesus the son of Mary (peace be upon him) because there [sic] normal way or tradition was to kill the prophets." Just like Suhaib Webb, the new ISBCC imam considers "effeminate men" to be "evil things" because "according to the Shari'ah they are a considered dirty and unclean." Once APT published this information, none of the Boston Jewish organizations said a word. Merchant did not even say anything about the homophobic statements, but he published a wildly dissimulating apology for the anti-Semitic statements. See, he was just translating material that was pejorative to Jews and publishing it online. It wasn't his personal opinion. This excuse did not work for Tarek Mehanna in federal court, but it worked like a charm for Merchant with Jeremy Burton.

•   •   •

On April 24, 2017, the David Project's erstwhile attorney in the ISB's lawsuit against its critics, Jeff Robbins, resurfaced into the narrative. Robbins had since left the dying David Project and continued his activism within the Jewish community by becoming the chairman of the Anti-Defamation League's New England board. He supported many of the organization's left-wing causes and would probably have wanted to keep his past representing Islamophobes like Charles Jacobs and Ahmed Mansour quiet.

But yet, it followed him wherever it went. In 2013, Robbins was invited to speak at the Northeastern University School of Law in Boston. Left-wing activists disrupted his speech and circulated a petition demanding

Robbins be de-platformed. Robbins's crime? Representing Charles Jacobs and the David Project. It didn't help that we continued to make the ISB's terrorist connections, which he found during the lawsuit, very public, no matter what he tried to do to block us. Robbins began to harm Charles Jacobs and APT.

On January 23, 2014, one of APT's largest donors received an email from Rabbi Howard Jaffe, the same rabbi who had organized the seventy-rabbi attack against Charles and APT and all but kicked us out of his synagogue. Our donor was a member of Jaffe's synagogue, and so was Jeff Robbins. Jaffe was trying to dissuade our donor from supporting us, and he asked the donor to meet with him and Robbins.

> To the extent that you are genuinely interested in learning more about why I say that Charles Jacobs takes things out of context," Jaffe wrote, "I would mention that Jeff Robbins, who, as you may know, and I may have mentioned before, successfully defended Charles in the lawsuit brought against him by the leaders of the Roxbury mosque, and knows him quite well, has offered to join us by telephone to share his sense of that. Of course, I am certain that you are aware that Jeff was one of the targets of the recent and perhaps ongoing tension with Charles and others, but I will tell you that, as I expressed in the letter that was signed by my colleagues and I, that I believe Jeff to be an absolutely outstanding and upstanding human being whose input would be valuable, if you are truly interested in having that particular conversation.

This "upstanding human being" was blatantly violating his ethical responsibilities to a former client under the Massachusetts Rules of Professional Conduct, Rule 1.9(c), forbidding a lawyer from using confidential information he gained while he represented a former client to harm that former client.

And yet here was Rabbi Jaffe, who hated Jacobs's guts, telling our donor:

"I trust that you are aware that Jeff was the attorney who successfully defended Charles against the leadership of the Roxbury mosque. FWIW, I do not want forget to mention to you that I think it is fair to say that [Jeff's] impression of how Charles presents that which he presents is very similar to my own, and that Jeff has asked me to mention to you that he would be pleased to meet with you as well, should you be interested. Again, please bear in mind that Jeff is someone who has not only worked closely with Charles, but defended him against that most significant lawsuit. I would hope this would not put him above reproach, but provide him with a credential that indeed, no one else has."

That largest donor stopped being our donor entirely shortly thereafter.

None of Robbins's behind-the-scenes treachery compared to what he did publicly in the spring of 2017. After President Trump was elected, Robbins jumped on the Democrat strategy of purporting to defend Muslims against the President's evil decrees. During the ISB lawsuit, Robbins had snagged the *Boston Herald* as a client. He also got a regular column at the newspaper. In a March 3, 2017, article ironically titled "Surge in anti-Semitism Spreads Fear," Robbins demonstrated why the legal profession gets a bad name sometimes.

As an implicit swipe at President Trump for supposedly spreading hate across America, Robbins flaunted his own virtue by embracing the people who sued his former clients: "In Boston shortly after the election," Robbins wrote, "two lawyers who had clashed bitterly over a lawsuit centered on the Islamic Society of Boston's Cultural Center in Roxbury buried the hatchet in a joint visit to the ISBCC....The two lawyers, both Jewish, decided to attend Friday afternoon prayers at the ISBCC mosque together in order to pay their respects to the center and to its Muslim worshippers, many of whom are immigrants. They were warmly welcomed by the imam and his congregation, who saw the visit as the message of reconciliation it was intended to be."

On April 24, 2017, Robbins violated Rule 1.9 again by writing, in a *Boston Herald* article titled "Islamic Center reflects U.S. Values":

> *Those of us directly involved in the case, who were passionate advocates for our respective sides, know that there were enough legitimate griev-ances on both sides to go around.* [Emphasis mine.]

Robbins claimed that that the ISB plaintiffs had "legitimate grievances" against his former clients and based that claim on privileged knowledge he possesses by virtue of being "directly involved in the case." Robbins also wrote to one of our supporters that the ISB's "legitimate grievances" against his clients included "[t]he feeling that their right to worship was being questioned." In other words, according to Jeff, one of the key claims made by the ISB in its lawsuit had merit.

And yet, while he was being paid by the David Project, Jeff sang a different tune: "It was difficult not to conclude that this was all about bullying and about intimidation, and not about any legitimate claim to have been defamed."

Not all lawyers do this stuff, but, unfortunately, the David Project picked the one who does.

• • •

The last straw for me fell on July 25, 2017, when, in what appears to be the first time in American Jewish history, an affiliate of a terrorist group that murders Jews was invited to solicit donations at a synagogue. The affiliate was CAIR, the terrorist group was Hamas, the CAIR representative was none other than Cambridge city councilor Nadeem Mazen. And the synagogue was none other than Temple Isaiah in Lexington, which was headed by Rabbi Howard Jaffe.

Mazen, feeling confident from the national attention that our Breitbart article got him, decided to run for Congress from the Massachusetts Third District, which covers the wealthy suburbs where Mazen's parents live, among them Lexington. The event was organized by JCRC and the ISBCC and, like the ISBCC rally with Elizabeth Warren, was seductively titled "Out of Many, One." It was billed as an important interfaith bridge-building affair. However, video of the event and printed materials handed out to attendees reveal that what the rabbi presided over was something quite different. It was a political rally where Islamist extremists pretending to be moderates sought to enlist Jews in their campaign to undermine U.S. government counterterrorism efforts, while raising funds for the Hamas-connected hate group CAIR—all in the name of "social justice" and interfaith harmony.

The rabbi's Muslim guests were Nadeem Mazen, a New England director of CAIR, the Council on American Islamic Relations, Stephanie Marzouk, the founder of a group called the Muslim Justice League (MJL), and Samer Naseredden, the director of youth programming at the ISBCC. The rabbi falsely presented his guests as people who are allied with the progressive values of his congregation. The Islamist speakers tried to act the part. The ISBCC's Naseredden, for example, claimed that he's as American as apple pie. In fact, the mosque's youth-training curriculum is used to radicalize the historically moderate Boston Muslim community.

Marzouk argued that American Muslims should refuse to give aid to law enforcement officials investigating Islamist terror plots against their fellow Americans. She handed out flyers that alleged, without evidence, a widespread conspiracy of "targeting Muslims through U.S. government policy" that "has occurred for many decades." Her fliers cited the case of Tarek Mehanna, whom she portrayed as a good boy unfairly prosecuted and stripped of his liberties by the Obama administration's anti-Muslim witch hunt.

CAIR director Nadeem Mazen, complained to the gathered Jews that New York cops embedded informants within MIT's Muslim Students Association when he was its president. But Mazen did not disclose any of the obvious reasons for them to do so: During the time Mazen attended MIT, for example, his spiritual leader, Suheil Laher, happened to run al-Qaeda's main fundraising base in the United States and was linked by the FBI to the 1993 World Trade Center bombing. Laher openly called for jihad against non-Muslims on his MIT website, and under his influence, Aafia Siddiqui became al-Qaeda's most notorious female leader, at one point being the most wanted and dangerous woman in the world.

The three honored guests seemed to count on the ignorance of Temple Isaiah's Jews. Mazen unleashed a string of howlers: "Of course, o percent of Muslims are doing violence in the Greater Boston area," he insisted. "I would argue that o percent Muslims are doing violence in America at large." According to Mazen, "it turns out that CAIR isn't Muslim Brotherhood." "I mean the Muslim brotherhood doesn't really exist in this country," Mazen told the congregation. "There's no political Islam," he said. All this in the face of significant amount of federal trial evidence and academic research.

Mazen then blasted Israel and the United States. He suggested that the congregation should "engage in difficult conversations" about the supposed "maleficence" of both Israel and the United States, whose governments "often subvert the will of the people and the natural democracy that it is owed."

As the program came to a close, the Islamists asked the Lexington Jews for money. "My project this year is I have to raise a million dollars," Mazen announced. "Don't send clothes, send money. I'm not afraid to say it anymore." "Go out and donate to any Muslim organization, ISBCC, CAIR, Jetpac, Muslim Justice League, come on, donate to us," urged Marzouk.

When I saw the video of this event, I was about to begin my last year in law school. For the previous two years I watched as the ISBCC and CAIR grew back like weeds after the pruning APT gave them in 2014–15. I had to do something, and Charles and I agreed to call Rabbi Howard Jaffe out for his absolutely irresponsible event with CAIR. In response, the JCRC and the Massachusetts Board of Rabbis issued yet another mass denunciation letter:

> We, the Executive Committee of the Massachusetts Board of Rabbis (MBR) and the Jewish Community Relations Council of Greater Boston, condemn in the strongest terms the recent attacks on our colleague and former MBR President, Rabbi Howard Jaffe, by Americans for Peace and Tolerance (APT) and its director, Charles Jacobs....Despite their claims to be standing up to extremism, Charles Jacobs and APT are the true face of extremism in our community: purveyors of hatred and division, they engage in outrageous attacks on communal institutions and individuals involved in the important work of building relationships among Boston-area Muslims and Jews.

The JCRC and the MBR then accused us of "verbal violence"—a favorite term of left-wing fascists, used by them to justify censoring speech they don't like by claiming it is violent. This was exactly where JCRC and MBR were going, getting down to the following demand:

> We call on all Jewish communal news organizations—including *The Jewish Advocate* and the *Times of Israel*—to refuse to carry Charles Jacobs' writings unless and until he ceases his defamation of respected Jewish communal leaders and vicious anti-Muslim propaganda.

But the sting of these letters was somehow gone. Like with most of the leftist outrage turned up to eleven in the age of Trump, people have stopped listening. Toba Spitzer, the lesbian rabbi and brave defender of homophobic Islamists told Boston's Jewish newspaper: "I don't see Charles as a part of the Jewish community...He's essentially alienated himself from the community. Americans for Peace and Tolerance is not a Jewish group." The Jewish newspaper responded with an outraged editorial, titled "Marginalizing disagreement is not Jewish." The editorial stated:

> With all due respect, no one—not even a member of our beloved clergy—is the arbiter of who belongs to the Jewish community....Asserting APT, which many members of the Jewish community support with their hearts, minds, efforts and dollars, is not a part of our Jewish community is absurd. If anything, it is more reasonable to suggest JCRC is far more selective and exclusionary. Regardless, APT clearly represents a significant segment of our Jewish community.

Corrupt rabbis have been trying to excommunicate Jews they disagree with politically since before Baruch Spinoza. Toba Spitzer will end up on the trash heap of history with them. Shortly after we exposed Nadeem Mazen's CAIR fundraiser with Rabbi Jaffe, Mazen dropped out of his race for Congress, citing inability to raise the right amount of funds. It seems like his Muslim Brotherhood campaign cash has dried up. Perhaps the higher-ups did not like him sleeping around on Tinder.

But, there are many more Islamist leaders and imams spreading their poisonous ideology, unchallenged, among the Muslim youth of New England. The ISB mosques remain terror factories. And treasonous leftist civic leaders in New England continue to support these terror factories and their grisly works.

In Quintus Smyrnaeus's *The Fall of Troy*, Cassandra, King Priam's daughter, has both the blessing of seeing the hidden truth and the curse of no one believing a word she says. When the Trojans brought the horse inside the city walls, Cassandra saw the Greeks inside. She tried to warn her countrymen: "Fools! ye know not your doom: still ye rejoice with one consent in madness, who to Troy have brought the Argive Horse where ruin lurks!" But the celebrating Trojan mob "cried shame on her, and said she spake but lies" with "a raving tongue of evil speech." Cassandra tried to burn the horse and chop at it with an axe, "but straightway from her hands they plucked and flung afar the fire and steel, and careless turned to the feast; for darkened o'er them their last night."

It's lonely and hard to be thrust into the role of Cassandra, like Charles Jacobs was when he spoke out about the ISB. But, unlike the Trojans, we are lucky. As President Trump's election showed, the curse of politically correct blindness to the obvious is being lifted from the eyes of more and more Americans. I knew that now was no time to stop. I had to come back to APT, now as Executive Director and with a law degree. Already, I have caught the ISBCC's new imam, Yasir Fahmy, spouting the same anti-Semitic and homophobic hatred from the ISBCC's pulpit as his predecessor, Suhaib Webb did before he left the city in disgrace. Stay tuned for the sequel.

CODA

I am confident—in fact I have seen it first hand in other cities like Nashville, Detroit, and Buffalo—that the events described in this book are occurring, more or less in the same fashion, in many other cities across America and the Western world. I am also confident, that in many of those cities, there are people like Bill Sapers, Charles Jacobs, Dennis Hale, and Ahmed Mansour, who see something wrong and who want to speak out. This book was written for such people. I hope you read about our experience in speaking out and fighting back, learn from our mistakes, improve on our successes, and reach out to us at APT, so that we may work together to keep America at peace.

ACKNOWLEDGMENTS

First and foremost, I am honored to thank my mentor and hero, Charles Jacobs, who, more than anyone else, has championed the principles and goals of the protagonists of this book. Neither this book nor the story told in it would exist without Charles's leadership, support, and patience. Whatever deeper thoughts I might have managed to convey in this book were most likely the fruits of discussions with Avi Goldwasser, whose wisdom has been an invaluable guide, and for which I am immensely grateful. Major thanks go to Professor Dennis Hale, who contributed his scholarly knowledge and his talents as a literary editor to a work that greatly benefited from both. I am also much indebted to the production and editing team at Encounter Books for the excellent results of their dedicated efforts, and for bearing with me on my first book. I would like to thank Bill Sapers for being the first to see the threat posed by the Islamic Society of Boston, to recognize the threat for what it is, and to say something about it, at considerable personal risk. Many thanks and great honor are due to "Rashid," who took an even greater risk to tell me about the threat "from the inside." I also would like to thank the men and women of the armed forces and law enforcement for taking the ultimate risk on behalf of their fellow Americans, and for keeping this country safe notwithstanding their political leaders' mistakes. I give the deepest thanks to my grandmother, who taught me how to read, write, and love both; as well as to my grand-aunt, who taught me about dissent.

INDEX